DUTCHMEN ON THE BAY

ETHNOHISTORY

A series edited by
Anthony F. C. Wallace and Lee V. Cassanelli

DUTCHMEN ON THE BAY

The Ethnohistory of a
Contractual Community

Lawrence J. Taylor

UNIVERSITY OF PENNSYLVANIA PRESS

Philadelphia • 1983

Copyright © 1983 by the University of Pennsylvania Press
All rights reserved

Library of Congress Cataloging in Publication Data

Taylor, Lawrence J.
  Dutchmen on the bay.

  (Ethnohistory)
  Bibliography: p.
  Includes index.
    1. Dutch Americans—New York (State)—West Sayville—
Social life and customs. 2. West Sayville (N.Y.)—
Social life and customs. 3. Oyster fisheries—New
York (State)—West Sayville—History. I. Title.
II. Series: Ethnohistory (University of Pennsylvania
Press)
F129.W704T39 1983   305.8'3931'074725   83-7029
ISBN 0-8122-7886-0

Printed in the United States of America

FOR MY FATHER, BEN TAYLOR,
with whom I learned to love the Bay

CONTENTS

ILLUSTRATIONS

FIGURES

PLATES (between pages 92 and 93)

FOREWORD

The art of writing community history, and not mere "local history," is to connect the community with the larger world, and to reveal in the detailed study of one small group of people social and cultural processes of theoretical interest to a discipline. This art has been well practiced in this book by Lawrence Taylor, as it was in the first contribution to our ethnohistory series by my co-editor, Lee Cassanelli.

Taylor has written an historical ethnography of a small Long Island, N.Y. community of oyster fishermen of Netherlands ancestry whose product was sold in an international market. He focuses chiefly on the nineteenth and early twentieth century, with due attention to the community as it is today, and addresses topics of general interest to historians and social scientists: ethnicity, class, religious factionalism, the "Protestant ethic," and—of particular interest to him—the relation between the pursuit of individual interest and the maintenance of community solidarity. The work has the holistic character of the ethnographic approach, attempting to bring together the ecology, the technology, the social structure, and the religion and ideology of a particular community; but he wisely does not confine his attention to his community alone, and takes note of economic and other forces in the "outside" world that affect West Sayville.

There is of course no competing study of the Dutchmen of West Sayville. There is, however, an extensive literature on a number of topics to which this work is relevant as a case study. The ethnicity and immigration literature is one such field but I think I would point to the genre of historical community studies as its natural home. There are a number of these by now that center on nineteenth- and early twentieth-century industrial communities of various kinds and vary from the primarily statistical (the new social history) to the largely ethnographic. The book makes a real contribution to the literature of ethnographically-oriented historical community studies and also to the general theoretical literature on the various topics such as ethnicity and class, factionalism, individual and group, etc. It should also have a particular interest to that anthropological subfield that specializes in the study of Western European and American coastal communities and, more generally, to the anthropology of Western culture.

But it is also an intrinsically interesting story, worth reading for the human drama that is played out in the lives of relatively obscure people. So, without further ado, let the curtain rise on *Dutchmen on the Bay*.

Anthony F. C. Wallace

PREFACE AND
ACKNOWLEDGMENTS

I did not spend my youth clamming or oystering, but I did pass a good part of it on, in, or alongside the Great South Bay—occasionally chasing one or another of its denizens, but most often simply watching its surface ripple between my home in Blue Point and Fire Island beyond. On those waters were the usual range of pleasure boats, but also any number of less pretty but more serious craft: clam boats from which a great many locals from all the south shore communities tonged or raked the bay's valuable shellfish. There were also more imposing craft to be seen: the bulky "drudge boats" that churned back and forth through the shallow waters, like great sea-harvesters, dragging thousands of clams from their soft, muddy beds. Most of these large craft were berthed a few miles to the west, where Green's Creek emptied into the bay. There, at the edge of the hamlet of West Sayville, a bulwarked basin was home to a row of shellfish companies: aquabusinesses that planted and harvested clams on leased or owned grounds out in the bay. In Green's Creek itself, however, dozens of little one- or two-man clam boats found shelter as well.

I do not remember whether I was struck by the proximity of such contrasting fishing styles. Probably not. I do, however, remember hearing, among the clammers of my own village, vague references to the "Dutchmen" of West Sayville. There were held to be extremely serious clammers, clannish, and religious—the very type of the "independent bayman." I did not imagine that these same Dutchmen were also the founders of those shellfish companies, the natural enemies of all independent shellfishermen.

Returning to the area as an anthropologist interested in maritime communities, I discovered that there existed no more fascinating example of life "following the water" than that of those Dutchmen of West Sayville, particularly in the years around the turn of the century. In those days oyster "was king," as the saying went, and West Sayville was a small but very busy port out of which the full range of working boats sailed and motored in search of not only oysters but also clams, scallops, and finfish. Oystering had lately become something like an industry, and a handful of wealthy planter/shippers battled with less well-endowed entrepreneurs and with "independent baymen" for the valuable and limited grounds under the Great South Bay. In that respect, West Sayville was a variation on the general range of shellfishing communities—somewhere between places like the Chesapeake (where large-scale entrepreneurs had made almost no headway against independent oystermen) and some of the European regions, which by that time had been transformed into virtual mill towns. The presence of these variations within the compass of one very small community, however, made West Sayville an especially appealing case study through which to examine the social and cultural impact of an industrializing fishery.

Turn-of-the-century West Sayville was interesting in other respects, particularly to an anthropologist. In the early years of this century, it was a culturally homogeneous immigrant village, the greatest number of whose inhabitants had come from a small number of communities in the province of Zeeland, in the Netherlands, beginning in 1849. Many of them were raised in the shellfisheries of that region, but they brought with them more than a proclivity for oystering. They came with a particular cultural experience, a set of values and institutions that were peculiarly Dutch. The most obvious of those cultural characteristics were those arising from the Dutch Calvinist churches, institutions that embodied not only a system of beliefs but also forms of association and interaction which greatly affected the adaptation of the Dutch to their new American environment. As a well-bounded immigrant community, West Sayville represented another kind of case study, for the Dutch experience is one that challenges some generally held assumptions about the adaptation of European immigrants to American environments. While some able historians have written on the Dutch settlements in the Midwest, their interests have been less comparative.

The ethnic culture of the West Sayville Dutch was not, however, exotic by American standards. In fact, the turn-of-the-century community might be taken as an extreme example of just those patterns of culture we view as American. The West Sayville Dutch were entrepreneurially inclined individualists bound together by voluntary associations into a strong moral community. As an example of what I, following historian Christopher Hill, call the "contractual community," West Sayville promised to be a case study of even more general comparative significance, shedding ethnographic light on Weber's thesis concerning the culture of capitalism.

These three comparative themes have guided the view of the community taken in this book, although it is the last that I have found most compelling. Accordingly, it is the "contractual community" that receives the most explicit theoretical attention. Other issues, equally plausible of investigation in the context of West Sayville, are given less direct consideration. These include the more technical issues of cultural ecology as well as the ever-continuing arguments concerning the relative assimilation of immigrants: the "melting pot" debates. These issues, and many others, are significant; that they do not receive lengthy treatment here is only a testament to the limitations of my interests and abilities. It seemed a better strategy to concentrate attention on those comparative issues to which the case might make the most interesting contributions.

These theoretical problems and possibilities have drawn me to the study of historic West Sayville, but so also have the people, living and dead, who are that community. The oysters are gone now, but clams have filled the gap. "God does not take away with one hand," as an elder put it to me, "but that he gives with the other." If not the scene of bustling industry as it was in those boom years before World War I, West Sayville is still a maritime community worthy of that title. The older men and women still live aspects of the life they told me about, and so do a surprising number of their children and grandchildren. It would be a disservice to that life "following the bay" and to most readers if the story were lost in a more opaque sea of social-scientific jargon. Although theoretical points are raised where appropriate, and a methodological appendix appears at the end of the text, I have endeavored to put the tale in a narrative format capable of holding the interest of the general as well as the specialized reader.

This book is the result of the unusual collaboration of a social anthropologist and a regional history museum. The first credit must go to Roger B. Dunkerley, director of the Suffolk Marine Museum, an institution located in West Sayville, chartered by the New York State Education Department, and operated as a division of the Suffolk County Department of Parks. Aware of the extraordinary local riches in lore, photographs, and maritime objects relating to the rise of the local shellfishing industry, the museum set about planning a major exhibit that would tell that story. With the support of a farsighted board of trustees, headed by David DeGraff, the museum acquired the period oyster sloop *Modesty* in 1974, and by donation in 1975 a 1908 oyster house whose structural restoration was completed in September of the bicentennial year. Mr. Dunkerley then had the good fortune to hire an extremely talented curator, Margaret Holsten, who took over the task of planning and putting together an exhibit on the rise of the shellfishing industry. The museum received a planning grant from the National Endowment for the Humanities, under whose auspices I joined the team. My own interests were as much in the structure of the Dutch immigrant community as in the shellfisheries, so that our final implementation grant proposed both a permanent exhibit on the shellfisheries and an ethnohistory of the Dutch immigrant community that so contributed to that industry. The project was generously funded by the Endowment (PM-0219-79), and the necessary matching funds were received from the enthusiastic and supportive local and regional community. The exhibit, "Oysters, Dutchmen, and the Bay," opened in May 1981 and is the very model of an interpretive exhibit of maritime life.

My own research in the community was conducted intermittently from June 1977 through the summer of 1981 and included three months' residence in the community and several weeks in Holland. Throughout that period, I was fortunate to have the constant assistance of the museum staff, including director Roger Dunkerley and registrar Gertrude Welte. Special thanks, however, are due Margaret Holsten, exhibit curator, and Jack Kochiss, research associate, both of whom were constant sources of data, direction, and constructive criticism. Other vital research aid came from Lucien DeMoor, and especially Hendrik Taatgen, who acted not only as translator and interpreter of Dutch manuscripts but also as tour guide in Holland and anthropological critic on both sides of the Atlantic. All my students should be thanked for their patient listening and sometimes astute questioning, but I am especially grateful to Phil James for his hours of painstaking assistance with kinship charts.

A large number of my colleagues at Lafayette College and other institutions added much to this study through readings, criticism, and discussion. My first debt in this regard is, as always, to William Arens of the State University of New York at Stony Brook, who continues as mentor long beyond the term of any formal obligation. Invaluable assistance was also received from Dan Bauer, Howard Schneiderman, and William Dobriner, all of Lafayette College, Bonnie McCay of Rutgers University, Ivan Karp of Indiana University, Jojada Verrips of the University of Amsterdam, Michael Kenny of Simon Fraser University, and Jane Schneider of the City University of New York Graduate Center. I am also grateful for the many helpful comments of academic audiences at Stony Brook, Lafayette, CUNY Graduate Center, and the University of Leiden. In addition to providing an atmosphere conducive to research as well as to teaching, Lafayette College contributed a summer research grant through their Committee for Advanced Study and Research, which I here gratefully acknowledge.

John McGuigan of the University of Pennsylvania Press, and series editors Anthony F. C. Wallace and Lee Cassanelli, both of the University of Pennsylvania, did much between them to make this book far better than it otherwise would have been. I count myself fortunate to have worked with them. A special debt of gratitude is owed Nancy McGuigan. The typing was ably done by Mary Jane Lutz and Joy Glock of Lafayette College. The illustrations were done by Tom Kraemer, and V. M. O. Hickey helped choose the photographs.

It is impossible to thank the people of West Sayville adequately. They were unfailingly kind and generous to me, and the degree to which my book is their work will be apparent through the ensuing pages. There are too many to thank individually, but I want to mention Ollie Locker, the late Arie Schaper, Ade Hoek, Marinus Verschuur, Janetje Ockers, Ed Ockers, Adriaan Daane, and Lester Seerveld, each of whom contributed especially significant pieces of the puzzle. In most cases their names and other names are replaced by pseudonyms in the text. In Holland, Isaac Daane, J. Glerum, W. E. P. Van Ysseldijk, and C. Pronk all deserve special thanks. This book would have been weaker without the access to local records provided by the New Life Community Church, the Christian Reformed Church, the West Sayville Hook and Ladder Company, the Ockers House Museum, and the Suffolk Marine Museum. I thank them all and hope that nothing I have written will be interpreted as a violation of their trust.

There are finally those thanks that are most impossible to express: first to my parents, Harriet and Ben Taylor, for having given me the self-confidence to embark on this and other projects. Last, and most, I owe to my wife Michiko, not only for her usual patience and perseverance but also for her constant aid, advice, editorial comment and general sustenance.

INTRODUCTION

In 1849 the families of Cornelius DeWaal and his brother-in-law, Cornelius Hage, left the village of Bruinisse in Zeeland, the Netherlands, for America. They arrived in New York City with the intention of moving on to the Michigan frontier, where many of their countrymen had already settled, but had instead what turned out to be a fateful change of heart. Oysters, they were told, were abundant in Long Island's Great South Bay, and having been raised in that pursuit, Hage and DeWaal decided to head for that nearer frontier. They boarded the Long Island Railroad and sped over its newly completed "central line" fifty miles east of the city to the terminus at Lakeland, with the intention of settling somewhere on Suffolk County's southern shore.

That short train ride brought them into another world, for as close as it was to New York City, much of Suffolk County remained as yet peripheral and underpopulated (see Figure 1). Most people resided in the small towns and villages along the North Shore and East End, to which well-harbored region their southern Connecticut Puritan ancestors had been attracted in the mid-seventeenth century. Though grown prosperous by the seagoing commerce of Long Island Sound, these communities had not expanded much, in two centuries, into the lands to their south. The center of the county, through which the new railroad cut its narrow swath, was level woodlands known by such unappealing epithets as "the pine plain" and "the barrens." Below that lay Islip's sandy and sometimes impenetrable marshy south shore. Even though the Great South Bay offered a variety of resources and another sea route to the New York market, the southern shore of Islip

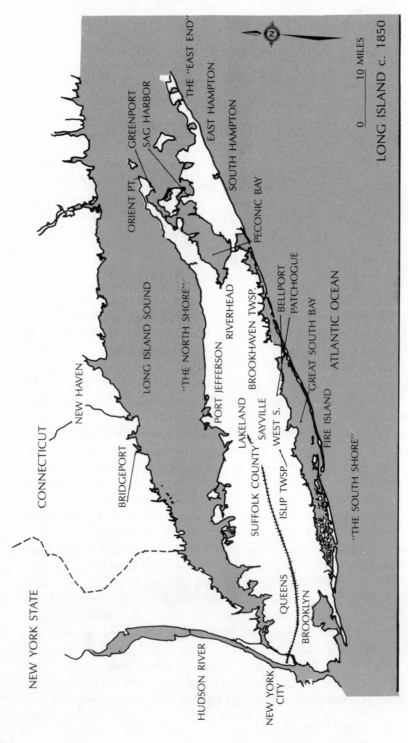

Figure 1. Map of Long Island, circa 1850

was still, in the 1840s, thinly settled, and "the barrens" to the north remained, to use a comtemporary phrase, in a "state of nature."

The appearance of a railroad betokened changing times. The wild lands of Suffolk had lately been released from the entailed estates of great landlords, and while Yankees from the east edged westward along the southern shore, land speculators in league with railroad interests were doing their best to attract more alien settlers to the less inviting lands of the county. Hage and DeWaal were among the first of these settlers, and they were able to find homes for their families near the tiny South Shore hamlet of Oakdale and a living there on both land and water. By 1865 enough friends, relatives, and neighbors from Holland had followed them there to form a distinct Dutch community, known eventually as West Sayville. To their north and east, the pine barrens were pioneered by a steady stream of central and eastern Europeans who settled into a new life based on farming and rural manufacturing. Thus did the population of Suffolk grow in number and diversity through the second half of the nineteenth century, with a concomitant development of the regional economy. By the closing decades of the century the Great South Bay, always a vital part of the local adaptation, had become the scene of a great maritime industry, and West Sayville was at the very center.

If the Dutch immigrants timed their arrival to benefit from that commercial development, they certainly contributed—arguably more than any other community—to the rise of the great shellfishery that made Blue Point Oysters a famous commodity on both sides of the Atlantic. Quickly adapting to the novel ecological conditions and technology of Great South Bay oystering, the Hollanders proved abler still in exploiting the entrepreneurial possibilities of the pursuit. They were among the first in the area to take good advantage of the new laws permitting the leasing of town-owned underwater lands for oyster cultivation and accordingly profited from the rising demand for oysters in New York. Several sons of the first settlers went on to become substantial oyster planters and shippers, always quick to adjust to the changing exigencies of production and marketing. By the turn of the century these men constituted a new industrial elite in the still-small immigrant community. One of them, "King Oyster Planter" Jacob Ockers, was in his time the greatest exporter of oysters in the world. Not everyone rose with the industry, of course, and toward the end of the century the ranks of the ordinary baymen and oyster shanty workers were swelled by new immigrants from an economically distraught

Holland. Though still hardly more than a hamlet, West Sayville was
by that time a bustling port, whose people, if united by maritime concerns, were divided into rich and poor, and if of common Calvinist
roots, were separated by walls of sectarian dispute.

The following chapters tell the story of the founding and growth
of that community and offer a detailed account of the most important
arenas of public life there in the boom days of oystering. Distinctive
in their entrepreneurial zeal and Calvinist religiosity, the West Sayville
"Dutchmen" were and are an interesting variation of the American
immigrant experience. The meaning their story has for us, however,
depends on the perspective from which we choose to view it: whether
as a local tale of singular peoples, places, and events or as an episode
illustrative of more general social and cultural processes.

ANTHROPOLOGY AND LOCAL HISTORY

From the "local" perspective, the tale of West Sayville may appear
largely fortuitous. Cornelius Hage and Cornelius DeWaal were headed
west to the newly established Dutch settlements in Michigan when
they "heard about" (according to Hage's daughter) the oystering on
the Great South Bay. As we shall see, the formation of a Dutch settlement in what eventually became West Sayville appears to have been
contingent on the ambitions of one local non-Dutch entrepreneur named
Sam Green. It was Green who sold the plots of land on which the
immigrants would build their village, who leased the waterfront prop-
erties to the growing oyster companies, and who dredged out "Green's
Creek," the small but vital sheltering water in which were harbored
the many small craft of the local baymen. As for the success of the
oyster industry, what would that have come to without the ambitions
of men like Jacob Ockers, whose relentless energy and commercial
acumen remain favorite subjects of the local folklore?

Even life in the churches, those other vital village institutions,
may seem a saga of singular events. The first Dutch Reformed church,
it could be argued, would never have been built, as it was in 1867, if
the immigrants had not begun to congregate around Green's Creek,
for there was nothing that would have kept the Dutch men and women
(or at least those without "separatist inclinations") from going to the
Methodists or Congregationalists. Once formed, life within that congregation may seem also to have been the product of local particular-

ities. The first few ministers were, by some accounts, moral degenerates whose accidental arrival in the community sparked a series of religious crises. Those fires were fueled, so we are told, by a small band of local "troublemakers," and the ensuing conflicts led to the schism of 1876 and the founding of the more orthodox Calvinist "True Holland Reformed" congregation (known eventually as the Christian Reformed Church). Confrontations, especially within that newer congregation, continued to trouble religious life over the following decades, and all of them could be attributed to the idiosyncrasies of one intransient fellow or another.

Events originating outside the community may also be viewed as singular accidents that happened to have dramatic effects on local life. The processes involved in oyster culture were developed elsewhere and introduced into the Great South Bay along with similarly alien notions about underwater land tenure. Labor relations within the local industry were upset when the speech of an "outside agitator"—the "walking delegate of the American Federation of Labor"—led to the formation of a local chapter of the Oystermen's Union in 1900 and eventually, in 1902, to a short-lived strike.

If a narrowly focused view tempts one to explain local events in such terms of happenstance and personality, social scientists are bound to see in such particularities evidence of more general economic, social, or cultural phenomena. They seek behind the idiosyncrasies of events and personalities for patterns, recurring structural features which indicate that incidents may be viewed as instances of some more general process rather than as utterly singular events.

An economic determinist, for example, might point out that if Jacob Ockers had not become the Oyster King, someone else would have, for when ecological and market conditions produce an environment conducive to such commercial enterprise, someone is bound to step up and take advantage of it. If Yankee or Dutch ingenuity was involved in the American development of oyster culture, our hypothetical theorist might go on to point out, then it was matched elsewhere in the world by a similar French and Japanese ingenuity, the common factor being the exhaustion of natural oyster beds and the consequent search for alternative ways of meeting the substantial world demand. As for the Oysterman's Union, certainly that was but a minor local instance of the national labor movement, which developed in counterpoint to the growing industrialization of craft industries. The Dutch baymen were probably discovering, as had their fellow immigrants in the coal mines of Pennsylvania, it might be argued, that their interests lay in defining themselves as workers.

West Sayville church life appears equally susceptible to analysis of a broader scope. The conflicts and schisms that so rent those local institutions were, after all, no different from those sundering mid-western Dutch settlements, for the schism of the True Holland Reformed Church was a national split, not merely a local one. The quantitative analysis of historian Robert Swierenga (1980), for example, has led him to explain that schism as a reflection of two different cultural orientations among the immigrants, which in turn he traces to the degree of urban influence in their region of origin in the Netherlands. To say that, however, is ultimately to link religious life to economic factors, for certainly the development of urban markets in Holland can be explained by their important role in the development of what Immanuel Wallerstein (1974) has called "the world system." Alternative but equally grand theoretical models may do similar damage to the significance of local events. The idealist historian of religion, for example, might see the doctrinal issues as paramount and as arising as ideas in the heads of particular critical thinkers (e.g., Calvin), but it is safe to say that such fonts of theological wisdom would not be sought in this tiny maritime hamlet. Neither a "great man" nor an economic determinist theory of history is likely to lead many scholars to the shores of the Great South Bay—from any such larger perspective, the relevance of an intensive look at West Sayville seems to evaporate, local events having been reduced to minor examples of already discovered laws or patterns.

There is a perspective that may be said to lie somewhere between that of a local historian—entranced with the particularity of a distinctive way of life—and the grand theorist, who is equally transfixed by the sweeping processes of universal history. That is the perspective of the anthropologist, who is well known for asking large questions in small places. Ethnographies, which are the anthropological descriptions and analyses of particular groups of people, are, at their best, dialogues between the hypotheses and assertions of social theory, and the richly complex reality of particular lived human worlds.

While still primarily associated with the study of preliterate or tribal peoples, the discipline of anthropology has for many years been sending its intrepid field-workers into the towns, villages, and cities of complex and industrial nations. Even the United States has not escaped the scrutiny of the anthropological eye. Ever since Lloyd

Warner and his students began their study of "Yankee City" half a century ago (Warner and Lunt 1941), anthropologists and ethnographically minded sociologists have been taking intermittent looks at American society in a variety of local settings. And these ethnographers have not been content to restrict their attention to contemporary communities. As far as the sources permit, the anthropologist is sometimes able to reconstruct a historic town or village and put to its people the same kinds of questions he might ask of living informants. Anthony F. C. Wallace's (1978) study of a mid-nineteenth-century Pennsylvania mill town is a good recent example of such anthropological history.

Whether they poach in the preserve of the sociologist or the historian, however, are such anthropological case studies worth the effort? The appropriateness of a community unit of analysis has been questioned, especially with regard to the study of complex societies (see Mills 1956 and, more recently, Bell and Newby 1972). Newly awakened to the pervasive forces of large-scale economic and social processes, some anthropologists have called for attention to larger and larger units—the ethnography of regions (see, e.g., Ennew 1980) or even nation states. Some critics go as far as to disclaim the very existence of local communities. The "community" is a fabrication of the fieldworker, this argument runs, born out of methodological error and perhaps the felt or unfelt need to discover an attractively simple and harmonious world in the midst of modern anomie and alienation (Ennew 1980, 1–6). Yet use of the word "community" does not in itself imply either simplicity or harmony; certainly neither quality could be attributed to life in turn-of-the-century West Sayville. We may, as an alternative, define "community" as a relatively bounded social field within which actors are, through significant local institutions, related more to one another and less to outsiders.[1] The local community may have a further subjective existence—as a category in the minds of the people. Insofar as the people believe there is such a thing, the "community" exercises a force in their lives worthy of anthropological attention. Thus, even if it is argued that these local worlds are epiphenomenal—merely the local expression of the pervasive forces of history—certain social and cultural processes transpire within their confines which help us understand the human character, if not the ultimate causes, of these allegedly determinative forces.

Our present argument goes further in asserting the usefulness of the local community as a unit of anthropological study, particularly those apparently swept away by the currents of history. An anthropological examination of historic West Sayville reveals a community that does not always fit comfortably into the grander accounts of the great historic transformations acted out on its small stage: (1) immigration and the attendant adaptation to the American environment and (2) industrialization and the attendant growth of class distance between capital and labor.

Until recently, the nineteenth-century European immigrant experience has been treated more or less in terms of the image so poetically limned by Oscar Handlin (1951) in his classic study *The Uprooted*. The key element in that experience, as Handlin depicted it, was alienation. The immigrant was in all senses uprooted, for in crossing the Atlantic he underwent a concentrated version of modernization. In a matter of months, the poor Irishman, Sicilian, or Pole was thus shuttled from *Gemeinschaft* (community) to *Gesellschaft* (society), from relations of status to those of contract, from villages based on kinship to either rural isolation or the anomic city. In other words, he had crossed the great divide with which the classical sociological tradition has imaginatively bifurcated all human history. This theoretical perspective seriously underestimates both the diversity of European rural society in the nineteenth century and the degree to which Old World social and cultural forms proved adaptable and even useful in American contexts (see, e.g., Yans-McLaughlin 1977).

While the historic enthnographies of particular immigrant communities will no doubt continue to correct Handlin's general model, most studies, as Lewis (1978) has recently pointed out, have so far concentrated on Catholic Europeans. Such Protestant immigrants as the Dutch Reformed have attracted less anthropological attention, probably because they appear less exotic, less removed from Anglo-American culture. Their distinctive characteristics, however, make for theoretically interesting case studies.

As Dutch-American historian Henry Lucas (1955) pointed out, the immigration, as much religious as economic in character, was very often markedly communal. Led by mininsters, congregations of immigrants settled many of the midwestern Dutch communities, which continued long after to be noteworthy for their corporateness. Such villages as Holland and Zeeland, Michigan, were far from being mere aggregates of farmer families who happened to have come from the same district of Europe. Institutions bound them together in strong communal association. Though not founded by any congregation, and in fact distinctly individual and entrepreneurial in its roots, West Sayville also came to constitute a well-defined community. The social and psychological alienation Handlin described is difficult to discover.

But, what of the impact of industrialization? By the turn of the century, West Sayville's oysters were harvested not so much by lone craftsmen-fishermen as by employees of several large shipping companies. The small village had become a mill town, the fisherman had become a worker. Was there not a commensurate alienation and growth of class consciousness, a final shift over the Marxist version of the great sociological divide? Not exactly, and here once more the particular circumstances of the community must be taken into consideration. In a manner that will be investigated at length, West Sayville's relative ethnic isolation, its social and cultural tradition, and the peculiar legal and ecological character of the shellfishery all conspired to mitigate the growth of class consciousness, if not of classes in an objective sense. The turn-of-the-century Dutchman was inclined to view himself as a "bayman" and an entrepreneur, no matter how many months of the year he labored for another, and regardless of how poor his prospects for self-advancement. This may be either a case of false consciousness or a creative response that allowed for entrepreneurial action when the opportunities finally did arise. In either case, the anthropologist's job is to explain how such a world view could have been maintained, even in the face of contrary experience. That task remains the most important challenge for the anthropology of complex societies, and its best opportunity to contribute to our understanding of the human roots and consequences of social and cultural change. It is best addressed by close attention to the structure of everyday life in such local worlds. There are theoretical stances and ethnographic methods developed through anthropology's comparative analysis of communal cultures and social systems which may throw a new light on such deceptively familiar communities as West Sayville and lead us to rethink the larger process they may exemplify.

THE CONTRACTUAL COMMUNITY

Following Christopher Hill (1964), we may call the essential character of such local worlds as West Sayville "contractual communities," a label that serves to remind us of the central "tension between individualism and collectivism" which Hill and others have noted as a salient feature of Calvinist culture (Hill 1964, 495). Local communities consciously contrived on such principles were highly corporate in some ways, exercising strong cultural construction and constriction on the individual, and yet were equally apt in the cultivation of a self-image rooted in "an ideology of individualism, of human dignity" (Hill 1964, 487). If such a tension between the individual and the group lies at the heart of all human experience, it is particularly well defined in such Calvinist contractual communities, the study of which thereby begs anthropological attention—the more so if, as Hill argues, these social forms lie at the historical as well as the logical roots of modern capitalist society. Seventeenth-century Puritan communities represent interesting cases in point, but late-nineteenth-century West Sayville is another more recent, and in some respects more accessible, object of anthropological inquiry.

Insofar as Calvinist theology may lie at the root of the contractual community, Max Weber's (1958) famous thesis concerning the relation of "the Protestant Ethic" to what he called "the spirit of capitalism" might prove relevant to our inquiry. The central concern of Weber's classic study was with "the influence of certain religious ideas on the development of an economic spirit, or the *ethos* of an economic system [and] the connection of the spirit of modern economic life with the rational ethics of ascetic Protestantism" (Weber 1958, 27). According to Weber, these "rational ethics" rested on the "ability and disposition of men to adopt certain types of practical rational conduct" (ibid., 26). In speaking thus of the "ethos" and "dispositions" involved in economic activity, Weber offered a cultural theory of capitalism, but it is a culture that is born in the minds of religious reformers, especially Calvin, and lived in the thoughts and actions of particular individuals.

For the anthropologist, what is missing from Weber's formulations is an understanding of how this rationalist culture is socially constructed and maintained. Does such a rationalism also include an essentially detached view of the self as an independent entity bound to others by free contract alone? If so, what forms of social interaction serve to inculcate such a view? Moreover, what of the other side of the Calvinist coin, the insistence on the great communal authority of the contractual community? While Calvin took care to assure the doctrinal base of that authority (see, e.g., Troeltsch 1931, 588), we are still left wondering about how such antithetical cultural directives manifested themselves in real life. How did the individual living in such a community balance these demands? Did psychological and social conflicts arise as a result? If so, what kept such a community

from constant turmoil eventually inimical to its very existence? Were
there cultural forms that ameliorated such conflicts? To pose such
questions is to put the Weberian problem of capitalist culture into an
ethnographic frame and to ask what is the structure of an actual
contractual community.

Conflict and confrontation were prominent features of everyday
life in early West Sayville, and their consideration offers an anthropological route to an understanding of the community. Questions of
conflicts in norms and behavior, and of the religious resolution of such
conflicts, are associated, albeit in radically different ethnographic settings, with the work of anthropologist Victor Turner. Interested in both
the internal and external sources of stress in the social life of the central
African Ndembu, Turner chose a series of social dramas involving
typical conflicts and subjected them to a careful analysis now generally
known as "the extended-case method."[2] By viewing these confrontations in their full local context, Turner was able to discover something
of the structural roots of interpersonal conflicts that might otherwise
be attributed to personality or other contributory, but not basic, factors.
The ritual resolution of such conflicts, on the other hand, often revealed
much of the "ideal" moral order that provided Ndembu with a conceptual framework affecting their vision of everyday life.

Two prolonged and structurally significant conflicts in West Sayville especially lend themselves to this kind of analysis: (1) the troubles
surrounding the founding of a short-lived oysterman's union around
the turn of the century and (2) the disputes within the community
churches. Each of these lengthy conflicts had its moments of dramatic
confrontation: the strike of 1902 and the schism of the Reformed
church in 1876. These signal events are taken here as starting points
for extended case studies, for they were social dramas in the full sense
of the term, replete with leading actors, semi-anonymous extras, and
even cameo appearances. Their investigation leads us not only to an
understanding of the structural roots of the conflicts, but also to an
appreciation of the character of interaction in the two local social arenas
that figured most in the public construction of the local culture.

An initial and important revelation of this approach to those events
is that the conflicts may not have been what they seemed or seem,
from the point of view of the participants or from that of certain theories. The labor disputes surrounding the founding of the union might
appear to be an obvious case of the typical turn-of-the-century confrontation of labor and capital. When the strike is viewed as only one

of a long series of confrontations over maritime resources, however, and when the relative involvement of Dutch and non-Dutch oystermen is considered, alternative interpretations suggest themselves. The real dispute may have been over enclosure, the parcelization and leasing of public oyster and clam grounds by oyster shippers, for the local workers were also oystermen in their own right, as long as the public grounds remained accessible. That struggle over enclosure was fought long before and long after the brief union episode. As Bonnie McCay (1982) has cogently argued, such struggles were essentially class battles, akin to those fought over the enclosure of English village commons in earlier times (see, e.g., E. P. Thompson 1966, 218). If so, the class fighting for its commons on the Great South Bay had and has a self-image significantly different from that ascribed to the European villagers. The Yankee oysterman who resisted enclosure of the watery commons did not do so in an effort to protect some vestige of a manorial peasant privilege. Rather, he understood those commonage rights to be inherent in town membership. The Dutch, as it turned out, were not much involved in the union struggle. There were a number of reasons, both material and ideological, why that should have been the case, but understanding the position of the Dutch workers on these issues certainly requires an exploration of the full round of their activities and identity as "baymen." The oral-history accounts of days spent oystering, clamming, eeling, and fishing tells us not only about the technical nature of such work, but also about its social and psychological character.

An extended case study of the church schism of 1876, based mainly on the consistory records of both churches, permits us to put that confrontation back into its local context and to view the total relationships of individuals both before and after that split. Here, once again, questions are raised about interpretations of church conflict based on other theories and data, in this case Swierenga's (1980) use of Merton's (1949) "locals"/"cosmopolitans" dichotomy in an argument that assumes that these conflicts originate in forces extrinsic rather than intrinsic to the contractual community. While an alternative view of the causes of the church conflicts is indicated by an ethnographic approach, the form and language of the disputes themselves suggests an expansion of the anthropological notion of ritual. The sacred words of the Bible constituted a religious device, with which a man or woman was able to convert any secular difficulty into a moral and hence sacred issue. The ensuing verbal confrontations may be viewed as fulfilling Turner's ritual function, for they provided occasions for the expression of moral rules which, though they did not determine behavior, constituted an ideal conceptual framework for interpreting experience, and one particularly resistant to alternative views of a rapidly changing social world.

Thus an anthropological approach to these extended cases not only leads to different conclusions about their local meaning, but also suggests a reinterpretation of the relation of such communal social dramas to the historical process of modernization. In both cases, analysis reveals a difference between the issues over which the battles were ostensibly fought, on the one hand, and their probable structural roots, on the other. For most of the Yankee fishermen involved, the union movement seems to have represented a fight for communal rights in the face of the increasing enclosure of underwater grounds. As such, it is better understood as a fight that used contemporary rhetoric in defense of an older and threatened understanding of property relations and social identity. The Dutch, however, were for the most part less willing to involve themselves in this movement, constrained as they were by a variety of economic, social, and ideological forces.

The conflicts within the Dutch churches are more revealing, both of the challenge of modernization to the local community and of the particular cultural forms that may evolve to deal with that challenge. Those factional disputes are similar to some discussed by historians Boyer and Nissenbaum (1974) in their analysis of the famous Salem witchcraft trials of seventeenth-century New England. In both the New England Puritan case and that of West Sayville, economic and normative conflict (individualism versus collectivism) seems to lie behind religious disputes. Those authors, like Swierenga in his analysis of the Reformed church schism, ignore the possibility that the economic/cultural dichotomy and tension that arises in such communities may be, to an important extent, internally generated.[3] Weber emphasized the individual-entrepreneurial aspect of Calvinism; Boyer and Nissenbaum in their study, and Swierenga in his, stress the communitarian and authoritarian side of the orthodox "Covenant." I argue that these opposing forces may be equally strong in such contractual communities.

In West Sayville it was possible to express the antagonism inherent in this contradiction through the factionalization that the Dutch call *verzuiling*, or "pillarization" (Goudsblom 1967, 118–19): a vertical

alignment along theological lines which obviates horizontal stratification by class (as culturally recognized realities). Thus most mani-
festations of modernity could be converted into repetitive, ritualized
conflict involving moral rather than financial resources.[4] These battles
were evidently far more appealing to the immigrants than the confrontations of unionization and strike, which were not only more dangerous in an economic sense but failed to disguise the ambivalence
members of the Dutch community may have felt about the industrialization of oystering. If they sympathized with their Yankee neighbors'
resistance to the encroaching enclosures, they also entertained visions
of themselves advancing in and with the industry. This "pillarization"
of West Sayville was specifically religious, but it was necessarily linked
to a conceptual framework that prevaded other realms of experience
and interaction.

THE CONTRACTUAL IDIOM

Such expressed conceptual frameworks may play a particularly central
role in the maintenance of the culture of the contractual community.
To bring anthropology once again to Weber's aid, we can argue that
in having denied men ritual the Protestant Reformation (in some of
its incarnations at least) condemned them to a life of theologizing. The
moral order, everybody's business now, required constant expression,
not alone in the specifically religious arena, but also throughout social
relations. In such communities is needed a conceptual language which
implies that there is no contradiction between the entrepreneurial,
egocentric individual and the authoritarian community.

    Such a moral language can be designated by the word "idiom" as
employed by anthropologist Evans-Pritchard in several classic studies
of African peoples (Evans-Pritchard 1936, 1940, 1954). In writing of
the Nuer of the southern Sudan, for example, he stressed the importance of a "lineal idiom"; social behavior was always spoken of as if it
followed a moral order based on the principles of lineage fission and
fusion.[5] Personal and political realities were conceptually and verbally
adjusted to fit this order. The village community, for example, was
represented by the Nuer, to themselves and to the inquiring anthropologist, as if composed of the members of a single lineage. The bald
fact that only a small percentage of any given community's membership was so comprised did nothing to shake the Nuer's adherence to

his ideology, for all nonlineal attachments could be explained as exceptions to the rule, arising from particular contingencies. In this way the moral order was maintained on the conceptual level, through invocation in specific instances. The Nuer, like the rest of us, like to believe that their social order is ultimately rooted in morality, even if, again like us, that morality is honored most often in the breach. Though he never gives the term a specific theoretical sense, Evans-Pritchard uses "idiom" in these cases to indicate a way of perceiving and speaking about the world by reference to a set of such related key concepts, which, when so used, lend an apparent coherence to lived experience even as they allow a degree of latitude to the individual.

Evans-Pritchard's ethnographic correction of Durkheim hearkens back, in fact, to an older, more concrete tradition of French social thought, one which began with Montesquieu and reached its empirical zenith in Tocqueville's *Democracy in America* (1945).[6] During his extended visit to America in the 1830s, Tocqueville searched for the moral basis of the new democratic culture, not only in such formal pronouncements as the Declaration of Independence but also in the actual use of moral concepts in everyday life. Throughout his "fieldwork," he showed an awareness of the cultural significance of ways of talking about the social world that comes close to Evans-Pritchard's sense of the term "idiom." His discussion of the persistence of individualistic explanations of behavior in American parlance is particularly interesting in this regard. In perfect inversion of Evans-Pritchard's Nuer, the Americans, Tocqueville observed, were unwilling to believe that they ever acted in any way other than in their own self-interest. That is because their notion of the social order was one of "voluntary association" founded on the principle that no contradiction need exist between enlightened self-interest and the commonweal. To use Weber's language, while the Nuer's "traditional" idiom masked any "rational" behavior, in America the "rational" moral idiom may have similarly masked "traditional" behavior. In America, the rational was the moral.

Tocqueville's observations, and our theoretical extension of them here, are relevant to the case of West Sayville. The communal culture of West Sayville was not exotic by American standards, but may be taken as an epitomization of certain key features of American culture. The Hollanders issued, after all, from a religious tradition closely akin to that of the Puritan New Englanders, and to the Anglo-Americans of Long Island's southern shore their new Dutch neighbors appeared like visitors from their own past, an extreme embodiment of their own ideals. Life within the well-defined boundaries of that community reveals the "idiom" we speak of in action. In keeping with the cultural definition of the community as a voluntary association, the life of West Sayville seems to have been pervaded by what I will call a "contractual idiom": a tendency to speak about all social relationships as if they were voluntarily entered into by free individuals. This idiom had its religious version, of course, in the Covenant, but its penetration into the many realms of social relations in West Sayville emerges in our exploration of life on and off the water and testifies to its general and central cultural significance. If that pervasiveness is a general characteristic of the modern world, as so many have argued, then its clear and extreme manifestation within such a small compass is the more interesting.

We begin with a view of the village today which both acquaints us with its feel and character and leads us to inquire into its historical roots. The following three chapters tell of the immigrant path that led the first Hollanders to their new home, and of the rise of the Dutch-American maritime community through the decades of rapid social change after the Civil War. The remainder of the book amounts to an ethnography of turn-of-the-century West Sayville, thematically organized around the conflicts of shorefront and church. Although somewhat frozen in time in order to discover the interrelations of daily life, the ethnographic portrait of West Sayville is by no means meant to convey a sense of stasis. Those were dynamic times, through which much of this nation was changing radically, and in this study of one small community we offer a lens for examining those transformations as lived by a particularly intriguing group of Americans: the "Dutchmen" of West Sayville.

1

WEST SAYVILLE TODAY

As the sun casts its first full light over the rolling waters, Marinus cuts the engine in the *Otis G* and strolls forward toward the bow. From this vantage he looks shoreward toward the landmarks whose positions relative to his boat tell him that he found his range. Below is the clam ground he has been working for several weeks now, ever since spring brought once more—perhaps for the last time—the urge to "follow the bay." Now it is nearly summer, and although the clam boats within sight are mostly familiar, it will not be long before the bay is crowded with all kinds of craft. "On some afternoons," Marinus likes to say, "you can just about walk across the bay to Fire Island and never get your feet wet." For the present, however, the bay is not yet choked with amateurs, and the soft lapping of the water against the boat's pitted flanks makes Marinus recall his earliest days on the water, when as a lad of ten he stood behind his father on the deck of the sloop *Cornelius,* feverishly pulling great oysters from the seaweed. Oysters then, clams now—but the work is not very different even if more than half a century has passed.

Like his father and grandfather before him, Marinus hoists the stout and work-smoothed poles of his "tongs." Sixteen feet each, they cross and end in metal teeth and baskets—a man's tool, and vastly superior in Marinus's view to the simple rake used by the less adept young men who call themselves "baymen." Leaning stiffly over the side of the boat, which is held in place by anchors allowing just enough movement on the water to work the grounds beneath, Marinus lowers the tongs through the shallow water to the sandy bottom and begins the laborious scissoring motion that pushes the toothed baskets toward one another. As they pass through the yielding sands the teeth gather clams, along with rocks and weeds, into the baskets. Having thus closed the baskets below and the poles above, he lifts the tongs over the side of the boat and dumps the contents on the deck. After several hours of repeating this maneuver and sorting the clams and debris, Marinus has filled two bushels and, putting his tongs back on their rack, turns the *Otis G* toward home.

A bit of breeze has blown up, and Marinus tacks his boat across the mildly chopping waters. Turning north and landward, Marinus's eyes rest on the gentle parklands and marshy streams off the port bow. Now county park and private school lands, these hundreds of acres have changed little since his father's time, when they were the back-yards of millionaires like Vanderbilt, Bourne, and Hard. The scene changes radically where the park ends. Here, where West Avenue comes down to the bay, begins West Sayville. It is a shoreline that bespeaks industry rather than leisure; a series of rambling frame build-ings line the coast, behind them crate-stacked loading docks, and before them bulwark-enclosed harbors. Each watery corral is home to one or several rather ugly but utilitarian metal hulks: dredging boats, or "drudges" as Marinus calls them. It is curious that such a boat and the *Otis G* could be after like prey, but that is the nature of the fishing industry, where the most ancient and modern of technologies may compete in the same waters.

Having passed the row of shipping companies, Marinus turns his boat into Green's Creek, the eastern boundary of West Sayville. In this reedy waterway too, man has improved on nature, for the narrow channel has been dredged out on several occasions over the past cen-tury. Inside its confines are moored dozens of clam boats more or less similar to the *Otis G*. Each of these inauspicious and ungraceful craft boasts a simple engine (inboard or outboard), a deck clear for working that sits sometimes only inches above the waterline, and some sort of one-man pilot house. Since clamming has attracted an increasingly large number of amateurs, some of the boats seem a bit makeshift, looking not unlike children's play rafts oddly sporting misplaced out-houses. But most of these simple businesslike craft are appealing for that very reason. Like the bustling shipping companies, they seem to mark a community with a more serious attitude toward the water than is evidenced in most of Long Island's pleasure-boat choked harbors.

Having tied up, Marinus—a sprightly seventy—hops onto the dock and walks slowly but purposefully up to a waiting group of fellow clammers. Some of these older gents have since retired, but they still make it their business to bicycle or walk to the shore daily. Conversation always begins with the amount "gotten" and proceeds to the weather and bottom conditions, where others clammed, what they got, and where Marinus should try next. They comment on the amateurs' ignorance of nature and of the unspoken laws of the water. "Why, Peter was tellin' me," offered old Cornelius, "that he broke down out by the West Channel—the engine just quit on him—and one of them speedboatin' clammers raced right on by. Didn't stop and give help. Now that's the law of the water. You got to stop and help the other fellow on the bay. Many's the time I gave up a good day's work pulling in some fellow broke down out there. You did too, Marinus." "Yes," Marinus replies, warming to the well-worn subject. "Well, times have changed. When did you have to take your tongs home with you in the old days? Why, you'd have to be crazy to leave 'em out on your boat now. If it's not nailed down they'll steal it, and if it is, they may anyhow."

Close by, the dock is now crowded with many men—some of them the sort suspected of the nefarious deeds, but many of them the sons, nephews, and cousins of Marinus, Cornelius, and the others. Thick-muscled and very often blond, these younger men sell their bushels of clams to the same buyers the old do, and if they are not as concerned with seagoing manners, they are just as anxious about the price of clams and their likely whereabouts. The day's clamming completed and the bivalves sold, the men stow their tongs and climb into their cars, whether old black Chevrolet or bubble-windowed, metallic blue supervan, and drive the short distance to home.

West Sayville is a very small town. West and Atlantic avenues run a half mile or so up from the shorefront to Montauk Highway, main street of this and most other South Shore towns. Several avenues run north another mile or so, perpendicular to the highway. These, and the smaller connecting roads, comprise the village. The streets are lined by closely placed wood-frame houses, most of them of modest proportions and nearly all of them neatly kept and well shaded by large maples or locusts.

The parents and grandparents of Marinus, Cornelius, and the others settled this village in the years between 1865 and the turn of the century. Oysterers, fishermen, farmers, and gardeners, these Dutch men and women had come to seize an opportunity not usually available to immigrants—to follow their old-country work in America. Wedged between the great estates of Oakdale and the village of Sayville, West Sayville (first called Tuckertown and Greenville) was a veritable Dutch colony. Little seems to be left of that Dutchness now. Generally proud of being American, the people of West Sayville do not trouble themselves with tulip festivals. On no occasion do bonneted maidens clomp the tarmac in wooden shoes, nor are the local shops hung with Edam cheese. In short, nothing here proclaims the hamlet's ethnic character, save perhaps the enigmatic legend gracing the volunteer fire house which reads "The Flying Dutchmen."

Yet the life on the bay has brought with it a basic continuity that seems to define the community in time and space. Perhaps the Dutchness of West Sayville persists at a more subtle level: in a world view that lies behind the bustle of the shorefront. The old men do refer to their ancestral nationality in stereotypes of self: "A Dutchman will turn a nickel three times" or "A Dutchman will work harder than ten men."

John is certainly such a worker. On a late August afternoon he sits with a group of friends under the massive maple that spreads in front of his rambling yellow house on West Avenue, close to the shore. He is a massive young man, thick-necked and barrel-chested, the sort of fellow that old Marinus remembers as more commonly found in the inevitably heroic bygone days, "The kind of man," he recalls, "that could lift one of them great barrels of oysters just like that and set it down on the old cart like it weighed nothing at all." Now John's huge and calloused hands do the delicate job of readying his nets for the coming season's eeling.

In September he will build his eel trap in the muddy shallows just off the bay shore a bit west of home, and it takes all John's formidable strength to set it. Standing in his small boat, he pounds a series of stout wooden poles, each about twelve feet long, into the soft bottom. The set poles form a line about one hundred feet long, perpendicular to the shore, ending in a ring of poles at the deep end. On these stakes John hangs the sturdy net so that it forms a wall of mesh and then a circle, a trap to enclose hapless eels by the thousands. John is one of the last eelers using these "eel pounds," as they are called, on the Great South Bay.

There's one fellow out in Moriches, and maybe another to the west, but I'm not sure if he's still at it. It does well for me. My grandfather Pieter set eel pound nets with his partners back around the turn of the century. My father, who's also called Pieter, followed him in that business. I followed my father, and now my young son is learning to help me. But it's a hard job, and I must do the setting myself. In a good year I may get ten, even twenty, thousand pounds of eels. I keep them in boxes under the water, and though I'll lose a few that way, most will live until a trucker from Babylon buys them in December. He takes them live in his tank truck to Kennedy airport, where an airplane takes them right over to Hamburg, Germany. That's who buys the eels today mostly—Germans and some other Europeans. In the old days the Italians used to come out from the city before Christmas and buy most of them. That was their big Christmas food, I guess—eels. The people around here ate them too. There used to be a lot of smoked-eel stands all around here, little sheds with a string of smoked eels hangin' up like laundry in front of them. People don't seem to eat much eel here anymore though, so they mostly go to Germany and other countries.

Across the Great South Bay from West Sayville and John's eel nets stretches the great barrier beach called Fire Island. A summer playground for millions, the island has a different meaning to the baymen of West Sayville, protecting the relatively calm and less salty waters of the bay from the open sea beyond. Not all the sons of West Sayville have kept to the bay, however, and through the years a number of seagoing families have trawled or otherwise fished in the Atlantic. Leonard still does. He and his brother run a fishing company, whose ocean "pound nets" are some of the last of their kind on the East Coast of the United States. Huge versions of John's eel trap, the ocean pound net stretches on huge hydraulically-set poles, ending in a circle of net that must be lifted by engine power.

Leonard's ninety-four-year-old great uncle Aage began the company in 1912 with his younger brother. Today Aage no longer ventures out on the ocean waters, but lives quietly with his wife. Born and raised in Friesland, a northern province in the Netherlands, his voice rumbles with the heavy accent of the old country. Aage's still-square shoulders and fiercely piercing blue eyes do not belie the strength of body and character once well renowned in West Sayville and in ports beyond. "Mine brudder and I worked so that we could get always a bigger boat. We had the second engine-powered sloop in West Sayville. We'd catch fish out there and run them into the Fulton Market, but prices were bad, and we were told that the fishing was better up in Nantucket— so we sailed up there and fished for ten years." Asked about the music or folklore of fishing, Aage replies, "We were too busy working." *"Frisia non cantata,"* as Tacitus long ago observed.

In all these pursuits, the technology has changed with the times,

and yet one is struck by the still-elemental quality of the contest between man and nature and by the apparent continuities of life-style
spanning the last century. Alone or in small groups, the West Sayville
baymen wrest eel, fish, or clams from the waters around them in ways
strikingly similar to those of their fathers and grandfathers.

The lives of the women have changed more over the years, however. The immigrant woman's childhood came to an early end. As a
girl, she helped her mother tend to the chores of caring for a typically
large family. Later she might go into "service," working as a maid or
housekeeper for any of the more prosperous Yankee families in the
area, or on the estates of the wealthy New Yorkers that summered on
the bay. Otherwise, there was the backaching work of the lace mill in
Patchogue, where many girls from the age of fourteen or so would
spend their days bent over yards of lace cloth, looking for deformities
in the weave. When a girl was married, if further outside work could
be avoided, she would devote her labors to her own household. Today
the mills have long since closed, nobody goes into service, and families,
here as elsewhere, tend to be smaller. Household work has changed,
and those women who work outside the home find kinds of employment very different from that of their mothers and grandmothers.

The character of West Sayville as a distinct community in touch
with its own past rests on more than the continuity of work. There are
institutions that frame the interaction of men and women, drawing
them toward one another and away from outsiders. Of these institutions, the most important are the Reformed churches. The Dutch
immigrants brought with them more than a predilection for things
maritime. They were Reformed Christians, some of them seceders from
the liberalizing established church in Holland and nearly all of them
religious in a personal as well as communal way. In each of the homes
of the fishermen we have met sits a huge bronze-clasped Bible. Brought
by their forefathers from the Netherlands, these massive tomes bear
the Scriptures in bold Dutch print and list, on the inside covers, chron-
icles of the family: births, marriages, and deaths. The first entries are
from Bruinisse or Yerseke; the most recent might record births in
Grand Rapids, Paterson, or West Sayville. In their youth the old men
and women of West Sayville heard their fathers read daily from the
Testaments, and most older folk remember spending the greater part
of their Sundays in one or the other of the two community churches,
listening to lengthy services in Dutch or English.

Though not as strong a secular force as they once were, the churches continue to play an unusually prominent role in the lives of many West Sayville people. Not only do most people attend church regularly, but the Christian Reformed families especially are accustomed to the regular visits of their pastor. Church-sponsored organizations enjoy the membership of many age-groups and thus continue to some extent the traditional role of the Reformed church as custodian of all social interaction. One still meets the occasional austerely Christian elder who reads the story of his own life by reference to the exploits of Old Testament prophets, not hesitating to credit business success to the will of Providence.

Then there is the volunteer fire department: ubiquitous symbol of small-town America. Since the 1890s "The Flying Dutchmen" have met in the firehouse to joke and talk in a manner reminiscent of men's associations all over the world. Fighting fires is serious business, of course, but much energy is devoted to preparation for battles of a more symbolic nature. In the still summer nights one hears the roaring of engines and screeching of brakes as the hook-and-ladder team practices in the school yard for one of an endless series of tournaments: hard-fought bouts of masculine fortitude pitting the honor of West Sayville against that of neighboring and distant communities. The importance of social bonds forged in this association are easy for outsiders to underestimate. The fire department not only offers a visible symbol of community where other symbols are now hard to find, it also defines the community in an essentially open way, for even if the organization is called "The Flying Dutchmen," there are quite a few more recent arrivals among its members. The outsider who has moved into West Sayville has in the fire department perhaps the best and easiest route into the community.

Thus framed and isolated by description, West Sayville seems the embodiment of a nearly lost American dream. Two of our most sacred mythic self-visions are rediscovered here: the "community" whose loss sociologists so often bemoan, and the equally beloved "rugged individual." Bound by a shared experience and understanding, and by the institutions of work, church, and voluntary association, the people of West Sayville seem to constitute a real community. There are clearly insiders and outsiders, and among those who are defined as members there is a sense in which individuals define themselves in terms of what they share with their fellows.

As for individualism, who better realizes our dream vision than Marinus, who in his seventies still stands and works alone on the deck of his own boat, or John, ramming stakes into the muddy bay bottom? Such men seem cut from the pioneer mold, but they are also entrepreneurs risking capital and labor in search of honest profit. All began with nothing, or nearly nothing, and through their own work reached whatever plateau of worldly success their efforts allowed. By some accounts the smart and industrious became shippers, and the best of them became the richest. If even the most successful of the entrepreneurs remained within the moral community and thus subject to the egalitarian controls of the democratic Dutch churches, and to the censure and approbation of valued neighbors, there is here the ideal America writ small: a small-town democracy composed of neighborly, God-fearing individualists.

While it is not my intention to dispel this idealization totally, I must through the following pages relate matters that detract from the naively harmonious and insulated character I have thus far attributed to the community. If, however, the actual character of life is thus less perfect than I have so far indicated, it is also somewhat more interesting and instructive, for if the ideal West Sayville approaches the ideal America, perhaps the real West Sayville may shed some light on the real America.

We may begin by widening our field of vision. The modern village of West Sayville exists at the sufferance of the surrounding social world. In search of another American dream, many hundreds of thousands of urbanites have crowded onto Long Island over the past half-century, and especially since the conclusion of World War II. The newer residents compete in countless ways with such old-timers as the West Sayville Dutch, for their interests and values are often at variance. Their very numbers threaten the baymen's life in a fundamental way, for the sandy soils of Long Island cannot contain the sewage of these millions, leaving it to seep into the bay. Each year larger areas of the bay are closed to clammers by government officials and their "polluted" clams declared unmarketable. While they may vent their frustration on these officials, most of the baymen know the real culprit.

The social integrity of West Sayville is equally at peril. Although its very smallness has saved the hamlet from becoming "a reluctant surburb," to use Dobriner's (1960) apt sobriquet, West Sayville may be justly compared to the famous village of Dutch folklore. Here the dike is built of social and cultural bricks, and the sea beyond is of new people and often unwelcome values. There are breaks in that seawall, of course, the most obvious being the arrival of new families even within the confines of West Sayville's quiet old streets.

"We used to call Rollstone Avenue 'Van Essendelft Boulevard,' " one resident of that street remarked, "because so many houses were of that family—all the families were Dutch then—and I can remember lying in bed at night and ticking off the families in my head one by one: Van Essendelft, Ver Schuur, Ockers. And I could name them all up one side of the street and down the other, and I knew all those people. Now there are families moved in here, I don't even know their names, I don't know anything about them." There is in this old man's words an element of xenophobia, the fear of strangers we all expect from the small town here or abroad. There is more to it than that, though, for behind the words lies the pain in a perceived loss of community, of the security that comes with simply knowing the world you live in and relying on a certain expectable run of behavior within it.

More insidious are the transgressions of values and perceptions. The Christian Reformed congregation sends many of their children to a local Christian school, and a fair number of young adults from both Dutch churches attend either Hope College or Calvin College, schools founded and maintained by the Dutch Reformed and Christian Reformed churches in the Dutch-American region of Michigan. Most attend the local secular high school, however, and the experiences of life have thrown the young people into contact with outsiders with increasing frequency since World War II. A man in his fifties today remembers the transitionary period in his own life:

When I was a small boy, I wasn't allowed even into Sayville on my own. According to my mother it was "Sin City," a place with bars and evil men. When I went away in the war, I met a lot of different people—Catholics and Jews, the kinds of people I never knew here. Even though there were some Catholics around, we never really knew them. Through some friends, I met the woman I eventually married—she's a Catholic—and I brought her back here to West Sayville. Life was difficult for us. People I knew wouldn't speak to me, and some of them still don't. They're not all like that, though. There are some real mavericks around here too, people who don't care what the others think and take a man for what he's worth.

Such ostracism came to many who crossed cultural boundaries. Uglier still was the period in the 1920s when many in West Sayville,

as in communities across America, focused their fears on the chimera
of un-Americanism and papal plots. Some local men donned white
sheets and marched through the woods of central Long Island to attend
Klan meetings in Huntington. "We were told to take different paths
through the woods. You see, the Catholics were supposed to be lying
in wait for us, and that way they wouldn't discover our route." A few
crosses were even burned on the local lawns. This particularly virulent
period did not last long, and the spirit of ecumenicism and tolerance
is far greater today than in the past. Still, a sense of internal cohesion
is to some extent purchased at the price of external enemies, real or
imagined.

Even the internal harmony of the community is illusory. Just
beyond the shipping companies on the shorefront stands a large barn-
like structure, the meetinghouse of the Independent Baymen's Association. As the existence of this institution shows, if the founders of
the companies have risen from their ranks, this does not mean that
interests do not separate those Dutchmen from others of their compatriots. In the last century the so-called independent baymen worked
part of the year for the shippers and certainly found themselves less
than independent in their control over working conditions. Today, although they work for themselves, the independent baymen still compete with the companies for the rights to the precious bay grounds.
Founded by two tough-minded clammers in the 1930s, the association
has fought before local government bodies and judges for increased
or continued access to the public, open grounds on which their livelihood depends. The shippers are wont to point out that the danger of
overfishing is controlled only on the "private property," or leased grounds
managed by their large companies. It is a fundamental battle which,
though over a century old, shows no signs of abating.

Other divisions run through the community. Though not as sharply
divided as they were many decades ago, the two congregations represent two traditions of Reformed Christianity not altogether approving
of each other's theology and practice. Within each congregation, and
within each of the associations that have characterized life in the
community, the very individualism we have noted has often expressed
itself in willful assertion and stubborn animosity. The sovereign individual does not easily or peacefully submit to communal censure, or
any embodied authority. "These Dutchmen are a very stubborn bunch,"
remarked one elderly and very Christian man. "It's hard for them to

get along. It's hard for one man to take orders from another, on the water or anywhere else."

Yet these conflicts, external and internal, are by no means inimical to the existence of a strongly bonded community. The perception of external, hostile forces naturally draws people together, but even the deep-seated conflicts arising from the very character of life within West Sayville may contribute to its integration. There is a tendency among social scientists, as well as others, to equate community with cooperation, but there is such a thing as a "community of confrontation." As Simmel (1955) realized, conflict of the sort that characterized life within West Sayville—the theological debates of church factions, for example—has an integrative function, for in the course of the struggle there is a public affirmation of the basic values that lie behind the disagreements.

Thus the essential harmonies and disharmonies of life are not, however we might wish to construe them so, solely the result of recent changes wrought by the collapse or slow disintegration of a mythically peaceful and traditional small town. Rather, they are largely inherent in the structure of relations within the community. The character of that community may be understood as the response of a particular social form to a particular niche in the American landscape and society. As with other immigrant groups in America, the Dutch of West Sayville are today the outcome of a continuously changing adaptation to an equally dynamic environment. The cultural heritage from which that adaptation originated is rooted in foreign soils: in the sandy lowlands of Zeeland, themselves often wrested from the sea.

2

THE IMMIGRANTS

In the month of May, 1849, my parents, Cornelius Hage, and a brother-in-law, Cornelius DeWaal, decided to take the journey to America. They took their family of four children each, not thinking of the hardships and privations they would meet and the heartaches they were to undergo. This always interested me, when so many years after, they would talk it over and I would listen and say nothing and wonder if it were possible when one would say "do you remember so and so" and "I wonder if this one or that one is still living" and what to them at that time was sorrowful as joy and merriment now.

So begins Almina Hage Terry's account of her family's odyssey, and so also the story of West Sayville. Although two other Dutch families were already resident in the woodland of central Long Island, it was the Hages and DeWaals who first sought settlement on the shore of the Great South Bay, beginning the relation of water and people that was to shape the fate of both for decades to come. By 1860 the census lists just under a hundred Dutch men, women, and children in the Sayville area. Large families and several spates of fresh immigrant families brought the number of Hollanders (including the offspring of immigrants born in America) to something like 600 by the turn of the century. By 1910, local newspaper estimates put the population of a still almost totally Dutch West Sayville at around 1,200, after which time immigration steadily slowed until nearly cut off by new American laws in 1922.

The growth of the Dutch community in West Sayville will be taken up in the following chapters; we must begin here with more fundamental questions. Who were these early immigrants who in many ways would set the pattern of life for those who would follow, and why did they leave Holland? Answers must be sought in both the objective conditions obtaining in Holland at the time of the first departures and in the words—such as we are fortunate enough to still have—of the immigrants themselves.

Certainly there is much in Almina's story that is familiar. How many of us have no ancestor among the 35 million souls that came from Europe to America in the century following 1820? In his classic account of this mass movement of humanity, Oscar Handlin (1951) emphasized the uniformity of the European immigrant experience. The story, as he tells it, is one of universal human alienation. Each wayfarer, driven by poverty and the threat of starvation, uprooted himself, very much against his will, from family and village—a world of egalitarian and kinship values—only to find himself thrust into an alien, topsy-turvy existence. Whether settled finally in the chaos of the urban East or the isolation of the rural West, Handlin argued that the immigrant confronted utterly novel circumstances demanding radically new strategies for survival and success.

It is true that the various immigrant groups experienced much in common. Handlin's depiction of extreme uniformity, however, as well as his underlying theory of social and cultural change, have been justly questioned.

Patterns of rural life in nineteenth-century Europe were, in important respects, quite variable. The large agro-town of the Mediterranean, for example, with its urban orientation and patron-client relations, encompassed a set of economic and social institutions and an ethos quite different from those of the Serbian Zadruga, the Scandinavian farmstead, or the west Irish hamlet. Not only did the motives for emigration vary according to these local circumstances, but so did the manner in which that step was undertaken, and the kind of cultural perceptions immigrants were likely to bring to their American adventure.

Despite the novelty of the American environment, the immigrant experience here has never been one in which the Old World culture was merely shrugged off, like an old and tattered coat, in favor of a bright new American one, better suited to the rigors of the New World. Culture, no matter how that term is defined, is worn a good deal closer to the skin. Insofar as relatively few immigrants of any nationality found themselves totally isolated in a sea of Americans, there developed ethnic settlements which, if nothing else, typically perpetuated language usage (in varying degrees) for some years. Within those languages lived a variety of perceptions, attitudes, and categories through which even the most novel of circumstances were interpreted and judged. The degree to which European attitudes and institutions did not fit new situations depended to a large extent on the precise nature of the local conditions to which the immigrants adapted. The social organization of work, for example, might make the "padrone" as useful in the American construction business as in the quarries of Sicily. Even the structure of familial relations might persist through taking on new functions (see, e.g., Yans-McLaughlin 1977).

We need a model of European immigrants which takes into consideration the fundamental ethos and key institutions of the newcomers and attends to their "fit" in particular environments. On both ends of this equation the mid-century Dutch settlers were in some ways very like those from other areas in western Europe, and in some ways peculiar. The personal accounts of Hage and DeWaal's journey may lead us further in such matters. Hage's daughter, Almina, continues:

ECONOMIC FACTORS LEADING TO EMIGRATION

In the year 1849, crops had been very poor in Bruinisse, the little town in Holland where my parents were born. Farmers and people in general were aware of the fact that times would be much harder than they had been, and something must be done to alleviate the suffering.

The hard times referred to in Almina's account were widespread in Europe. A general economic depression had followed the conclusion of the Napoleonic Wars, and the effects were felt throughout the continent. Distress in peripheral regions was particularly acute, however, and while poverty may have been common, seasoned travelers had no trouble distinguishing levels of destitution. The situation in Ireland, for example, contrasts significantly with that in Holland. Sir Walter Scott's observations of the former unhappy land in 1825 are typical:

Their poverty is not exaggerated; it is on the extreme verge of human misery; their cottages would scarce serve as pig-styes . . . and their rags seem the very refuse of rag-shop . . . then for their food, they have only potatoes, and too few of them. (Anderson 1972, 1)

When those potatoes Scott speaks of rotted in the earth with the great blight that began in 1845, the position of the already marginal peasants

became more than desperate. Even so, it was not so much their extreme poverty that led millions of Irish to seek American shores as
their landlords' boot. Changes in the international market had made
stock-raising more attractive, with the result that large landowners
began to see their lease-holding peasantry as an impediment to modernization. Thousands of Irish cotters were accordingly cleared off the
land, making way for cattle as their Scottish cousins had for sheep.
In eastern Europe the capitalization of farming had similar results,
dislocating massive numbers of peasants who were then forced to seek
employment in the cities or emigrate.

The situation in the more economically central regions of Europe
was somewhat different. In England, France, Belgium, and Holland,
the decades following the conclusion of the Napoleonic Wars saw rising
competition in internal industrial development and for the control of
overseas markets. Long a trading nation, the Netherlands had lagged
behind Belgium and England in manufacturing, and in the 1830s and
1840s found itself inundated with foreign goods. Failed local industries
and various state economic and military ventures steadily increased
the tax burden on the considerable numbers of farm laborers and
unskilled workers.

Whatever the picture elsewhere in Holland, that part of Zeeland
which was home to the early immigrants (see Figure 2) had by the
1840s made a specialized maritime adaptation. Hage and DeWaal's
Bruinisse, for example, although rural and insular and—like much of
the province of Zeeland—somewhat culturally isolated from the cosmopolitan seaboard to its north, was hardly the classic peasant community depicted by Handlin. From at least the seventeenth century,
Bruinisse was one of the most active fishing communities in a shéll-
fishing region dominated by the market in Zierikzee. The entire
Oosterschelde estuary was home to banks of natural oysters and mussels, and their harvesting had been for centuries a local subsistence
and market pursuit. No less than thirty mussel sloops fished the mussel
banks close to Riemerswaal in the second half of the seventeenth
century, taking approximately 200 tons of the shellfish each day. Oysters, too, were to be had in local waters, particularly off Yerseke, where
Bruinisse fishermen competed with others from the many estuarine
communities in the area (van Ysseldijk 1973, 487ff.).

Local entrepreneurs among the region's shellfishers, however,
were by the eighteenth century no longer relying on the supply of
local natural growth oysters. In Zierikzee and Bruinisse, where harbor

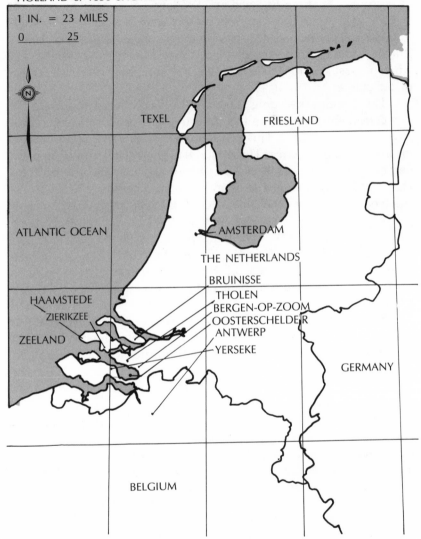

HOLLAND c. 1850 SHOWING TOWNS IN ZEELAND

1 IN. = 23 MILES

0   25

N

TEXEL   FRIESLAND

ATLANTIC OCEAN   AMSTERDAM

THE NETHERLANDS

BRUINISSE

THOLEN

HAAMSTEDE   BERGEN-OP-ZOOM

ZIERIKZEE   OOSTERSCHELDE R

ZEELAND   ANTWERP

YERSEKE

GERMANY

BELGIUM

Figure 2. Map of The Netherlands, circa 1850, Showing Zeeland Villages

facilities were adequate, enterprising locals imported thousands of tons of young oysters from England and Scotland each year. One-year-old "breed" and two-to-three-year-old oysters were replanted in beds out in the estuary or in enclosed "pits" in the harbor area. These replanted British oysters were believed to grow faster in Zeeland waters, and when harvested in the fall and winter they brought profits in the active oyster market.

The decades preceding Hage and DeWaal's decision to emigrate saw considerable growth in this industry, but with a concomitant increase in competition and in the distance separating the various classes involved in the fisheries. Those who had the capital and equipment necessary to farm British oysters as well as catch and market local shellfish favored national legislation which, beginning in 1805, restricted the pursuit to Zeelanders and thus excluded the Belgian competition. While less well endowed local fishermen in the various Oosterschelde communities were happy enough to see such "foreigners" excluded from their banks, those who hailed from towns like Yerseke, with rich banks just off shore, wanted to see access yet more restricted, for they were no happier to see fishermen from neighboring Zeeland communities on "their grounds" than they were to find "Brabanters stealing mussels" there. Thus, when the fishermen of Tholen sailed onto Yerseke grounds in 1837, they were met by a fleet of angry local skippers. A mini naval battle ensued in which, the report states, "the Tholen men had guns" (van Ysseldijk 1973, 493). Yerseke itself, however, had been the subject of a series of complaints from representatives of surrounding communities. Some of the Yersekers were evidently happy enough to come to personal terms with the outlawed Belgians, allowing the outsiders to catch mussels on Yerseke banks in return for buying the local catch as well (van Ysseldijk 1973, 491–92). There were also those Zeelanders who, although without the means to become proper fishermen, depended for part of their subsistence on mussels and oysters gathered by hand from the dikes and exposed tidal flats just off the shore. Their major fear was exclusion from this very limited harvest through either the removal of those shellfish banks from the public domain or the constant rise of government licensing fees. Not only did such a boatless "gatherer" have to pay three florins in 1830 for the same license required of a sloop-skipper, but his accessibility while scurrying along the dikes and harbor flats for shellfish made him a far easier target for the law than the skipper afloat out on the estuary (van Ysseldijk 1973, 492).

The gradual depletion of natural beds of shellfish, and the usual fluctuations of weather and market, took their cumulative toll on the fishery. While the larger skippers and shippers had more capital at risk, they were less vulnerable to variations in price and supply that might ruin the marginal fisherman or "gatherer." For the poorer classes life became increasingly difficult after 1840. A contemporary report for Yerseke in 1841 reads:

This was a bad year with bad consequences around here. Fishing, mainly for oysters and mussels is an important part of the living—and this was a bad year. Most of the oysters were frozen in winter, so little or none were caught. The people hope it will get better, but poverty is widespread. (Van Ysseldijk 1973, 497)

The European potato famine of 1845 and 1846 added further hardships, once again especially for the marginal classes who depended on them for subsistence. Already driven onto public assistance through high prices and taxation, the poor now found themselves with only turnips and cauliflower to eat. In many parts of Holland, riots in bakeshops and granary break-ins followed, and in Zeeland the ranks of the dependent poor swelled. While some good shellfishing years followed, the undependability of the market, coupled with the undoubtedly shrinking supply of local shellfish and the constant competition of locals and outsiders, brought many to the point of considering emigration.

No doubt anxious to shorten the welfare rolls, the Dutch government looked into the possibility of sending emigrants to the Dutch colony of Surinam in South America. Some took that route, but typically with disastrous results. Further suggestions of settlement in the Dutch East Indies, a region equally inhospitable to Northern European agriculture, met with little enthusiasm. Dutch eyes then began to turn to a land to which a small but steady number of emigrants had been going over the past several decades, a land with which the Dutch had long been familiar and in which they had sometimes prospered: America.

If the push of economic disaster was strong enough for some, it certainly was not sufficient to propel the multitudes, as was the case in contemporary Ireland and Germany. Nor was massive eviction the rule, as in those less fortunate nations. As Swierenga and Stout (1976, 299) note, the very smallness of the number of Dutch emigrants in these years, both absolute and as a proportion of the population, suggest that the compulsion to leave cannot have been so overwhelming.[1]

What of the pull to American shores? This is certainly a central theme in Almina's account. She goes on:

They had heard of the discovery of gold in California. In 1848, the cry was America, the land of wealth. The news flew in every direction.

Pamphlets described the possibilities offered by virgin farmlands cheap and ready for the plow in America's Midwest, and by mercantile markets in expanding cities. Though sometimes puffed up with exaggeration and outright lies, these leaflets were generally accurate. The United States was expanding agriculturally and industrially, and the emigrant would be in a position to take advantage of either—if he had the means to do so. By her memory, Almina's family was of that entrepreneurial temper which is willing to undertake risk for the proper reward. Certainly there were plenty of shellfish entrepreneurs at home in Zeeland as role models. This theme of self-improvement is one we shall hear reverberating down the decades in the history of West Sayville, and we do well to consider its roots in the very adventure of emigration. If to leave one's native land and community was such a terrible "uprooting" as Handlin's account would have it, why did families like the Hages and DeWaals choose to undertake it?

Almina continues:

Many tearful goodbyes were said, but their great desire to better themselves and their families gave them courage and perserverance. . . .

Go on they did, and through the typical harrowing series of storms and doldrums.

The ship tossed in its fury . . . sudden lurches made it uncertain whether their food was in their mouths or in their eyes.

Six weeks and many episodes later, the welcome sight of land was announced.

. . . After preliminary rules . . . passing the Doctor and Inspector, they at last arrived at Castle Garden which was then the landing place. . . . They were in America, the land of their dreams and ambitions.

RELIGIOUS MOTIVATIONS

Further motivations are revealed in the memories of another of West Sayville's earliest settlers, Bastiaan Broere, whose reminiscences were taken down by a friend. Broere, born in the Zeeland village of Yerseke, was more concerned with relating his religious experiences than the details of secular life—though the nature of his faith made that boundary difficult to draw. After a youth spent in anxious efforts to save himself through good works, Broere (1887, 2–4) had the obligatory transforming experience:

... Suddenly an unexpected and raging storm struck the house of my hopes and crashed it to the ground because this house had been built upon the sand. ... The words of Romans 3:20, "Therefore by the deed of the law there shall no flesh be justified in His sight," were shot into my soul as a bullet of lead. ... Gone was all my false confidence: vanished all my hope of salvation. ...

After fourteen days of following my ways as a wanderer driven forth by a storm, it was as though a voice called to me, "Look unto Me and be ye saved, all the ends of the earth, for I am God and there is none else [Isa. 45:22]." In my utter simplicity and ignorance of the Holy Scripture, I answered, "Who art Thou?" And again, I heard the voice, "I am the end of the law for anyone who believeth."

Oh how great a mercy was then poured into my soul for with that word the light of faith began to rise in my soul. ...

This intensely personal revelation did not, however, have the effect of isolating Broere from his fellow Christians:

Now I experienced a sincere attraction for God's children and I felt ... I was being drawn to them. Nor could I forego, tho' it be secretly, to follow them when they went to neighboring villages to hear Rev. Budding, van der Meulen, Line, and other preachers. ...

But Broere was far from being through his religious crisis, and his account goes on to tell of the battles between God and Satan fought with torturous effect over his soul. A great but, as the many pages of his saga reveal, far from final resolution of these difficulties came with a second epiphany:

Once more it pleased the Lord to heed my prayer and to fill my heart with his love and joy. Now I did not wish to delay, and in a short time I was accepted as a member of the Christian Reformed Church in Kruiningen by Rev. Gardener on confession of faith. Thereupon I consciously experienced the approval of God in the peace I enjoyed and in the partaking of the holy deeds vouchsafed to the church by the Lord. (Ibid., 8)

The religious perception of the world evinced in his account is of course a personal one, and indeed Broere may have been among the most pious of the early immigrants to Long Island. He was, however, hardly unique in the general character of this world view.

Along with its economic and political dislocations, Holland was, in the decades following the conclusion of the Napoleonic Wars, undergoing great religious upheaval. The spread of Napoleonic arms and influence had also brought an extention of the French enlightenment and the profoundly secular, rational view of the world it embodied. Under this influence, postwar Calvinism grew increasingly distant from the religiosity of the Reformation church. In Holland, as elsewhere, disseminators of this new essentially deist enlightenment religion saw themselves as the simple instructors of good morals. This change in theology was combined with a political reorganization of the institutional church. The original governing units of the church dating from the sixteenth century—parish, consistory, classes, provincial boards, and synods—were retained but were now controlled by the king through his annual appointment of a presiding officer over the national synod. Thus liberalization of church doctrine was combined with growing state absolutism (Lucas 1955, 42–43).

In the 1820s and early 1830s, several Dutch intellectuals came under the influence of a conservative reaction to the enlightenment church in Switzerland and Scotland. In their rekindled interest in the ascetism of the early orthodox Calvinist church, they were evidently returning to a faith that had never disappeared from large sections of the population. Henry S. Lucas, the authority on the religious roots of the Dutch emigration, tells us:

The common people in many parts of the Netherlands intently read the ancient authorities on Reformed theology, the *oude schrijvers* as they fondly called them. Devoutly they poured over the States' Bible, memorized the Heidelberg Catechism, and reverently sang the rhymed Dutch version of the Psalms. Their reading was in the books written by the school of theologians who drew their inspiration from Gijsbertus Voetius (1588–1676) who . . . advocated a puritanic conduct being opposed to dancing, theatres, overindulgence in eating and drinking, luxurious furnishings, attractive headgear, cosmetics, games of chance, the use of organs accompanying congregational singing and other practices. (Lucas 1955, 45)

While these sentiments and practices may have survived among portions of the population, including men like Bastiaan Broere, it required a number of strong organizational hands to marshal such individual predispositions into a religious-political movement challenging the very authority of the crown-controlled state church. Those hands were supplied by a number of young ministers fresh from university and led by Pieter Scholte. Beginning in 1834, Scholte, Hendrik DeCock, Antonie Brummelkamp, Simon Van Velzen, and Albertus Van Raalte, among others, each broke with the state church and led their congregations into secession. Together they formed the new "Christian Reformed Church" (*Christelijke Gereformeerde Kerk*), calling for a return to the basic doctrines of the old Reformed faith as stated in the Belgic confession, the Heidelberg Catechism, and the Canons of Dordrecht. Thus even as the Reformation of the sixteenth century was understood by its leaders to be a return to the basic Christianity of the time of Christ and the apostles, so these nineteenth-century reformers considered their movement to lead not forward but back to the Christianity of Calvin and the founders of the Reformed faith in Europe.

The king and the government, however, were not content to allow such a break with the state church and explicit challenge to their own authority. Meetings and services of the "seceders," as they became popularly known, were outlawed unless each meeting was petitioned for with a full list of intended participants and their purposes. Even when they did meet such conditions, these congregations were unable to function as true religious organizations, because they were forbidden to carry out any sacraments. If the religious sentiments of the seceders were widespread through the common people, there were also many who were distinctly averse to such religiosity. Not only were ministers harassed and arrested by government officials, but religious meetings were very often disrupted by crowds of stone- and abuse-hurling "worldlings." It was in this atmosphere of religious-political turmoil that Bastiaan Broere grew up in Zeeland, where van der Meulen, an important seceder minister, preached a return to a more puritan faith. Hearing him and others, Broere tells us, led him eventually into the Christian Reformed Church.

The seceder church did not remain an outlaw church; in 1846 it finally made its peace with the government. Broere's reaction to this is interesting:

I had always cherished a high admiration for these men whom I viewed as fathers in Christ endued with light and wisdom from God and ardently faithful in the carrying out of their pledges. But now I could not reconcile the fact that such men should lower themselves to ask an earthly king for pardon to worship God. It is very evident that this circumstance exercised a great influence upon my heart and mind to lead me to go to America as many others in that day were going. There, surely, for such were the reports, was freedom of worship, and many pious people had already gone there: Rev. Budding wrote a letter from America which was so enthusiastic that my heart opened up and I rejoiced over the prosperous condition in which the congregation there found itself, because it seemed to me that Netherland was falling away from the truth more and more and was forsaking God. This and this alone was the reason I felt moved to leave my fatherland. (Broere 1887, 8)

Could it have been that the legal acceptance of their church also inclined the leaders of the Christian Reform Church to emigration? A charisma that feeds on the opposition of the established order may have lost its glow in acceptance. Perhaps the ministerial leaders like Van Raalte and Scholte felt the need for a surrounding wilderness and in leading their flocks to the American frontier were replacing a secular enemy with a natural one. In any event, after their persecutions had ended, and in the face of a debilitated and declining economy, the leaders of the seceders began to look with favor on the prospect of going to America. In 1846 they began. Scholte led a party of nearly one thousand across the Atlantic and up the Mississippi to the plains of Iowa.[2] Van Raalte led his followers to western Michigan, where he was followed by van der Meulen and others.[3]

We have seen two important sources of the Dutch exodus to America: the economic and the religious. Much has been written by historians arguing the prominence of one or the other as a motivation for emigration. Such a question is certainly difficult, if not impossible, to answer. Even where their words and memories survive, which is rare enough, how can we gauge the conscious or unconscious motivations of these men and women? At best we have an indication of how a few of them may have viewed their own actions at a particularly retrospective stage in their lives. Moreover, the question of prominence of motivation is itself artificial and misleading, assuming as it does a clear distinction between economic and religious feelings. Although Broere talks about his "temporal" affairs as distinct from his religious motivation, his autobiography is quite thoroughly religious. Everything that happens to him—sacred or secular—is interpreted as the action of God or of Satan. In such a world view, as Weber (1958, 98–99) has taught us, the belief in predestination keeps people constantly searching for signs of their own salvation or election. Worldly success is just such a sign.

This connection between what Weber called "the Protestant Ethic" and the "spirit of capitalism" was true of Hollanders in the sixteenth century, and it was true again of their reawakened descendants three hundred years later. The coherence of at least these aspects of that world view is perhaps most concretely manifest in the lives of such ministerial migration leaders as Van Raalte and Scholte. While intent on leading their congregations into a wilderness safe from corrupting influences, these men were just as concerned with making the best possible purchase of land and with choosing settlement sites that afforded good trading possibilities. In West Sayville as well, concerns for salvation and entrepreneurial success were by no means perceived as antithetical. Broere, for one, strived hard for both.

ASSOCIATION

The Dutch immigrant, distinctive in his entrepreneurial and religious views, differed from most of the contemporary European immigrants in one other important respect. There was in Holland a long tradition of associational communities largely absent from other European nations. Even in the Middle Ages, organized associations were not limited in Holland to the familiar guilds but included rural communities organized for the purpose of reclaiming interior boglands for cultivation. More familiar are the communal enterprises of the coastland, where dikes were constructed and huge stretches of sea bottom laboriously taken into cultivation. Zeeland is particularly notable in this respect, more than half of it having been wrested from the sea. The notion of success is in that province's provincial motto: "Luctor et Emergo" (I strive and I rise) (Vlekke 1945).

In these social contexts, where communities were understood to be based on the contractual association of free agents, the theology of Calvinism was introduced. As church historian Ernst Troeltsch (1931, 590ff.) has pointed out, and as Broere illustrates in his memoir, the doctrines of the Reformed church taught that the elect should experience not only success at their callings, but also a compulsion to join with other Christians in the community—for the glory of God. This political dimension of Calvinism made sense in Holland, where associational communities were already a standard social form.

The nineteenth-century seceders also felt the necessity of practicing their reawakened faith in the company of like-minded individuals. Bastiaan Broere's memoirs are largely concerned with the discovery not only of his own religiosity but also of the properly religious community to practice it in. The leaders of the seceder church were not content to leave that search in the hands of their individual followers, however, and preferred to communalize the immigrant enterprise from the start. Van Raalte, for example, organized the *Christenen voor de Nederlandsche Landverhuizing naar de Bereenigde Staten van Noord-Amerika* (Rules for the Society of Christians for the Holland Emigration to the United States of North America), so that membership was open to any man twenty years of age regardless of income. The society consisted of two committees, one in Holland and one in America. Concerned with more than the moral state of the proposed American colony, it was a central purpose of this organization to buy land collectively, in order to keep the colony together and to prevent the location of outsiders within communal bounds. This notion of a community as much more than a loose association of neighbors is typical of the seceder movement, as is the formalization of associational bonds through economic and political confederation. Financed by gifts and land purchases, the society was further supported by labor obligations: two days of each year for the benefit of the colony (Lucas 1955, 59–60).

The community of Zeeland, Michigan, was in this way organized even before the migrants left the shores of Holland. An association was created in the form of a congregation, which then proceeded to elect a consistory of elders and deacons. The leading elder, a wealthy landowner named Van Luyster, advanced the passage and the land purchase money of many of his former employees. The congregation left Holland together, traveled across America together, and finally purchased the farmlands they would need to build the settlement in Michigan. Other minister-leaders followed similar strategies, such that "congregation" was synonymous with "community" and "covenant" with "contract"—for the members were tied together from the start by religious concern, political duty, and occasionally financial debt.

Many of the individuals who came to America on their own sought out these communities as places where land could be purchased and, perhaps most important, Dutch was spoken. Thus the seceder immigrants, even where they were the eventual minority, had set the patterns of communal association. In West Sayville, which was not a minister-led congregation, independently religious men like Broere urged the formalization of communal ties. Once the first church was formed in 1866, the political association was also established.

What can we conclude about the experience of emigration for these Dutch newcomers to America? Certainly it was disjointing. It is difficult to imagine a watershed more abrupt in the life of any adult than the radical transition necessarily involved in emigration. For each man and woman, the departure, the journey, and the arrival must stand together as unparalleled events separating his or her life into two distinct halves, perhaps a rite of passage akin only to that personal rite of being "born again" which Broere speaks of. This is certainly the sense emigration holds for those now relatively few living men and women of West Sayville who made and remember the journey. Aage, a Frisian immigrant who is ninety-five years old as I write, expresses no surprise at the desire of others to hear the story of "how I came to America," for in that tale he sees true drama, a drama that transforms his voice into that of the ancient reciter of heroic tales. The protagonist of this saga, however, is neither folk hero nor biblical character but he himself. So must the experience of emigration, or the memory of that passage, have propelled the peasant and the shopkeeper into their own folklore, for where else lived such a vision of adventure?

Even thus uprooted, the Dutch emigrants of the mid-nineteenth century did not much resemble the universal portrait penned by Oscar Handlin, nor is their social and cultural world easily categorized in terms of the traditional theoretical dichotomies. Their social roots were as much contractual and associational as they were based on the hoarier traditions of kin obligation. Their notion of self, their identity, was already entrepreneurial in some measure, and they were more inclined to see worldly success as a sign of salvation than a sign of damnation. When they could, these Dutch emigrants came in the company of like-minded others and founded small, church-centered communities in rural America. When they came alone, they often sought out such communities or, as in the case of West Sayville, soon formed them. Indeed, this associational factor is perhaps most vital, for it is only in the context of the community that a culture can be sustained, even one that is apparently individualistic, and the degree to which the world view described in this chapter still survives in Dutch Americans is closely linked to the extent to which those distinct communities have persisted.

So far we have reviewed the character of Dutch immigrant culture in order to understand how their world view affected their adaptation to conditions on Long Island's southern shore. West Sayville did not,

however, develop only as an expression of those cultural predispositions. The structure of local life there was also constrained by the
character of the niche in which the Hollanders found themselves. In
this respect, the Dutch of West Sayville were quite different, not only
from the mass of European immigrants but also from most of their
fellow countrymen.

3

DUTCHMEN ON THE SHORE

Despite the bustle and confusion of the big city, Almina's account tells us, the Hages and DeWaals were somewhat reassured by the apparent Dutchness of New York. Familiar architectural styles, such as the gabled brick mansions of Manhattan and the Dutch farms of Brooklyn, were comforting sights. Language, however, was a problem, and they were accordingly relieved to be directed to a hotel on Greenwich Street where they met a "Holland Jew." This "trusted and true friend," as he was remembered, was able to direct the two families to Hunter's Point. There they were to take the Long Island Railroad out to Lakeland in Suffolk County and from there make their way down to the shore—for the Dutchmen had told their new friend that they were anxious to go where there was water, and "some way or other they heard of the Great South Bay."

While the landing of any immigrant on our shores was bound to be a confusing and perhaps dangerous experience, it must be remembered that the various ethnic groups hardly found the same reception. Africans and Asians have had to fight racism as well as economic deprivation. As for the European arrivals, some were looked on much more kindly than others, typically as a function of their distance from Anglo-Saxon language, custom, and appearance. With the exception

of the Irish–Northern European and largely English speaking, but
Catholic and long the subject of a very special antagonism with the
English—the northern and western European immigrants fared better
than the later arriving southern and eastern folk.

This rule certainly applies to the Dutch. The Netherlands was
neither exotic, dangerous, nor unknown to nineteenth-century American minds. Holland was, in fact, a nation familiar to most Americans,
and one which they believed figured prominently in their own history.
Particularly in the Northeast, of course, Holland was known to every
schoolboy as the first haven for the Pilgrims and the predecessor of
the English colonial presence. Furthermore, the colonial Dutch had
by no means vanished from the landscape.

More important than the architectural survivals that caught the
arriving Dutchmen's eye were the descendants of colonial Hollanders
that had not only survived English conquest and American independence but prospered through all. The old patroon aristocracy of the
Hudson Valley, Albany, New Jersey, and some parts of New York City
still held positions of economic and political power, and individuals of
that class proved to be valuable assets to the Dutch immigrants of the
nineteenth century. Before setting foot on ship, Van Raalte, the leader
of the Michigan settlement, was known by reputation to several distinguished Dutch New Yorkers. Thomas DeWitt, minister of the Reformed Church and pastor of the Collegiate Church, met the immigrants
at dockside and introduced Van Raalte to a number of Dutch-speaking
Americans, thus facilitating his initial arrangements for transport to
the Midwest. That journey led Van Raalte and his company from one
helpful Dutch American to another. Arriving in Albany, they were met
by the minister Isaac Wyckoff, into whose hands a copy of Van Raalte's
open letter, "Appeal to the Faithful in America," had fallen. Well received by the Reformed congregation of that city, the party made their
way to Rochester, Buffalo, and finally Detroit, at each stage making
vital connections with well-established Dutch Americans. Even where
they did not deal with fellow Hollanders, the Dutch immigrants had
the advantage of being generally viewed as desirable newcomers. They
were, after all, Protestants of a familiar creed and seeking religious
freedom even as the Yankees' ancestors had. Accordingly, they were
aided, not alone by Reformed ministers but also by churchmen generally. Having arrived finally in western Michigan, Van Raalte was
much helped in his search for land by a local Presbyterian minister.
In Iowa, Scholte was similarly guided in his negotiations by a frontier

Baptist. The local lay population were also typically impressed by the familiar biblical puritanism of the immigrants (Lucas 1955, 166–67).

The relative prosperity of some of these newcomers also made for a better reception here. Although many individuals may have been very poor indeed, there were in many incoming congregations men and women of substantial means and education—contrasting mightily with the starved and unwashed bodies of less fortunate immigrants crowding onto the New York docks. Scholte's group traveled up the Mississippi to Iowa, leaving behind a veritable trail of gold and good impressions.

There is a difference, however, between such impressions made in passing and the relations among long-standing neighbors. The Dutch who made for the Midwest, helped by Yankees and Dutch Americans on the way, settled much by themselves, especially in the forests of western Michigan. There the problems of getting along with Americans were faced only by those young men and women who ventured outside the village community for seasonal labor on American farms. The difficult adjustment was not so much to culture as to nature. These Dutch farmers were far from familiar with the tasks of forest settlement and experienced numerous difficulties in clearing and farming the land. Though aided by the few pioneer Americans in the area, the settlers of "De Kolonie," as it came to be called, still weathered a number of disasters.

THE NEAR FRONTIER

In contrast to their countrymen pioneering the Midwest, Hage and DeWaal found their new homeland on Long Island less threatening but more circumscribed. Problems of social adaptation, they and their followers would find, would be more complex than adjustments to any natural conditions. It is easy, however, for those who know Long Island today to underestimate the wildness of Suffolk County—a mere fifty miles east of New York City—in the late 1840s.

Though only hours long, that train ride must have disconcerted the immigrants. Once in Suffolk County (see Figure 1) the locomotive followed its newly laid tracks not from town to town but through an apparently barren wasteland of sandy soils and scrub pine forests. Parts of the county had long been settled, for the northern shore and eastern end of that part of Long Island provided sheltered harbors for numerous

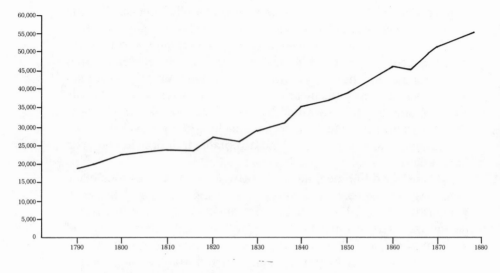

Figure 3. Suffolk County Population, 1790–1880

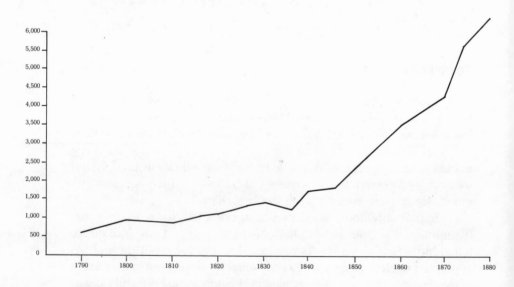

Figure 4. Islip Township Population, 1790–1880

small but prosperous farming/maritime communities of colonial vintage. For those villages, Long Island Sound was the principal highway to the markets of New York City; the new "central line" of the Long Island Railroad was constructed with future, rather than already established, communities in mind. In fact, much of this central barrens had been recently purchased by land speculators who, in collusion with railroad magnates, hoped to make a good deal of money by attracting new settlers to the area and thereby developing a region that would be dependent on the railroad for all manner of transportation. Whether or not Hage and DeWaal were lured to this near frontier by railroad propaganda it is impossible to say. Having arrived finally at the terminus of Lakeland, however, they were evidently surprised at what they beheld. Almina Hage Terry relates:

. . . Their hopes were almost crushed and they thought that their good friends had misled them. As far as they could see for miles, there was nothing but woods. Seeing no houses and the question of water still being uppermost in their minds, they looked this way and that, but nothing but woods met their eyes. On walking around they saw at a distance a young man with a yoke of oxen loading a flat car with pine wood. Even this was a welcomed sight. This man proved to be the late Carman Seaman of Bayport. They explained to him that their object was to go where there was water. They placed great confidence in human nature. Again good fortune overtook them. He told them to get in his wagon and he drove them through five miles of woods, which seemed very dreary, thinking that any minute bears or wolves would jump at them. They thought they would never get there. They never forgot the turn in the road where at last Seaman stopped at a house where they could stay. This house was owned by his father. The two families occupied one house. There were very few houses in sight, and much woods. In fact, there were more snakes than people. That was new to them. Some were very poisonous—rattlesnakes, milk snakes, and numerous black snakes. There were also wild cats. John Rhoad, a respectable resident of Oakdale, had the distinction of killing the last panther. It was only a few weeks before that the last tribe of Indians had left.

Ignoring Almina's somewhat suspect folk naturalism (milk and black snakes are not poisonous), we can still imagine that for Dutchmen used to the neat villages, open fields, polders, and dikes in Zeeland, the pine forests around Lakeland would not seem a promising seascape. A good portion of the barrens, as this woodland was then called, lay within the bounds of Islip Township, which stretched from the center of the island south to the bay, including within its bounds the adjacent portion of that body of water, and the barrier beach protecting it from the Atlantic Ocean (see Plate 19).

Even below the pine forests around Lakeland, Islip Township was throughout colonial times not surprisingly quite underpopulated. The north offered early colonists fertile glacial moraine farmland and a number of good natural harbors from which they would cross the deep waters of Long Island Sound to the ports of southern New England. The East End had also its early settlers—attracted there by good land and direct access to the Atlantic Ocean. By contrast, however, the southern shore of Islip was a vast marshland, very difficult to cross from east to west and indented by streams offering shelter only to small craft. To reach New York, local mariners had to escape the Great South Bay through one of the treacherous inlets that broke the barrier beach and led into the ocean.

There was also a social impediment to the settling of Islip in colonial times. Unlike the lands on the North Shore and East End, which for the most part had been purchased from local Indians by corporate communities in the seventeenth century, most of Islip was the property of a single patentee: the Nicoll family. As with the other expanses of unsettled lands in central and southern Long Island, the Nicoll estate had been crown lands which colonial governors of New York were permitted to grant in large tracts—very much against the practice and values of the New England–stock villagers on the northern and eastern shores. The surveyor-general, Cadwallader Colden, probably spoke for these Long Islanders when he said of this arrangement: "It is most injurious as to improvement of the country, the owners will not improve and others will not become tenants or vassals, for one great reason of people leaving their native country was to avoid the dependence on landlords and to enjoy lands in fee" (Nicoll 1865, 546). Such lands were typically held under entail laws, which prohibited the sale of any portion. Until these laws were suspended in the 1780s, prospective settlers could take up farms only under lease, and only few—as Cadwallader predicted—were so willing.

Accordingly, the population of Islip Township always lagged far behind that of neighboring regions. The first town meeting, held in 1720, was attended by a mere 30 freeholders, representing an estimated total population of 150. By 1776, the population had reached only 600. An act of legislation in 1785 permitted the Nicoll family to sell portions of their estate, including sections that were eventually to form the villages of Bayport, Sayville, and West Sayville. While these sales gave some impetus to the growth of the area, incoming settlers were few, and in 1820 there were still only 1,156 souls in the whole township, making it the most sparsely populated in a still lightly peopled county.

Town records from this first century reveal something of the population and its early concerns. The local social world can be loosely divided into four "classes." There were first the very few large landowners, descendants of colonial patentees like the Nicolls. Beneath them were the active farmers, originally leasees of Nicoll but after 1785 sometimes substantial landowners in their own right. Much less apparent in the records were the farm laborers, and the slaves, who provided the work force for some larger holdings. It was the substantial farmers of the second rank, men like Terry, Green, Edwards, and the Seamans mentioned in Almina's account, that took the largest part in the early township government. Farms were largely subsistence-oriented in this period, only the larger of them producing something of a surplus for sale in the city. In the early period town legislative concerns were accordingly agricultural. Endless effort was spent in countering the evils of "trespassing hoggs" and free-roaming cattle.

MARITIME RESOURCES

The town's governing body was also concerned with their common resources, which included a disputed portion of the Great South Bay due south of the community, and of Fire Island, the barrier beach separating the bay from the Atlantic Ocean (see Plate 20). For example, the town's annual rental of fodder land on the barrier beach was evidently an important event, attracting enough purchasers so that the town felt it necessary to limit their numbers to Islip residents. Of special interest to our concerns here are the early legislative measures affecting the bay resources, specifically shellfish. As early as 1765, Islip began imposing fines for taking shellfish by nonresidents, thus following the suit of neighboring townships, each of which was coming to regard its section of the bay as a valuable piece of corporate property. By 1815 the new version of this bill read:

Noted that any person not being a resident in the town of Islip not catch or carry out of the town any clams under the penalty of $10.00 for every offense. (*Islip Township Records*, 1815)

This measure went on to include, under the same provision, other denizens of the town's common waters, including fish and fowl. This

concern for bay resources reflects the varied adaptation to the local
environment that the eighteenth-century "farmers" of Islip's southern
shore had achieved, and important local notions of common property.
In addition to farming, fishing and oystering contributed in an important way to the subsistence of the early residents. "Progressive
farmers" (Howell 1949, 323) constructed sloops or two-masted schooners during the quiet winter months; whenever the agricultural cycle
allowed, they would run a load of oysters west to New York. When the
natural oyster beds began to run out in the 1790s, such enterprising
men began to run pinewood and charcoal into New York, hence Carman Seaman's pine cutting as reported by Hage and DeWaal.

The rapid rise of New York City in the early decades of the nineteenth century probably did much to spur the growth of maritime
activity all over Long Island, and the growth of population (see Figures
3 and 4) in Suffolk and Islip within it, reflects this development. A
nineteenth-century authority tells us that the number of sloops carrying wood and produce on the bay increased from twelve in 1785 to
thirty in 1800 to fifty by 1830. Such vessels would continue to carry
the great bulk of such materials to the city until competition from the
railroad began to have its effect after the 1840s. From the 1820s on,
larger-scale trade was also carried out of the South Bay ports by 150-
to 300-ton schooners sailed by Brookhaven and Islip men who made
for such southern ports as Savannah, Charleston, and Richmond (Reeves
1885, 62–63).

The fisheries of the Great South Bay also prospered and grew
through these decades. With seine nets, lines, or tongs, men all along
the South Shore took whatever finfish or shellfish the season offered.
The easy access of such fisheries to the southern shores of Brookhaven
and Islip townships, and the fluctuation in supply and value of the
catch, encouraged most of these "baymen" (as they styled themselves)
to remain only part-time fishermen, and there is accordingly little
indication of a landless or totally nonagricultural population in the
region before the middle of the century. The situation was very different among the seagoing fishermen of the North Shore and East
End, where, after the demise of whaling after 1820 or so, fleets of
smack fishermen set out for ocean banks of cod. These men were of
necessity more specialized and less likely to follow the varied seasonal
rounds that characterized the life of the South Shore baymen.

While the fishing smack skipper of the eastern North Shore carried
their own fish to market, most baymen had neither the time nor the

vessels for such an enterprise and relied instead on those entrepreneurs who specialized in such traffic. These were, for the most part, the same sloop or small-schooner captains who took pinewood and charcoal to New York. Yet even such mariners typically had interests in local stores and/or farmed or fished themselves. The only truly specialized trade to arise from this early maritime growth on the South Shore was shipbuilding. For the builders of Patchogue and Bellport, the years between 1825 and 1860 were, in the words of a contemporary, "the palmy period of this business. . . . Some of the finest and fleetest vessels . . . built anywhere were built by 'Bosses' (as the shipbuilders title went) Hiram Gerard, Perry Smith, the Post brothers, . . . and one or two others" (Reeves 1885, 62–63). Such "fine and fleet" vessels were the large trading schooners piloted up and down the Atlantic Coast, but numerous smaller fishing boats were also produced by such builders, particularly as the demand for seagoing schooners fell off after midcentury.

Such development was fairly confined to Brookhaven's shore, however, and until the late 1830s Islip remained thinly settled by families occupying farmsteads either isolated or gathered in small groups along the roadsides and creeks. Nothing deserving of the name "village" yet graced the area that the Dutch immigrants were soon to settle. Although the small population of baymen around Brown's River were assigned a post office and the name "Sayville" in 1836 (according to the folklore, a clerical mistake; the application had been for the name "Seaville"), the real beginning of that village can be dated at 1841, when W. J. Terry opened the first general store. That was in response to the then recent revival of oystering in the area, linked by some to the seeding of the bay in that area with young oysters brought by a trading schooner up from Virginia.

Regional development was also accelerated by the completion in 1844 of the Long Island Railroad's central line. Land speculators, as noted, had bought tracts in areas like Lakeland, having been assured by the railroad officials that any settlers of these lands would receive bargain rates for the transportation of their produce. These frontier communities were eventually founded in the ensuing decades, but they did not fare well for some time.

Despite the encouragement of scientific agriculture and the improvement of the barrens—including special premiums offered at the county farms for the produce of "the pine plain lands adjoining the Long Island Railroad" (A. G. Thompson 1850, 301)—Suffolk County,

and Islip within it, remained a distinctly maritime region both in settlement and preoccupation. In 1854 Samuel Thompson, then presiding
over the soon-to-become-defunct Suffolk County Agricultural Society,
attempted to explain the local situation to the evidently exasperated
officers of the state society, far away in Albany.

I think very little attention has been paid to the scientific aspects of farm
cultivation, as the value of our produce is based in part on our nearness to
New York City. Our market (however) is at home mainly . . . this would seem
to tell not very well for our agriculture, but it must be recollected that our
situation is peculiar; we are surrounded by waters which afford abundant and
profitable fishing. The fishermen who are employed in procuring fish for the
New York market are dependent upon the farmers for their food and many of
our farm products, instead of being sent to New York for market, are sold to
the merchants at the principal fishing points, and are resold by them to fishermen receiving that money which has been received from the city for fish
and other products of the water. (S. L. Thompson 1854, 640)

Thompson somewhat self-righteously concluded with this observation:

It has been stated as a fact that more money is received from the sale of fish,
oysters, etc., from the waters of Suffolk than from all the products of some of
the most flourishing agricultural counties of this State; but I presume it would
be better for our agriculture that we were denied these seeming advantages.

By the 1840s the inhabitants of Sayville and its environs were
fully enmeshed in this complex regional economy. The local stores
provided the vital point of exchange in the more localized flow of goods,
including marine products. Samuel Terry of Sayville, for example,
though a mariner, bought and sold the shellfish of the local baymen
as well as cartloads of the "moss bunkers," mussels, and seaweed—
all of which were the principal fertilizers for farmers all over Suffolk
County. While this local market development allowed for a degree of
regional and personal specialization greater than that possible in more
totally agricultural climes, it would be a mistake, as we have seen, to
assume too great a division of labor. In fact, most shellfishermen around
Sayville in the 1840s were also landowners, men who went out for
small amounts of oysters and fish in the fall and winter when agricultural tasks were less demanding. They called themselves "baymen"
and thought of themselves as practical opportunists, willing and able
to take advantage of "whatever was going."

Such a varied ecology and economy was probably particularly
appealing for landless immigrants like Hage and DeWaal, for the Great

South Bay offered opportunities to anyone who could find a way to harvest its natural bounties. Perhaps they had heard in New York of the "California bed," as a large bank of oysters discovered off the Islip bay-shore was called in 1848. At any rate, it was stories of abundant oysters that led them to seek settlement away from all their countrymen in the woods of Michigan and Wisconsin.

ARRIVAL OF THE DUTCH

The two families made their way to Oakdale, then but a row of five farms that had grown up around the estate of William Ludlow, the last local scion of the Nicoll family. Of the two men, it was DeWaal who had been a seafarer in Holland and who was accordingly anxious to take advantage of the burgeoning oyster trade. Evidently possessed of some small capital, DeWaal was able to buy a sloop with which to catch clams and oysters and take them to New York. His niece remembered:

He ran a great risk as the way was not open as it is now, and having as his only companion his nine year-old boy. When people found out what he was doing at so great a risk, they said: "Why man, you will kill yourself." He repeated it several times, keeping it in memory, thinking he had acquired some very important thing in the new language.

Hage, on the other hand, had been a farmer or farm laborer and sought work on the "fine residence of W. H. Ludlow," the gentleman farmer of the area. Although refused at first, his persistence was eventually rewarded with a position: farm laborer at seventy-five cents a day.

In these first few years of life in Oakdale, the Hages and DeWaals were joined by the Verweys and Hiddinks, who had also followed the immigrant trail to Lakeland, where they had lived for some time in a "surprisingly comfortable sod home." Bastiaan Broere of Yerseke had made his way to Oakdale as well, after a series of misadventures in the Michigan forest and on eastern canals. He too had heard of the oystering on the Great South Bay and, "having been raised in that pursuit" in Yerseke, was convinced he would fare well there. The 1850 census lists the large and growing families of these Hollanders. The young Broeres (for Bastiaan had found a wife in New Jersey), were as yet childless. DeWaal, at this time thirty-three, and his wife Maria, thirty-one, already had four children, ages eleven to two, the youngest presumably born in the year before departure. Hage was by then thirty-seven, and his wife Nanke was thirty-five. They had four children, ages three to nine. The Verweys, Anthony (fifty-six) and Anna (forty-nine), had presumably passed their childbearing years, but had been blessed with nine surviving children ages nine to twenty-nine. Such a family size would prove common.

In economic adaptation to the local resources, these first immigrants had established a pattern that forthcoming Hollanders would follow. DeWaal and Broere each attempted to make a living on the bay. DeWaal's capital allowed for the purchase of a sloop and hence some marketing as well as oystering activity. Broere presumably had less means, and we have no record of how he initially went after shellfish, whether on his own or in company with others. Hage, as we have seen, had found work on the Ludlow estate, and this pattern of labor on the area's large estates was to become increasingly important as the number of such places grew in the second half of the century. Of the Verweys, we know only what the census tells us—that the father was a merchant and that his eldest sons, respectively, were clerk, baker, and two engravers. Where these trades were plied we cannot say.

In the decade following 1850 the Dutch population of the area grew to around 92. Relatives were the first to hear about the opportunities afforded by the bay. Cornelius DeWaal's brother, Jacob, left Ravenna, Michigan, in order to join the prospering oyster trade. More often, however, it was relations through women and marriage that formed the immigrant network. Hage and DeWaal, we remember, were brothers-in-law, and Hage "sent transportation" for his wife's sister's family, Hannah and Arie Beebe, also of Bruinisse. We will find this in-law link to be of prime importance in later migrations and also in continuing community relations.

New arrivals were hardly restricted to relatives. Most came, as far as it is possible to ascertain, from the Oosterschelde region of Zeeland—Bruinisse, Yerseke, Burgh (see Figure 2) and perhaps other of the villages engaged in the area shellfisheries. The 1860 census reveals some of the important characteristics of these immigrants. By that time, the 92 Dutch men, women, and children occupied 30 households. They were comprised overwhelmingly of young families: 12 young couples without children and 13 young couples with children. As the number of households indicates, there were few extended-family households. Only 6 households are listed as including more than nuclear family members, most of those having one widowed parent in company with a young married couple. Evidently this early immigration was predominantly of young families, men and women in their twenties and thirties as yet unburdened with more than one or two children.

While most of these families found homes around the Ludlow estate in Oakdale, others of them were scattered around the edges of Sayville. Of the 40 Dutchmen with listed occupations, 14 are designated "farm laborer" or "laborer" and 26 as "baymen." In 1860 the average age of the laborers was forty-seven, while that of the baymen was thirty-one. Most of the young arrivals were evidently able to engage in the fishery that had probably attracted them there. Bastiaan Broere probably spoke for many when he said, "I feared I might have to make my living in America by farming, and I cordially hated farming seeing that I had been at sea since childhood" (Broere 1887, 9). His experience in the Midwest did not alter these sentiments, and other Zeelanders either contemplating life in the American Midwest or already settled there or in less maritime sections of New Jersey were only too happy to relinquish the spade in favor of the oyster tongs. For those with either no means to fish or no inclination to follow the bay, Cornelius Hage's success on the Ludlow estate presented other opportunities. By the diligence of his toil, as his daughter tells the story, Hage had risen from laborer to manager of the farm and was hence able to offer employment to more than a few incoming countrymen.

Although linked by propinquity and kinship or provincial association, these first families of Hollanders did not yet constitute a closed immigrant community. In these early years the trend was toward assimilation, for their work did not tie them together and their social life was necessarily a function of preexisting institutions. There being no Dutch grocer, for example, one had to go to Sayville for coffee, sugar, and the other necessities of life. Almina reports the typical trials and tribulations of immigrants attempting to make themselves understood there: "At one time, wanting starch, they rapped the clerk's shirt front to give him the idea." Their knowledge of English naturally grew through these encounters. The degree to which their occupations involved interaction with the locals must also have made for a faster progress in the English language than was possible for the isolated farmers of the Midwest.

Most critical to their assimilation was the schooling the Dutch children received at the hand of one Miss Hawkins from Islip. Almina remembers initial difficulties encountered when the Holland children attended class dressed in their native costume. Then, as now, children were intolerant of such deviation and offered "much criticism" on that score. Anxious to fit in, the Dutch children soon conformed to local usage, and being quite young for the most part, made the linguistic transition as well, undoubtedly with greater facility than their parents.

Finally there was church life, so important in the life of the Dutch immigrants of this period. Although Broere had been a seceder, the DeWaals, Hages, and Verweys were not, and these families were evidently content to attend the local Methodist Episcopal church in Oakdale. Built in 1769 to suit the local gentry, St. John's well reflected the local social structure. "The pews had doors with silver plate and the number of the pew inscribed on the plate. In the gallery on both sides, the slaves and help were supposed to sit." By the mid-nineteenth century, Almina reports, "the people were old-fashioned Methodists. They would sit with closed eyes and suddenly rise and shout and were very much serious and earnest."

On Sundays a gloom seemed to settle on the place and everything else. The meals progressed in silence. Even the ornament on the mantlepiece had a stiff and unfamiliar look. According to my childhood ideas, I wondered if my parents loved me. If I read, it had to be a religious book and I was glad to welcome the time for Sunday school and church. I thought I was a lost creature like Adam. I had disobeyed, common with the human family. I would walk home at a snail's pace. In the afternoon we were allowed to walk, generally in the graveyard, and in the condition of my mind I was willing to be an inmate of the place.

Even so, things were evidently not serious enough for Broere, who although happy with the plentiful oysters he found was considerably less pleased with the company:

There were two Holland families not far from our house, but already I had discovered from their words and from the loudly spoken oaths as though His name were a mere byword, that I could not associate with them on friendly terms.

Broere evidently lived alone with his convictions, not much associating with his Holland neighbors. Feeling it pointless to attend services conducted in a language he did not understand, he and his wife stayed alone with their Bible on Sundays, very much missing "friends with whom I could speak, sing, pray."

With the exception of Broere's stubborn isolation, these as yet few Holland families would have seemed at this point in time to be headed straight for complete americanization, for in all these significant institutional settings, the Dutch were following a pattern of increasing incorporation into local life. Between the Methodist-Episcopals and Miss Hawkins's three R's, little would have remained of their children's Dutchness, and even less of their grandchildren's. Circumstances, however, were to change. More Hollanders were on their way, and there would soon be a number sufficient to establish their own institutions. Moreover, relations with certain sectors of the local populace were to encourage a concentration of Dutch settlement, and closeness of households is often conducive to the maintenance of community bonds.

4

"STRIVING AND RISING"

The half-century following 1860 saw the rapid growth of the Dutch population (including those born of Dutch parents) around the Oakdale-Sayville area, as it did the growth of the region as a whole (see Figures 3 and 4). The dramatic rise, the result of both birthrate and escalating immigration, is certainly a good indicator of the absolute extent of a potential Dutch community, but a community does not arise from mere aggregates of individuals. Communal association depends on institutions—places and situations that provide stages on which local social dramas can be regularly acted out. In that sense of community, it was the twenty years or so following Hage and DeWaal's arrival that were critical, for if the number of players was to continue to grow rapidly after the 1870s, they would find the stage already erected, the scenery in place, and the play well under way.

Some of the elements of that set were hardly unique to the community, but rather bore a resemblance to configurations elsewhere in the region, the nation, and even abroad. In the eastern United States, the second half of the nineteenth century saw the rise of a large number of regional industries, many of them run by immigrant labor. This newly expanded industrial capitalism no doubt imposed a new class structure, similar in some of its basic features, on all such regions. The precise nature of the work, and the structure of local social relations before the development of such industries, however, might also contribute in an important way to the character of life as it developed. This was especially the case in the industrialization of fisheries, where the transformation in productive and distributive practice went through a series of complex stages—from traditional subsistence pursuit to limited market cottage industry to increasingly capitalized and mechanized industry—with odd combinations prevailing at any given moment. Questions of "sea tenure" (see McCay 1982 for a good anthropological view of this general problem) were also typically complex and troublesome, arising, as they did, like the productive techniques, from local traditions that did not always give way easily or completely before the forces of progress.

As for the Great South Bay fisheries, the consumption and sale of such sea and bay products as "bass, black fish, cod, chequet, eels, flounder, flat-fish, frost fish, mackerel, perch, porgies, shad, sheepshead, tom-cod, oysters, clams, crabs, lobsters, escalops, mussels, and winkles" had long been an important part of a regional economy, responsive to local and distant market fluctuation. While the post-1860 decades saw a rise in the number of men employed in such fisheries, an improvement in the caliber of vessels and gear and an escalation of the value of their take, the fin-fisheries remained, for the most part, the affair of independent men with relatively little capital, using the labor of only a small crew.

Menhaden, an oily fish related to the herring, was the only fish that lent itself to anything like industrialization. A process was introduced in the post–Civil War years for rendering tons of these fish into either "scrap" or oil, either of which could then be sold to various markets for industrial use. The operations involved in this process necessitated an investment that evidently attracted a number of entrepreneurs who saw substantial profits, especially in the 1870s. While three such works were built on the Great South Bay, an 1885 report lists fifteen "factories" on the Peconic and Gardiner's Bay. These latter plants processed close to 154 million fish that year, producing over 387,000 gallons of oil and 11,500 tons of dried scrap. The South Bay menhaden industry was far less capital intensive and employed fewer men, but it involved more sail vessels, indicating that more small-scale fishermen supplied these works than those around Greenport. The South Bay factories did not, in fact, fare very well, and menhaden achieved the status of an important local industry only in those communities around the Northeast with easy access to Gardiner's and Peconic bay sources, and to the sea route to Connecticut and New York markets (Reeves 1885, 72–73).

It was oysters that transformed the maritime life of the Great South Bay, and there alone among fisheries did the opportunities exist for a much more thorough capitalization and industrialization of the once household pursuit, for oysters could be planted and harvested, as well as mass packaged and marketed. While the small fishing village of 1840 became a bigger and better equipped fishing town by 1880, the oystering village of 1840 might become a virtual mill town in the same space of time—for the industrialization of oystering meant a total reorganization of the forces of production—and consequently a great transformation of local social and cultural life.

Yet such changes do not transpire in a vacuum. The particular path any such industrialization takes depends on more than the exigencies of the technology. Not every community responds in the same way to such pressures and opportunities, and the consequences of any local industrialization may also depend in some measure on the previous relations of locals to one another and to the resources on which any such industry must rely. As for the Dutch settled around Oakdale and Sayville in the 1850s, a number of critical events transpired in the years following the arrival of the first immigrants which were to complete the stage on which the Dutch would experience the transformations that were to follow.

In 1851 the town of Brookhaven began leasing parcels of underwater bay grounds for the farming of oysters. That legislative change amounted to a radical alteration in notions of property, initiating the "enclosure" of the watery commons. A victory for private property and enterprise, leasing laid the absolutely necessary groundwork for the transformation of oystering into a full-scale industry. When newer immigrants arrived after 1880 or so, the gold-rush days of freebooting on the natural beds were already drawing to a close. A small number of the earlier immigrants had by that time become "planters" and "shippers," employing their countrymen as workers and making large profits by exporting thousands of barrels of shellfish. The life of the bayman now followed a complex cycle of work for himself and work for others, with accordingly complex patterns of association and identity.

The other set of changes amounted to an equally important transformation in local life—the consolidation of the immigrant community achieved through the impetus of two decisions, one reached by a local American entrepreneur and the other by the Hollanders themselves. In 1865, Sam Green, proprietor of a general store on the outskirts of

Sayville and owner of about two square miles of land stretching from the bay to the north, just west of Green's Creek (see Plate 21), decided to sell small parcels of land to his Dutch immigrant customers. Beginning with Willem Tucker, they took up these plots, and the once scattered Hollanders found themselves cheek by jowl in a veritable Dutch village. That village founded its most important institution in 1866, when thirty-one men and women gathered in the home of Nicholas Tucker and formally organized the first Dutch Reformed congregation of Sayville. While many of the immigrants had been personally religious, and even given to meeting in one another's homes for Sabbath worship, the organization of a congregation with a minister and consistory of elders and deacons furnished the Hollanders with their principal local political institution. The church bound them, by covenant, into a contractual community, tied them to an American Reformed church, and separated them forcibly from their local American neighbors.

These changes on the edge and at the center of what would eventually be called West Sayville set the critical parameters of the community—not a simple or egalitarian or harmonious community, but a community nevertheless. On the water, in the streets, and in the church, it was a social world in which the tension between individualism and communalism was graphically manifest. Some of that tension, as we have seen, was already inherent in the cultural and social forms imported by the immigrants to America, but there were peculiar aspects of their new circumstances that may also have contributed to the particular form taken by this contractual community. To separate out these threads and attempt an understanding of how and why West Sayville took the path it did, we need to take a close look at the early decades of growth and change.

THE RISE OF THE SHELLFISHERY

The circumstances governing the conduct of the Great South Bay shellfisheries were, as in fisheries everywhere, ecological, technical, and legal (see Power 1970). The last dimension is inevitably the most complex, and for the social anthropologist it is often the most interesting, but it is better to begin with the less abstract matters of waters and boats.

While other aspects of the local landscape were unfamiliar to the Zeelanders, the seascape itself was less foreign. Indeed, as he cast his eye over the bay for the first time, Cornelius DeWaal must have been comforted by the familiarity of the surrounding vista. As at home in Bruinisse, he saw a gentle, sandy coastline without great hills or bluffs, cross-cut by numerous small rivers and creeks running through Long Island's glacial outwash plain and emptying their fresh water into the bay. That body of water stretched before him—not a dangerous open sea but a comfortably proportioned lagoon. Across the mere five or six miles of water to his south, DeWaal no doubt espied the other stretch of sandy, reed-choked coastline of the barrier beaches that separate and protect the bay from the ocean beyond. To his east and west, the bay seemed shallow and undramatic, disappearing into uncertain horizons of land and water. Apparently the Great South Bay was much like the estuarine waters at home in which he and other Zeelanders had fished the natural oyster and mussel beds with profit.

There were, however, important differences. In America the flow of seawater into the bay was not as dramatic as in Holland's Oosterschelde, with its huge tidal flows and occasional floods. Even so, the apparent permanence of the Great South Bay was misleading. The action of tides was constantly, if imperceptibly, filling up inlets and washing away sand from the barrier beach, irresistibly changing the outline of the distant shore. More than that, great hurricanes periodically blew up, not only whipping the calm bay into tempestuous fury but sometimes wreaking more dramatic changes on the land and seascapes by breaking new inlets through the always fragile barrier beaches. These were local conditions to which the Dutch would adjust, even as their Yankee predecessors had.

Even the internal uniformity of the bay was illusory. There were really two bays, known colloquially as "The East Bay" and "The West Bay." The approximate boundary ran from Nicoll Point to Fire Island (see Plate 22) separating two distinctive ecological zones whose differences were basically a function of relative salinity. The East Bay was completely sheltered (at that time) from the ocean by the barrier beach of Fire Island. Thus closed off from the sea and fed by the many freshwater streams that ran through the marshy southern shore of Long Island, the East Bay maintained a relatively low level of salinity. To the west, however, the bay was open through several inlets to the Atlantic and was accordingly far saltier. This difference was crucial to the local shellfish populations and hence to those humans who wished to harvest them. The lower salinity of the East Bay meant an easy time for baby oysters, because such conditions wére unsuited to the prop-agation of their most serious natural enemy, a snaillike creature called "the oyster drill." Low salinity, however, was not conducive to the fattening of these young oysters or to the growth of that other important shellfish, the hard-shell clam. Circumstances were reversed in the West Bay, where the saltier water was good for drills and clams, and the prevalence of the former creatures made it difficult for the vul-nerable baby oysters to survive. Older, more developed oysters grew well in this sector, however, fattening nicely in saltier waters.

The accessibility of these two zones lent itself to the practice of tonging the young seed oysters in the East Bay and planting them in the West Bay, where they could grow to marketable proportions. Most of that bay bottom was public grounds belonging to the bordering townlands, and hence the fishery was at first open to any resident. The vessels in this pursuit were simple enough. Skiffs or sharpies—nothing more than open rowboats—were adequate to the task. Larger, sail-powered craft such as catboats and sloops were preferable, how-ever, conferring greater mobility and carrying capacity. In all cases, the oysterman simply anchored over the oyster grounds and, with a pair of tongs, scraped the oysters off the surface of the bay bottom.

Such a pursuit was attractive to immigrants like DeWaal and Broere not only because of its familiarity but also because of the min-imal capital investment it required. According to the Reverend Hoff-man, an old boat could be purchased from a neighboring American for $100 to $150 (Hoffman 1898, 3). While the purchase price of a sloop was initially beyond the means of most, many Dutchmen could manage some kind of craft, either alone or in partnership, or at least find a place on the boat of a fellow countryman.

The pursuit was thus simple enough technically, but legally it was increasingly complicated. Wherever fishing is done close inshore on particular spots or locations, the question of property rights naturally arises (see McCay 1982). In the case of marine creatures actually planted on a particular spot, the question obviously becomes more crucial. For the enclosed Great South Bay, both ownership and use rights became more and more critical issues as the industry grew profitable. Indeed, these difficulties can hardly be said to have dimin-ished today.

Who owned the water and the bay bottom beneath it? The answer to that question is linked to the special history of the region. Settled at a time when Islip was inhabited only by Indians, Brookhaven Township had enjoyed rights over the Great South Bay, not only off its own coast but off the eastern half of Islip's shore as well. As the market value of oysters rose in the 1850s, this became an increasingly aggravating issue to the governing body of Islip Township. The source of their irritation was not the inaccessibility of the shellfish, for residents of Islip were free to tong oysters and clams on Brookhaven's public grounds. The issue between the towns was rather one of revenue, for in 1851 Brookhaven had begun to lease grounds in the West Bay, off the Islip shore.

This leasing was no doubt in response to the growing pressure on the increasingly lucrative oyster trade and to the desire of men who had gone through the work of tonging seed oysters on the public grounds in the East Bay and planting them in the West Bay. Naturally such baymen wanted some guarantee that the crop they had so laboriously planted could not be reaped by others. Beyond those concerns was the desire of the township to garner something of this newly rich harvest. Within the specified area, two-acre lots were laid out to be leased for five years at two dollars per year, paid in advance. In order to preserve this pursuit as a truly public one, not more than one such lot per lessee was allowed.

Not all the bay ground was under town control. A large section between Nicoll Point and Bayport to the east (see Plate 20) was the private property of "the Smith heirs," descendants of the colonial patentee William Nicoll, who along with his vast dry-land holdings owned (by license of the English crown) a large tract of bay bottom as well. These rights were not lost in the American Revolution, and in 1850 "the Smith heirs" claimed legal control of this vast section of now extremely valuable bay bottom.

Islip fought Brookhaven's control of the bay bottom off its shore through repeated attempts at legislative change in Albany. All efforts at wresting Islip's bay from Brookhaven's control failed, however, until 1880, when a delegation of Islip board members was able to conclude a settlement with the Brookhaven trustees. As far as the Smith property was concerned, Brookhaven was content at mid-century to share the management and proceeds of the shellfisheries on their portion of the bay bottom.

Islip had meanwhile proceeded to lease those portions of the bay bottom off their shores not owned by either Brookhaven or the Smith heirs. In 1857 the first set of Islip Township oyster regulations were passed governing the oystering between Nicoll Point and the Huntington town line. Men owning or leasing land that bordered on these waters were allowed to plant oysters in the waters opposite their respective lands extending from the low-water mark to no further than 500 feet into the bay. The rest of the bottom remained "open" or public grounds, on which any resident could plant oysters with the exception of certain channels used as clamming grounds. Planters designated their planted lots by driving two or more stakes into the bottom at the extreme corners and by putting up a marker on the adjacent shore which could be used as a "range" for relocating the spot from the water. Records of these beds were kept on town maps, and the fishery was further regulated by a prohibition against the taking of oysters from June through August.

All this legislation and regulation bears witness to the growing importance of the nascent oyster industry in the 1850s, not just to the Dutch immigrants but to all the residents of both Brookhaven and Islip townships. These baymen were happy to add the profits of oystering to their diverse farm and fishing income. Those that could, better availed themselves of the shellfishery's potential by leasing the best possible bottom land. The amount of bay bottom they could so lease was limited, however, not only by the township regulations but also by their own willingness to specialize. Most of the non-Dutch baymen were dry-land holders to whom the bounties of the water were never sufficient to tempt them into full-time fishing. On the other hand, the 1860 census lists only one Dutch "farmer." As we have seen, most Dutchmen were listed simply as "baymen," which we may take to mean oystermen not averse to clamming, musseling, or fishing as the seasons allowed. These immigrants, having so little to lose, were in a better position to take a greater entrepreneurial plunge than many of their Yankee neighbors may have been willing to dare.

It is therefore not surprising that Brookhaven lease records show a disproportionate Dutch involvement in the leasing of bottom lands by 1865. Although they were residents of Islip, these Dutchmen were allowed to lease lots from Brookhaven in the area lying off their own shores. Leasing was by then no longer limited to one acre per person, and lots ranged from two to twenty-six acres in extent. Among the Dutch names that appear are Jacob Ockers and Henry Ockers, Joseph and Leonard Verspoor, Leonard Van Houden, and Willem Scherpenisse (already Anglicized to Sharp). Most of these men leased only small lots, and often in combination with one another. Such holdings were probably sufficient to provide them with a fair oyster crop but not large enough to warrant an investment in shipping. The crucial position in the industry was as yet not in production but in marketing.

In the 1850s the oyster trade was not in the hands of any shipping companies but instead passed through Samuel Terry Green's general store. The local general store was much more than a simple retail outlet. Surviving account books show that Green not only bought and sold oysters but was engaged in planting them as well. This activity was, in fact, only one part of his general regional exchanges, for the shopkeeper also bought other fruits of the baymen's labors, such as mussels, clams, and large amounts of fish. Most of these fish were "moss bunker," an important fertilizer for the more prosperous local farmers, who bought them by the cartload. In addition to these relatively large-scale marketing activities, Green's store was the source of all ordinary consumer goods; foods, cloth, tobacco, shoes, and ropes were also available there. Thus standing at the very heart of the local economy, Green was buyer and seller of industrial as well as household supplies.

But the oysters still had to be carried to market, and that was the job of coastwise trading vessels until a southern railroad line was completed in 1867—and to a degree for several decades thereafter. Sloops owned and operated by local mariners still plied the bay and ocean between South Shore ports and New York City. Such mariners were typically oystermen as well, for a man could tong from a sloop as easily as from a smaller craft. Taking advantage of their larger holds, these men bought the oysters of their less well-equipped neighbors and ran the cargo through the inlet into the ocean and west to the city. Such activity was not without its risks. The voyage itself was often hazardous, especially the transit through the typically troublesome inlet leading to the open sea. Certainly the mariner's craft was more easily lost on this fifty-mile run than was the bayman's small boat on the quieter waters closer to home. A disaster on the bay was not only less likely, it also represented a financial loss perhaps more easily recoverable than that of a larger and much more expensive craft.

In 1860 only one Dutchman was among these mariners: Almina's uncle Cornelius DeWaal. Almina recollected the concern of neighboring Americans for the safety of her uncle, who was making this hazardous voyage with only his very young son. Perhaps the fear of competition lurked somewhere behind such warnings, for it was not long before this oyster shipping was dominated by immigrant mariners. In general, these men were not satisfied to limit themselves to marketing. DeWaal and his nephew, for example, were in 1865 the largest lease holders in the bay, their twenty acres of oyster grounds safeguarding their shipping business with an assured supply of oysters. This pattern was soon followed by others successful in this stage of the industry. Such entrepreneurs were by no means investors of money alone. Although some funds were necessary to the purchase of the sloops used in making the New York runs and in advancing the yearly rents on the larger oyster plots, investment was at this stage as much of labor as of money. DeWaal and the others were in no position as yet to hire men to work for them. When they were not making New York runs they were tonging oysters themselves. The difference between these shippers and those whom we have called baymen was minimal, however, and the two groups did not as yet constitute classes in any socioeconomic sense. Indeed, at this early stage all the baymen were to some extent entrepreneurs. Those who restricted their risks to renting oyster plots may have done so because they lacked the necessary funds for further investment, not because they lacked the spirit.

That spirit, as we have noted, was deeply rooted in the Dutch, and especially Dutch-Calvinist, culture, and one cannot help wondering to what extent that view of the world gave the Hollanders an edge over their American neighbors in this period, when the risks still appeared to outweigh the assurances. Certainly the most successful of these early entrepreneurs was a Dutchman, Jacob Ockers, whose fabulous career in the industry was to earn him the title "the Oyster King." Jacob, born in Bruinisse in 1847, arrived in Oakdale with his father, Hendrik, in 1851. Attracted by news from Hage and DeWaal, Hendrik followed the pioneers to Oakdale and wasted no time getting into shellfishery. Evidently aware that the future lay as much in transporting oysters as in catching them, he invested in a small sloop and began the marketing runs to New York City. Jacob soon began to accompany his father on these voyages, and by 1865, at the age of eighteen, was renting oyster lots in the bay along with young Gabe DeWaal, to the extent of sixteen acres. At the age of twenty-five, Jacob purchased his own oyster schooner, a larger, safer vessel able to carry more oysters than a sloop, and over the ensuing fifteen years he managed to make substantial profits.

By the 1870s several such men were making the more profitable runs possible with the large schooners, buying oysters from the independent baymen and expanding their own lease holdings to the point where their needs exceeded their own labor capacity. Among them, Wolfer Van Popering was typical. Born in Zeeland in 1844, he arrived as Jake Ockers had in 1851, a small child with his family. Laboring for his father as a young man, Van Popering, again like Ockers, was put in charge of a sloop, at the age of twenty-two. By the end of the century he was in control of seventy-five acres of oyster beds on the bay bottom and was also exporting oysters to European as well as American cities. The same pattern was followed by others: Van Wyen, Vander Borgh, Westerbeke.

The success of these men required rapid adjustments to the changing circumstances of the times. At each transitional stage the furthest advanced was in the best position to adjust. The example of vessel size is a good one. Those who were willing and able to purchase the larger schooners (rather than sloops) were not only able to carry more oysters into New York but also in a position to obtain their own seed oysters when these became available in large numbers off the Connecticut shore later in the century (see Chapter 6). As their holdings increased, men like Ockers required nonfamily labor to cull, or sort, the oysters for barreling, and by the 1870s the shippers were building sheds on the shorefront for that purpose. In this enterprise, relations with the local gentry were crucial. Ludlow, whom we remember as the last of Nicoll's descendants and an employer of Dutch labor on his estate, leased shoreland on Great River (see Plate 19) to several of the Dutchmen, on which they built their oyster shanties.

Other technological as well as organizational changes of far-reaching consequence lay ahead, as we shall see in Chapter 6. Even in the 1870s and 1880s, however, it would have been plain to any observer that oystering was growing rapidly not just in economic importance but concomitantly as a focus of local political, social, and cultural attention. For the Dutchmen, the consequences would seem to have been at once integrative and divisive, for as they would be drawn together by these common concerns and endeavors, so might they be separated by not only competition but also by incipient class divisions. As they climbed the ladder of maritime success, men like Ockers certainly began to outdistance their neighbors in other respects as well; they built larger houses, they wore better clothes, and so on. And if class differences began at this date to separate the shippers from their workers, that distance was widened by the arrival later in the century of large numbers of new and typically very poor Hollanders.

COMING TOGETHER

But the integrative and divisive effects of the rise of oystering can be understood only in the social context within which that rise occurred. While at first dispersed through the area, the Dutch immigrants had already begun to come together into a community capable of generating and maintaining its own cultural forms. That community was as much a product of a local American's entrepreneurial efforts as it was of the Dutchmen's desire to form a compact settlement.

In 1865, Samuel Green, proprietor of the general store mentioned earlier, divided a portion of his extensive landholdings into small plots, selling the first of them to Willem Tucker. One by one the other immigrant families relocated on neighboring plots, so that the region alongside Green's Creek slowly took the shape of a Dutch village.

While the opportunity to buy land and build their own homes near the water was undoubtedly welcomed by the Dutch families, Green was certainly acting in his own interest as well. The growing population of the area and the value of house sites so near to the bay, and hence the shellfisheries, combined to make such small house sites expensive. A still agriculturally oriented local Yankee population may well have been less likely to buy such lots, insufficient for cultivation beyond small household gardens, than these Dutch families whose main interest was easy access to the bay. Few if any of the Dutch purchasers were able to pay cash for the land and the house they were to build on it, and for financial assistance they turned once again to their benefactor. Green supplied the mortgages for these purchases and in so doing not only profited from such interest charges as accompanied these loans, but ensured the patronage of his debtors as well. As was typically the case where local general stores sold on credit, those owing substantial sums felt obliged to continue shopping where they owed. This obligation was no doubt much exaggerated when the debt was not just for groceries and supplies but also for mortgages.

It would be unjust to picture Green as entirely calculating in this interaction or unsympathetic to the Dutch. Indeed, it is impossible to say what his motivations were, but it is interesting to note that his continuing relations with the Dutch community were more than sim-

ply economic. His financial dealings with the immigrants changed his
social as well as economic position in the area. Before the late 1860s
Green's store was one of several in the Sayville area servicing the
general needs of the surrounding agricultural and maritime region.
After 1865 his store drew its clientele increasingly from the Dutch
settlement growing up around it and more and more provided a social
center for that community. Many locals remember passing such little
leisure time as the Dutch allowed themselves in Green's store, where
the proprietor took a lively interest in matters of purely local concern.
In these early days Green was perceived as a powerful patron, with all
the ambivalence that typically accompanies such a perception. He is
remembered as benevolent and praised for his knowledge of the Dutch
language and customs, or for the list of outstanding mortgages and
debts he kept prominently displayed in the store. Some tension is
certainly revealed in the contention over the name of this new community, known to the Dutch as "Tuckertown" after its first Dutch
resident, but as "Greenville" to outsiders after the original landlord.
As we shall see later, the economic and social prominence of Green
and his store were much reduced in ensuing decades by the rise of
the great oyster shippers and opening of several small Dutch-owned
shops in the area. Green's store, however, was still an active and important local institution through the early twentieth century.

The growth of a Dutch neighborhood—eventually village—did
much to increase the Dutch perception of themselves as a distinct
community. It also greatly facilitated continuous contact with one another, allowing for the continuation of Dutch patterns of village social
interaction. A formal institutional basis for that interaction was still
missing, however.

The observations of anthropologists and historians have shown
the critical importance of churches in this regard in the early life of
many American immigrant communities. The importance of the church
as a source of social as well as religious order was particularly pronounced with the seceder Dutch communities in the Midwest. The
early Dutch settlers of the Oakdale area had come individually, however, and hence without their church. Even so, they were not long in
establishing one, and the influence of that institution on the tenor of
life in the late nineteenth century is difficult to overestimate. Even
today, when asked about their ethnic identity or about the most distinctive feature of local life within West Sayville, older locals typically
reply in religious terms. Dutchness was expressed in Reformed Prot-

estantism, and membership in the Dutch churches was in large measure coincident in people's minds with membership in the community.

We remember that in the earliest days of the colony many Dutch
families worshiped with their American neighbors in the local Episcopal church. However, the need was felt for religious activity that
was Dutch in form and language, and several of the families gathered
in each others' homes on Sundays to read the Bible and pray. Bastiaan
Broere (1887, 19) remembered,

O how I rejoiced to have found a friend on the road to the Heavenly Canaan.
We soon agreed to meet on the Lord's Day, in obedience to the warning of
the Apostle, "not forsaking the assembling of ourselves together" [Heb. 10:25].

While no doubt satisfying in many ways, this form of worship did not
fully answer the charge of Reformed Protestantism, which called on
people to form an active congregation to govern their moral lives and
do God's work on earth. It was thus with great satisfaction that the
growing Dutch community received the Reverend Jongeneel, sent by
the northern Long Island classis (the regional governance body) of the
Reformed Church in America. With his help the first Dutch Reformed
church was built in 1867 on Montauk Highway near Green's store.

While the new church drew the immigrants together in worship
and provided an institutional basis for all sorts of interaction, harmony
among the communicants rarely prevailed. As we shall see later, life
within the Dutch Reformed Church was actually quite strife-ridden,
especially in the early decades of the local congregations' existence.
In 1876 a number of people separated themselves from the religious
community, founding what would eventually become the Christian
Reformed congregation of West Sayville. But that schism did not end
the trouble within either church. With or without their problems, however, the immigrant churches were at the heart of the newly forming
community, and guarding its edges as well. As with the fisheries, the
form this institution took through the late nineteenth century was an
adaptation of Dutch cultural forces to a new environment, though in
the case of the churches a conscious conservatism was especially active.

Thus the decades following Willem Tucker's move to what would
be called West Sayville saw the rapid growth of a Dutch American
community. The shellfisheries were the principal magnet, offering
employment for the many more immigrants that followed, and
entrepreneurial opportunities that were relatively rare in immigrant
experience. The fisheries certainly drew the Dutch together in geo-

graphical as well as social and cultural orientation. What might have become a mere region of Dutch settlement became with Green's help an immigrant village. What might have been a village with only proximity of habitation in common became a maritime community, a community with a shared way of life.

But the growth of the fisheries, as we have noted, also engendered an increasing stratification of the Dutch population. If the immigrants of the late 1880s found, on arrival, a well-defined and largely Dutch-speaking community, they also found a community internally divided into social strata with markedly different life-styles. They found a religious community, but a religious community already rent asunder. The two congregations were separated by more than religious ideology; they also comprised two different reactions to the forces of acculturation and assimilation—one seeking solace in increased isolation and preserved tradition, the other more accommodating to the pressures of the surrounding American world. It was a village community where the closest bonds may have been the sometimes bitter oppositions that linked its people in contention, moral and political confrontation in the church and economic competition on the water and shorefront. That conflict and competition are often not antithetical to the bonds of community association is a fact well known to anthropologists and sociologists. The nature of that world is unfolded in a closer look inside the domains of everyday life in the community, which is the object of the following chapters.

5

THE STRIKE

On the twenty-first of August 1902 an unusually distraught Jacob
Ockers called an emergency meeting of the Blue Point Oyster Shippers'
Protective Association. The equanimity of "The King Oyster Planter"
had been disturbed that morning by the refusal of five of his shanty
workers to put in the expected ten-hour day. In itself this job action
hardly threatened Ockers's livelihood; the shipping season would not
commence for another two weeks, when these five men would constitute an insignificant proportion of the sixty or so he regularly employed in season. But Jake Ockers recognized this minor rebellion as
a threat to the authority he enjoyed in his own place of work.

Ockers had warned his inexplicably complacent colleagues about
the evil of unionism when the local chapter of the Oysterman's Union
had organized two years before, but even he had underestimated the
seriousness of the movement. Talk had been going around that some
of the men were not fully satisfied with the $1.75 per day they were
paid in the shanties and the $2.00 a day on the boats. But those wages
were no lower than those paid in other oystering centers, nor was a
ten-hour day unusual in that industry or in other laboring occupations.
No, Ockers and the other shippers were convinced that they had always
given their workers the squarest of deals. Had they not often lent them
the money to buy their own boats and houses and in many other ways
contributed to the general welfare of the local community? They were
accordingly amazed at the turnout when that local "rabble-rouser," as
they put it, Bill Collins, had called a meeting to discuss unionization

in early March 1900. About one hundred men had shown up to hear Collins speak of the advantages of combination and to be reminded that they were, after all, skilled workers and consequently not easily replaced, and deserving of higher wages and better working conditions. Collins was elected president of the local chapter, which according to American Federation of Labor rules needed seven charter signatures to qualify for official status. Collins had no trouble drumming up twenty-seven signatories.

The local newspaper reported that several of the shippers had decided to "take the bull by the horns" and immediately discharged employees known to be active in the union movement. As a result of that action, when Daniel Harris, the labor organizer sent out from New York to speak to the newly organized chapter, arrived at the firemen's hall in Sayville the next Saturday night, he found two or three hundred men waiting to hear his exhortations. Harris's speech evidently suffered from a misinformed notion of local conditions, but when the meeting closed, fifty-one men added their names to the union roster. On the following Monday morning, several of the shippers discharged more men—and there was talk of little else in the shops, streets, and waterfronts of the area. Sayville's paper, *The Suffolk County News*, rushed to provide professional coverage of its first industrial crisis, and along with the story of the union meeting, the March 16, 1900, issue published the responses of the concerned shippers to the new state of affairs. Their reactions varied in an interesting way. Jake Ockers's characteristically blunt reply came first:

I don't want to have anything to do with any union. They are continually stirring up trouble. I have always gotten along well with my men . . . and I would rather raise wages 25¢ a day of my own accord than to be driven into paying 5¢ a day more. . . . I now have sixty men and as far as I know only two have joined the Union. They have been discharged. I can get twice as many men as I want and if necessary to make a fight will hire non-union men and pay them more. This organization hasn't the right men at the head of it and I am not going to let those kind of fellows run my business.

Edward Westerbeke, the second largest shipper in the area, revealed in his answer a line of thought even more typical of the shippers' world view:

We began this business in a very small way and as poor as any of the men and I think they are satisfied. . . . If they have grievances I am always ready to listen. . . . I am a working man myself and when I have to oppress the poor man I will quit business, but I am not ready to have a master workman or a walking delegate step in and tell me what I must do. We have about forty men and only four or five, so far as we know, have joined.

The other Dutch shippers responded in a similar manner; none of them wanted anything to do with any union, and each reported that very few or none of their men had joined the organization. While James Herring, manager of Lewis Blue Point Company, followed Ockers and the others in their stiff opposition, the other area non-Dutch shippers (LeCluse, Brown, and Rogers) all adopted a much more conciliatory stand, and while none of them seemed to think a union was a good idea, they did not fire any joiners, which they numbered as "quite a few."

By April 4 the *Fishing Gazette*, a national trade magazine, reported that the Oysterman's Union of Sayville had a membership of one hundred. It was not until August 1902, however, when Jake Ockers called the meeting of the association of shippers, that the local industry was troubled by anything worthy of the name "strike." In refusing to put in the required ten-hour day, the five workers at Ockers's establishment were acting on the decision to seek nine-hour days and a 50-cent-per-day pay hike for its members. Even more important, the chapter sought official recognition from the shippers, for in its two and a half years of existence, the union had made no headway in transforming the oyster companies into union shops.

The Protective Association, which was called to order that August, was just one year old itself. In 1901 the Dutch planter/shippers of West Sayville and Oakdale had joined forces with their Yankee counterparts in Sayville. Though competitors, all these men shared certain concerns, such as the availability of leasable lands, the state of local transportation, and competition from other oystering regions. The international market for Blue Point Oysters was good enough that this last concern was paramount. The demand was such that all the local shippers could make good profits, provided the Connecticut growers, in particular, were unable to muscle in. Some of these New Englanders had been marketing their own oysters as "Blue Points," and the association had been busying itself registering a BP's trademark to prevent such incursions when the trouble with the union had begun.

It was April 1902 when Bill Collins requested that the association officially recognize the union. The oyster shippers voted unanimously against any such recognition, but they did appoint a committee of five to meet with a delegation of union members to find out what demands they proposed to make. While the shippers seemed willing to compromise on issues of specific conditions, they continued to resist recognition of the union, informing its members that they intended to run independent shops next season, the same as in the past, adding, in apparent amelioration of their former position, that they "would not discriminate against union men."

If the shippers had hinted at concessions, their announced wages for the coming year were the same as the year before; nor did the ten-hour working day from 6:45 A.M. to 5:15 P.M. (a half-hour off for meals) represent any change. The response was the strike of five workers in Ockers's house, with the issue of hours evidently paramount. The shippers called together that August evening decided to stand by their previous wage and hour decision and further agreed not to employ any of the men employed by Ockers in the previous season without his consent. The union remained adamant, however, and even though the shippers, after much internal argument, offered a pay hike of 25 cents and a reduction of hours to nine and a half per day, the union refused to compromise. No doubt the real issue of union shops was motivating them most strongly, and the shippers rightly recognized that as by far the most dangerous demand. After a few weeks of meetings with representatives of the union and the rejection of all their compromise offers, the shippers decided to give up on the union altogether and hire new men at the improved wages. They evidently had no trouble finding them, and the strike was effectively broken. Although there are indications in the association minutes of occasional harassment of nonunion workers by union men, these incidents are no longer reported by the time the season was in full swing that autumn. The strike was short-lived, and the union itself receives no further mention in any local accounts, having presumably died the quick death of neglect.[1]

If the strike of 1902, and indeed the whole local labor movement, was of so little apparent consequence, why tell their story? Because conflicts of this sort are likely to be symptomatic of the general state of a social system. A close look at the causes of the conflict, the way in which the sides were drawn, and the possible reasons for its outcome may reveal much about the character of life in this maritime community around the turn of the century.

Certainly, confrontations between labor and capital were common enough in the period. The late nineteenth century had seen the culmination of the process of radical change in many American industries. Mechanization and the division of labor had enhanced the productivity of many industries, but they had also effected a virtual revolution in the relations between workers and employers. Former skilled crafts-men often found themselves reduced to cogs in the new machine, subject to both economic insecurity and a newly abased notion of their own worth as individuals. Where confronted, such alienation and eco-nomic weakness might give rise to labor union movements that had as their psychological counterpart the development of a working-class consciousness. As United Mine Workers President John Mitchell put it in 1903, "The average wage earner has made up his mind that he must remain a wage earner. He has given up the hope of a kingdom come, where he himself will be a capitalist, and asks that the reward for his work be given him as a workingman" (Brooks 1964, 114).

In many respects, oystering in the Sayville area had followed the general pattern of land-based industries, for the two decades previous to the strike had seen increasing mechanization and specialization, amounting to a transition from a cottage system of production to some-thing very like a factory. Were Ockers and his workers being swept willy-nilly along with the great currents of national and international change? If so, then modernization and industrialization had in a short space of time managed a radical transformation of what had been a close-knit, church-centered immigrant community, for it must be re-membered that, unlike most American industrial communities, West Sayville's bosses and workers were alike immigrants, from the same area of Holland in this case, and apparently from the same class. If we knew nothing more about local life in the period, the account of the strike might lead us to suppose that the Dutch immigrant com-munity of West Sayville had become both Americanized and modern-ized—that is to say, the shippers were as drawn by class and cultural interests to their Yankee fellows as the Dutch workers were to Yankee workers. The existence of the Blue Point Oyster Shippers' Association seems to attest to the first, as the union does to the second.

There are reasons to question such an interpretation, however. Many of the Dutch shippers, as we shall see, could be characterized as cosmopolitans, men whose broader view of affairs gave them more in common with fellow businessmen than with fellow immigrants. With the exception of Jake Ockers, however, they were all members of one of the two local Dutch churches and typically "pillars" within them. The churches and other institutions, which remain out of view when only the workplace is considered, still served to bind the Dutch shippers to the other immigrants. The Shippers' Association can be justly interpreted as representing a union of Dutch and non-Dutch shippers to protect their common interests, but it does not represent a general cultural identity any more than most international alliances do. These men had united to wage a battle against common foes, whether the enemy turned out to be the oyster cartel of Connecticut or the union in Sayville.

That the union and strike testify to a common working-class consciousness that had overcome the differences between the Dutch and Yankee workers is even more doubtful. We must first view this apparent labor movement in the local context, for the strike of 1902 was neither the first nor the last confrontation between "small men" and "large" on the shores and waters of the Great South Bay. Warriors against shippers in former and later battles rarely styled themselves "workers," however, but rather, "baymen," a word, it can be readily imagined, with very different connotations. The bayman was an "independent fisherman" who "followed the water," which meant that he pursued a variety of maritime activities with the seasons, one of which might indeed be work for the shippers. As the bayman saw it, his freedom was contingent on the continued existence of a "free bay," uncontrolled by the shippers, and it was for the persistence of these public waters that he associated with his fellows and fought. Considering that the principal issue of these associations was the retention of a free bay, it makes more sense to view them as "antienclosure" movements than as fledgling unions. Men like Bill Collins and Captain Ketcham may not have been the vanguard of a workers' movement so much as conservatives fighting the forces of private property on this last, watery frontier. If the free bay continued to exist, the independent local bayman would always be able to make a varied living on the water, with or without seasonal employment in the oyster shanties. Perhaps the antienclosure mentality did correspond to a kind of class-consciousness, insofar as the watery commons was always the refuge of the poor. If so, however, then the class involved did not see themselves through Mitchell's lens, and if men like Collins used the union rhetoric of the day, that should not lead us to assume that it was the idiom of the rank and file. Their world view is better revealed in the court cases so often brought against the shippers through the decades, wherein the key words are always "free bay" and "independent bayman" (see McCay n.d. and 1982).

The Dutchmen, however, were conspicuous by their relative absence from the union rolls, although they certainly formed the great majority of the work force in the large oyster houses of West Sayville and Oakdale. Any theory of rising working-class consciousness must account for their apparent reluctance to join the union and take part in the strike. There were actually many reasons, and as we shall see later, some arising from the objective position of Dutch workers in the oyster company, including their more economically dependent relation to their boss than that of their American counterparts in Sayville or Patchogue.

There may have been other barriers to the association of union, at least as that social form was defined here in the United States. In Holland, industry and unionization followed a distinctive path. According to Lijphart (1968; 97–98), the industrial revolution did not begin in the Netherlands until around 1870, and a large industrial proletariat did not emerge until the years around the turn of the century. Thus, late in its industrial development, Holland may have been equally distinctive in its social structure. The ruling class had for centuries been comprised more of merchant princes than of landed gentry, and if the lack of a strong nobility meant that the workers of Holland were deprived of the buffer between management and workers provided by the aristocracy of England and Germany (Lijphart 1968, 98), they were also less subject to the sort of "class as natural order" ideology that prevailed in lands so blessed with a dominant landed aristocracy. Holland was a thoroughly bourgeois nation, and if industry was slow in coming to nineteenth-century Zeeland, for example, there was by then a long history of trade, of the rise and fall of minor and relatively major entrepreneurs. Perhaps the poor could always hope for some such entrepreneurial future for themselves. Whether or not such hopes were and are delusive, it is interesting to note that although "the objective inequalities between classes . . . are relatively high in Holland . . . it is difficult to assess the relative strength and persistence of class loyalties and class antagonisms in twentieth-century Holland. As Johan Goudsblom points out, 'social stratification is seldom made the topic of public discussion . . . even sociologists have tended to shun the topic' " (Lijphart 1968, 19–20; Goudsblom 1967, 63).

This lack of a class-focused ideology and idiom may be attributed to competing ideologies and associations—in particular, the *verzuiling,* or "pillars," which continue to divide Holland into vertical associations of individuals ranged under church and sectarian banners. As Lijphart points out (1968, 90), "Religious and class lines in Holland run at right angles to each other. If the class cleavages are represented as horizontal lines, the religious cleavages are almost perfectly vertical lines." Such pillars have penetrated all realms of association and public activity, from political parties to television programming, and insofar as they do they necessarily militate against other ways of dividing up and, more subtly, of viewing the social world. Those unions which succeeded in Holland came, for the most part, under sectarian banners. So far from disrupting religious association in favor of class alignment, such unions reinforced the old religious loyalties.

As for the immigrant Dutch of West Sayville, preexisting patterns of association and ideology may have militated against any working-class consciousness in their new home as well. If he sympathized with those American baymen fighting for the retention of the "commons," the Dutch bayman may have been at least somewhat ambivalent about the issue of property, for if he entertained hopes of a great entrepreneurial future for himself, he must have known that such a fate hinged on his ability to hold, by secure tenure, underwater acreage. An unlimited future required unlimited acres so held. The local communal culture reinforced this entrepreneurial self-view through a contractual idiom, while its churches provided arenas in which personal ambivalence and interpersonal antagonisms arising in the increasingly stratified world of West Sayville could be expressed in a dramatic, but essentially less dangerous, ritualized form. In exploring all this in the following chapters, we will witness the resilience of a community and its culture adapting to rapidly changing circumstances. Those changes, as we have already seen, began with the growth of the oyster industry in 1860s and 1870s, but the path taken in those years had led, by the time of the strike, to a local world that would have been unrecognizable to the youthful Hage or DeWaal.

6

OYSTER IS KING

Around the table with Jake Ockers on that August morning of 1902 sat the other shippers of Sayville, West Sayville, and Oakdale: Ed Westerbeke, Case and Leonard Beebe, J. A. Cochrane, Wolfer Van Popering, Nicholas Vander Borgh, Ed Brown, and James Herring. Herring was the manager of the Lewis Blue Points Company, a large operation that was the local arm of a Connecticut oyster firm. Ed Brown ran a small, recently opened Bayport shipping firm, and Cochrane headed a middle-sized operation in Oakdale, soon to move farther west to Bayshore. The rest were Dutchmen, as were most of the other members not attending that particular meeting. Together their shore-side plants dominated the coastline from Oakdale to Brown's River, though by that time all the major shippers but Ockers were located around West Sayville's West Basin. The oyster king would join them there in 1908.[1]

On the bay these men held leases on many hundreds of acres and worked them with small fleets of power- and sailboats. They were sharing in the general prosperity the oyster trade was enjoying at that time, for by 1901 the oyster accounted for half the value of the New York fisheries, amounting to 1,768,713 bushels of market oysters and another 545,075 bushels of seed oysters (whose use will be explained below). These $2 million worth of shellfish were largely the result of the rise of cultivation in New York. The Blue Points of the Great South Bay accounted for a good share of that revenue, and any visitor to West

Sayville in 1902 would have had little difficulty discerning the major occupation and preoccupation of this village whose streets were paved with oyster shells. The organization of the Blue Point Oyster Shippers' Association signaled a certain maturity in the growth of that local industry, but not yet its peak development. Several years of expansion and growth still lay ahead—until around 1910, when various circumstances would enter the picture to curtail the boom. More on that ending later. Our present task is to explore the rise of the industry— how it passed in the brief space of a few decades from the expanding cottage industry of the 1860s to the agro-business of 1902. The story of that development is one of constant advances in the assertion of human control over the forces of nature, and of the equally vital imposition of notions of private property on the once-public domain. These were processes begun elsewhere, only belatedly making their way into the Great South Bay, so our story really begins on other shores (see Ingersoll 1881).

For centuries oysters had been a popular food in both Europe and America, and shellfish had been gathered by the millions with various techniques from natural beds on both continents. As with many another abundant natural resource, the supply of oysters seemed inexhaustible, an appearance that faded rapidly when the vastly increased consumption of the mid-nineteenth century began to take its toll.

In some regions the drop in the wild oyster population was dramatic. In Zeeland, for example, whence all the early immigrants to West Sayville area had come, the oyster merchants were handling 3 million oysters in 1861, one-third of those gathered by Zeeland fishermen, the rest brought in by English and Scottish oystermen. In 1864 the same dealers saw only 50,000 oysters, and the two hundred or so Zeelander crews who depended on the trade found themselves in desperate straits. The situation was much the same in the other oystering districts of western Europe and in the northern fishery of America as well. While the tremendous natural beds of the Chesapeake promised to supply oysters for years to come, the heavily fished waters of Long Island Sound along the southern shore of Connecticut were by the 1860s showing rapidly diminishing returns. Meanwhile, the demand for oysters showed no signs of abating, so a powerful incentive arose for the discovery of alternative means to secure adequate numbers of that shellfish.

EUROPEAN METHODS

For the Hollanders back home in Yerseke, the answer came from France, where recent research had built on the oyster culture practiced centuries earlier by the Romans. It was generally understood that oysters propagated during the summer by releasing millions of eggs and sperm into the surrounding water. Astronomical numbers of larval oysters resulted, but of these the only survivors were those lucky enough to alight on a hard, slime-free surface to which they could affix themselves and grow. For the vast majority, the soft mud or shifting sands brought an immediate end. The French method involved placing cleaned ceramic tiles in tidal areas where natural oysters were thought to spawn, thus supplying an artificial home for the spat. When the young seed oyster had reached the proper size, the tiles could be easily collected by hand when exposed by the ebbing tides. The young oysters were then scraped off their artificial home and placed on the muddy bottoms of their natural estuarine environment to grow to marketable size. In Yerseke the tiles were placed in oyster pits, basins constructed out of stone into which the tides of the Oosterschelde River were allowed to flow. The spat were eventually transferred from these artificial nurseries to the muddy bottom of the river, from whence they could be gathered, once again by hand, when the twenty-foot tides left thousands of acres exposed.

The introduction of oyster culture to Yerseke required a redefinition of property relations. Before 1870 all the lands of the Oosterschelde River were in the public domain, available for the use of any and all inhabitants of the region. The practice of oyster culture described above depended on the ability of culturists to privately control those portions of the river bottom on which they wished to plant seed oysters. The national government was willing to encourage the industry, and it immediately divided the lands in question into parcels, five to ten hectares in extent, which were leased at a public sale. These leases ran for five years, but were renewable, and that was enough security for the entrepreneurs who bought up the rights with alacrity. By 1887 nothing remained of the free fishery on the Oosterschelde, for every parcel was under the lease control of one of several wealthy investors, who by then ran a lucrative local oyster industry (Glerum 1953). Given the methods, the Yerseke industry was labor-intensive, so that if the livelihood of the free oysterman had disappeared, hundreds of jobs for men and women were created by the new oystering methods. For the rest, there was still the mussel grounds, though these too were destined to be divided into leased lots (van Ysseldijk 1973, 500–501).

AMERICAN METHODS

Developments in America during the same period had proceeded differently, owing to both ecological conditions and a more complex set of property relations. In southern Connecticut in the 1860s, several oystermen had devised their own version of oyster culture. Instead of placing tiles in tidal flats, as the Europeans did, the Yankee oystermen simply dumped thousands of bushels of clean oyster shells on the estuarine bottoms at the propitious moment in July when those waters were aswarm with the microscopic larvae of the natural growth oysters. If done properly, this method resulted in abundant crops of young oysters, with far less labor and hence expense than the European methods incurred. There was here, as in Europe, however, need for private control of such planted grounds, and thus the state of Connecticut, under whose jurisdiction most of the grounds came, began to lease lots in this period.

Back on the Great South Bay things were moving more slowly. Although Brookhaven and Islip townships had followed Connecticut's lead by leasing lots in the West Bay beginning in 1851, it was not until the late 1870s that the need was felt to make even indirect use of the seed culturing that had developed in New England. The slowness in this regard had nothing to do with any reluctance to innovate on the part of the West Sayville shippers; it was simply that local natural seed had remained available. Indeed, there had been enough not only for their own limited needs but also for shipment to New England planters. But the growing demand for Blue Points, particularly in Europe, coincided around this time with a steadily diminishing supply of natural seed oysters in the East Bay. The hundreds of boats tonging these grounds yearly must have taken a toll; probably enough grown oysters were taken before they could spawn to impair the natural population increase. In any case, one obvious solution to the problem would have been to use the East Bay for the artificial cultivation of oysters by Connecticut methods. But such a move would have required the carving up of those public grounds into privately leased lots, and the hundreds of voting baymen who had come to depend on these grounds for at least part of their income would not have happily countenanced that.

A more costly solution, but one very productive in the long run, did present itself. For various reasons, the Connecticut growers were beginning to find that although their seed crops propagated well and grew nicely, their grown oysters were experiencing difficulty in the market. The rising demand for seed oysters in the Great South Bay encouraged several Connecticut growers to specialize in their production. The Oakdale shippers were happy to buy this seed and happier still to discover that the yield in adult oysters was much better than with Great South Bay seed.

The Oakdale shippers saw to their own seed supply. Those who could afford it purchased whole or part interests in schooners that had capacities for a few thousand bushels. Their intrepid captains took them each spring around Long Island to the Connecticut shore to purchase seed from growers there. Back and forth they sailed from April through June, until each of the shippers had all the seed oysters they needed. About 500 bushels of seed would be shoveled onto each acre of bay bottom, so that the requirements of the larger planters were considerable. Already in 1879 the Oakdale shippers were planting about 200,000 bushels of seeds between them. While something like half that amount still came from the East Bay, each year saw a steady growth in the use of Connecticut seed and a concomitant reduction of the local product. Thus the baymen who tonged those young oysters on the public grounds found themselves reduced to a far less important role in the local industry.

The 1880s saw a near-constant advance in the productivity of the Oakdale companies, most of which were officially incorporated in that decade. By 1890 Ockers's plant employed about thirty men and shipped over 15,000 barrels of oysters a year. The more modest operations of Van Wyen, Westerbeke, Vander Borgh, Van Popering, and W. S. Biggs (the only non-Dutch shipper in the area by then) did about one-third of that business each. The "Blue Points" grown from Connecticut seed (for so they were still called) were evidently finding great favor in the world market. Indeed, the local paper was pleased to report that Queen Victoria had the good taste to prefer Blue Point oysters over competing American and European types, even if she did require their rough shells to be sanded smooth before allowing them past the portals of Windsor Castle.

Shipping to Europe or elsewhere depended on getting the oysters into New York in good condition. That task was considerably facilitated by the completion of the southern line of the Long Island Railroad in 1867. After that date, thousands of barrels of oysters could leave Sayville station each week by express trains, although the shipment of shellfish by boat continued through the beginning of World War I, providing a competition with the railroad that kept the freightage charge down.

Even greater advances were made in harvesting. In that end of the enterprise, the shippers had two principal requirements: more land to grow their oysters on and more efficient and dependable means to get them up as needed. The land question was primarily a legal one. With the rise of cultivation, a distinction had been made in many American oystering and clamming regions (including the bay) between areas devoid of natural growth oysters, which were leasable, and those with such beds, which were retained for public use. In practice, however, much land fell ambiguously between these two poles, for small numbers of oysters or clams might be found anywhere at all, leaving it to the officiating body to decide whether such grounds were leasable or not. Many a battle was fought through the "oyster commissions," with lobbying and electioneering from both sides. In the Brookhaven waters a further complication had been the claim of a body of private citizens known as "the Smith heirs" to ownership of a substantial portion of the West Bay. These were valuable grounds which the shippers wanted available for lease and which many baymen were equally anxious to keep public. A civil suit brought by the heirs in 1899 ended with a division of the disputed area (see Plate 20) in a way that rendered to the complainants a full 13,000 acres of grounds, which they in turn leased to the shippers.

Meanwhile the harvesting of the large planters' ever-expanding holdings was facilitated in 1893 by the repeal of the laws prohibiting dredging, which had been on the local books since 1870. Even though operated by hand at this date, a sloop armed with a dredge could harvest far more than one with two tongers aboard. Antidredging laws still prevailed on public grounds, however, so that the free bayman was denied this much more efficient means of gathering shellfish, ostensibly in the interests of conservation.

By far the most important innovation in the harvesting operations was the advent of the gasoline engine-powered boat. The engine had in fact two important functions in the oyster fishery; not only could the boats themselves be engine-powered, making it possible to use much larger craft with a far greater carrying capacity than the sloop, but the dredges could also be lifted by engine power, so that dredges with 21-bushel capacities might replace the much smaller hand dredge. Jake Ockers was naturally the first planter to float an engine-powered dredge boat; the year was 1896 and the boat was the *Jacob Ockers*. The future plainly lay with power, and every planter of any size followed suit, so that by the year of the strike, 1902, every large planter had at least one "oyster steamer" and Ockers had several.

By the time of the strike, the shipping companies had come a long way. Beginning in 1889 they had moved their shoreside operations to waterfrontage rented from Sam Green, where by 1902 all but Jake Ockers's plant crowded along the West Basin. Ockers farmed something like 800 acres in the West Bay by that time, from which he shipped over 30,000 barrels of oysters with the help of something over sixty workers and a veritable fleet comprising several power-dredge boats and many more sloops. Other large shippers, such as Westerbeke and Vander Borgh, each planted several hundred acres and employed around forty men. By that time they each had at least one power dredge. Their workers must have had a difficult time swallowing Ockers's complaint that "things weren't too good in the industry just then because the price of seed has lately risen very high."

Ockers was telling the truth. The rising price of Connecticut seed oysters around the turn of the century had, however, provided the impetus for yet another expansion of the South Bay shipping industry. By 1902 Ockers and Westerbeke had already purchased their own seed-growing lands in the Long Island Sound and were about to expand into the Peconic as well (see Figure 1). By the closing years of that decade, the other large shippers had all followed suit, and marvelous "sets" were being reported on the shells they had dumped on their new eastern and northern grounds.

There were other signs that the industry was thriving, for several new shipping companies had sprung up in recent years. William Rudolph, destined to become one of the most successful local planters, had only begun his operations in 1896. In 1902, the very year of the strike, T. H. Dykstra commenced his business, specializing in the open-stock trade which, though long a big part of the Connecticut business, had only lately become much in the bay industry. Ed Ockers (unrelated to Jacob) started a small firm in 1903, as did Frederick Ockers, Jake's brother, in 1904. Each summer nearly all these shippers either expanded or improved their operations, floating more vessels or adding opening or culling houses or storage facilities. There were, of course, setbacks. Harsh winters killed thousands of oysters or rendered them inaccessible under the ice. Theft also took its toll. Against nature, though, the Dutch shippers waged an ever more successful war. If they could not tong the oysters through the ice, they would use their dredge boats, copper-sheathed for the duty, as ice-cutters smashing through the coastal ice to the free water beyond. The shorefront told a clear story of an industry that was doing very well indeed.

The shippers did not really deny their success, they proclaimed its legitimacy. As Ed Westerbeke had put it, "they were working men themselves." From Jake Ockers in the 1870s to William Rudolph in the 1890s, the lives of these men had followed the same pattern. They began by skippering their own sloops on the bay, from which they purchased oysters to run themselves to the New York market. It was a life of hard work, and not without real risks. Having achieved some success, few men of that stamp are likely to keep much distance from the workplace, and most of these Dutch oystermen were no exception to that rule. Ockers, Rudolph, and all the others were typically to be found at the shore, not just behind the desks of the shipping offices but walking the work areas, casting a careful eye on the culling, opening, and barreling of their product. Frederick Ockers was famous for his concerned presence at his shorefront operations. One day, as the local paper reported, he was pacing the timbers that formed the floats in which the harvested oysters were put in order to drink fresh water and plump up. So preoccupied was he with the pressures of the business that he stepped off the end of the float and into the water for an unsought-for drink himself. His brother Jake was even more notorious. Many a surviving bayman remembers his ability to pay off his workers each week totally from memory, having kept track of his sixty workers presences and absences through the week.

However intimate their knowledge of the workers and their labors, by 1902 neither Ockers nor Westerbeke would be found hauling a dredge or topping a barrel. For an understanding of the nature of the work itself, we are better off viewing it from the perspective of those who did it.

Plate 1. Bastiaan Broere, Early Immigrant from Zeeland

Plate 2. Jacob Ockers, "King Oyster Planter"

Plate 3. Three of Long Island's Most Extensive Oyster Planters

Plate 4. West Sayville Basin Showing Floats, Oyster Houses, and Sloops

Plate 5. Oyster "Steamer," with Dredge Up

Plate 6. Inside Jake Ockers's Oyster House, Early 20th Century

Plate 7. Oyster House Crew

Plate 8. Tonging Oysters Through Cut Ice, Early 20th Century

Plate 9. *A Severe Winter Brings Piled Ice and Broken Floats and Piers, Early 20th Century*

Plate 10. *Loading Barrels of Clams*

Plate 11. 'Cobus Kwaak, "Independent Bayman," Tonging

Plate 12. Catboat on the Bay

Plate 13. Green's Creek, Oystering Vessels

Plate 14. Setting a Pound Net in the Bay

Plate 15. Ladies Posing on a Sloop

Plate 16. Women on the Dock

Plate 17. Heading for Fire Island, Fourth of July Picnic

Plate 18. West Sayville Hook and Ladder Company

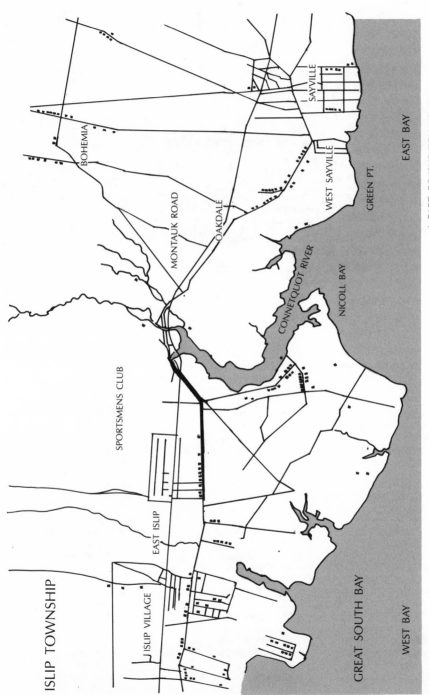

ISLIP TOWNSHIP

ISLIP VILLAGE

EAST ISLIP

SPORTSMENS CLUB

BOHEMIA

MONTAUK ROAD

OAKDALE

SAYVILLE

WEST SAYVILLE

GREEN PT.

CONNETQUOT RIVER

NICOLL BAY

GREAT SOUTH BAY

WEST BAY

EAST BAY

A PART OF ISLIP TOWNSHIP. 1895

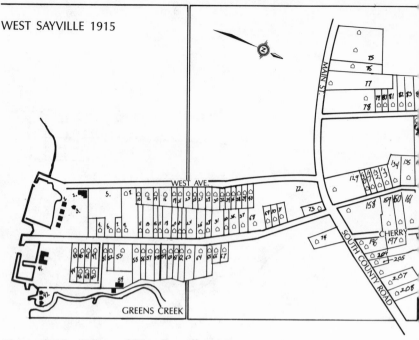

WEST SAYVILLE 1915

Plate 20. The Village of West Sayville, circa 1915

Key to West Sayville 1915

1.,2.,3. Oyster houses
4. G. Goldsworth
5. J. Van Wyen
6. Van Wyen
7. L. Van Vessen
8.,9. Van Popering
10. DeWaal
11. T. Buys
12. Mrs. M. Zegel
13. Mrs. J. Otto
14. C. Kahler
15. Mrs. M. Zegel
16. Mrs. Nellie Locker
17. Mrs. Wm. Slager
18. McLellan
19. J. DeWaal
20. J. DeWaal
21. R. Schaefer
22. Mrs. M. Zegel
23. Van Wyen
24. Van Wyen
25. M. Zegel
26. Miss C. Rudolph
27. Wm. Van Popering
28. Mrs. Vander Borgh
29. L. Van Vessen
30. J. Van Vessen
31. Christian Reformed Church
32. J. Newhouse
33. Mrs. DeRonde
34. Wm. Barkenbush
35. Geo. Rudolph
36. J. Buys

37. Otto Kahler
38. Wm. Van Wyen
39. C. Zegel
40. J. Bevelander
41.,42. Oyster houses
43. Paul Zegel
44. no name
45. C. Zegel
46. Peter Zegel
47. C. Griek
48. Wm. Griek
49. J. Dykstra
50. T. H. Dykstra
51. no name
52. H. Brandt
53. J. Stein
54. Dykstra boatyard
55. Wm. Tucker
56. O. Simpson
57. T. Zegel
58. John Colson
59. S. P. Green
60. Mrs. Simpson
61. J. Tucker
62. S. P. Green
63. Wm. Rudolph
64. Ed. Rudolph
65. Van Vessen
66. G. Vander Borgh
67. Wm. Barkenbush
68. DeGraff
69. Mrs. E. Van Vessen
70. Mrs. C. Van Vessen
71. J. Beebe
72. E. Edwards and Mrs. Strong

73. R. C. Tucker
74. Mrs. David Van Popering
75. Case DeGraff
76. S. P. Green
77. Mrs. M. C. Strong
78. F. G. Bourne
79. T. Zegel
80. D. Kwaak
81. J. Kwaak
82. Jacobus Kwaak
83. Wm. Kwaak
84. Daniel White
85. Mrs. F. DeGraff
86. Walter Brown
87. C. Vanderwender
88. Wm. Seerveldt
89. G. Van Yseldyke
90. P. Kaan
91. P. Verbeek
92. P. Zegel
93. Ed. Van Essendelft
94. J. Sanders
95. Hiran Sebree
96. A. Otto
97. F. DeGraff
98. P. Kwaak
99. C. Broere
100. D. Hoek
101. Wm. Van Essendelft (shop)
102. L. Good (?)
103. L. Candreye
104. J. Hoek
105. L. Kwaak
106. Adrian Hoek
107. C. Locker

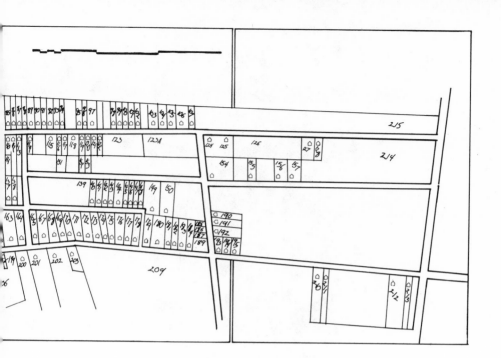

108. J. Verizer
109.
110. Leeman
111. DeGraaf
112. Ed. Seerveldt
113. Frank Newhouse
114. Jacob Simpson
115. C. Zegel
116. M. Van Essendelft
117. J. Kaan
118. Great South Bay Water Co.
119. J. Van Essendelft
120. no name
121. F. DeGraff
122. J. Van Essendelft
123.,123A. Wm. Smith
124. Miller
125. Raymond
126. Edw. Schell estate
127. no name
128. F. Losee
129. Burke
130. S. P. Green
131. J. Buys
132. J. Van Essendelft
133. J. Bakelaar
134. Chas. Marsh
135. M. Van Popering
136. Mrs. C. Smith
137. O. Washboe
138. no name
139. Tyler
140. C. Vander Borgh
141. J. Vander Borgh
142. Wm. Van Essendelft

143. W. Van Essendelft
144. J. Buyse
145. J. Coleman
146. no name
147. S. Leuwen
148. no name
149. M. Paauee
150. Town sand pits
151. Wetherland (?)
152. H. Van Vessen
153. no name
154. C. DeGraff
155. P. DeDrew
156. J. Newhouse
157. A. Vander Griek
158. S. P. Green
159. S. P. Green
160. DeGraff
161. J. Brandt
162. M. Van Popering
163. Dutch Reformed Church
164. P. Van Vessen
165. Mrs. Ed. Westerbeke
166. Fred Ockers
167. Wm. Otto
168. Mrs. Thames
169. Westerbeke
170. Gustav Albertis
171. P. DeReaux
172. Wm. Westerbeke
173. J. Seerveldt
174. H. Vander Borgh
175. Miss L. Vander Borgh
176. H. Vander Borgh
177. A. Paauee

178. Kwaak
179. S. P. Green
180. J. Blom
181. M. DeReaux
182. Ed Ockers
183. Th. Thomas
184. J. Hoek
185.–188. no names
189. Mrs. Thompson
190. J. J. Hoek
191. Ch. Pagels
192. J. Wessels
193. Mrs. Stahl
194. M. Evisdyke
195. C. Dykstra
196. J. Mott
197. H. Otto
198. G. Rose
199. H. Otto
200. L. Howe
201. L. Brandt
202. Westerbeke
203. no name
204. Mrs. Strong
205. S. P. Green
206. Mrs. J. D. Green
207. Wm. Westerbeke
208. Edward Westerbeke
209. no name
210. Abraham Wessels
211. M. Evisdyke
212. C. H. Hansen
213. R. A. Smith
214.,215, Edward Schell estate

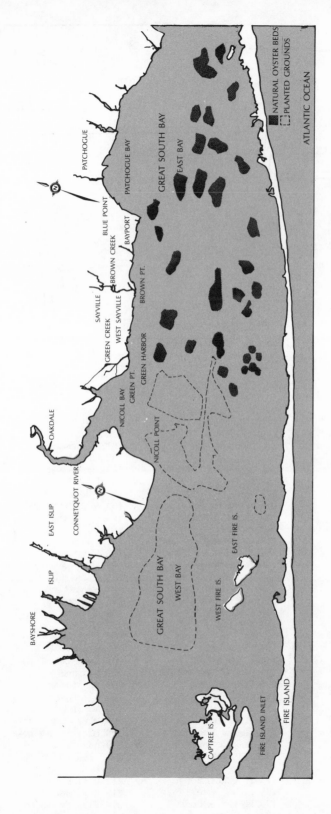

Plate 21. The Great South Bay Near West Sayville

7

BAYMEN AND WORKERS

It is easy to appreciate Ockers's entrepreneurial view of life and work in 1902, for his own career and that of his fellows seemed to bear witness to the fact that anyone might rise through hard work and perhaps some shrewd investment. What, however, of the workers of that era? Certainly the wretched fellow bent ten hours a day over a bench culling or opening oysters could have harbored few delusions about the golden opportunities of a life on the Great South Bay.

THE SECOND WAVE

Perhaps he did, though, for the view people hold of their work is never simply based on its objective character.[1] Human beings judge the present in the light of their remembered past and expected future, and from that point of view the work in the oyster house might be a very different experience for the newly arrived Dutch immigrant than for the Yankee bayman. By 1902 a large share of the West Sayville work force was composed of immigrants recently come from Zeeland and elsewhere in Holland in a second wave that had begun in the 1870s. These families were by and large a destitute lot, drawn to West Sayville by the promise of employment in the booming local industry. Many of them came once again from Yerseke, where their own famous oyster industry had suffered some setbacks.

Unusually harsh winters in the early 1890s had killed a large part of the oyster crop in the Oosterschelde. Being exposed in low tides, the oysters were more vulnerable to the cold than the shellfish of the Great South Bay, and a number of businesses had closed as a result. The real blow, however, seems to have come in that period with the gradual loss of the British market. In these same years the erstwhile sons of Yerseke and Bruinisse, now of West Sayville, were busy expanding into the very same market. The queen, we remember, preferred Blue Points.

With the decline of the industry, and the hard life of the few independents, life in Yerseke was difficult indeed in the closing years of the century. Adriaan Daane remembers:

My father owned a small boat with a flat bottom. While the tides were high everything was fine, but if you didn't make port before the tides receded, you were left high and dry until the incoming tide allowed you to proceed again. While the tide was out, you anchored your boat and then you could walk and pick up mussels, "kruikels," or periwinkles. You could also spear eels or fish in the puddles. . . . Many fishermen and women worked in the oyster shops and for the shellfish companies. The companies bought the fish and shellfish from independents and paid as little as possible. Many townspeople walked out from the mainland when the tide was low and gathered whatever was possible to make a few dollars. One particular danger for those gatherers was the North Sea "fog" which comes up very fast. Many times people drowned because they lost their direction in the fogs. . . . The winters were at times very severe, cold and miserable and much unemployment. If you didn't work you didn't eat. The government doled out a bit of food or credit once in a while if you were a member of the Dutch Reformed [state church] in good standing. . . . My father was getting tired of the unemployment and living from hand to mouth in Holland, so he went to the village square one day to read the enticing propaganda about colonization in South America. . . .

Adriaan's father did consider emigration to tropical climes, but hazards suffered by relatives in Brazil convinced his mother that the family would be better off in North America. One of her sisters was married and living in West Sayville, and she encouraged Adriaan's father to come there, promising a job and even offering to borrow money from the Sayville bank to bring over the rest of the family. Ade's father left Yerseke for West Sayville in November 1908. Two days after his arrival he was working for Westerbeke Brothers oyster company at $2.50 per ten-hour day. While that wage may have been less than acceptable to the strikers six years earlier, it was enough for the newly arrived immigrant to send money home to his wife and children. Adriaan recalled, "Whenever he sent back a few American dollars we started to live like kings. That following winter . . . we even had real butter once in a while and two slices of bread for every meal."

No wonder that men like this, who comprised a large part of the work force in 1902, were more than willing to line up for work that September when the season opened. Westerbeke Brothers was not the only oyster company willing to help their countrymen over. Certainly it was in the interests of the shippers to bring over such loyal workers. The money would be paid back after all, and in the meantime they had men who were in their moral as well as financial debt. Nor did the financial relation typically stop there. If a worker wanted to buy a home, where was he to seek the mortgage? There was the Sayville bank mentioned by Daane, but the Oysterman's bank, as its actual title read, was in fact an extension of Jacob Ockers's (and others) interests, so that one way or the other the mortgage seeker came to the door of one of the shippers, and typically to that of his employer. A loan of that size really served to cement the bond between employer and employee.

Not all aid to immigrants came from the shippers, though; some were able to secure emigration loans from local shopkeepers or from the Hollander's Benevolent Association. It would be wrong, furthermore, to conclude that the bond between the immigrant workers and their employer was only financial in nature. It must be remembered that the situation in West Sayville was unusual with regard to their relationship. Immigrant labor was common enough in the America of 1902, but immigrant bosses were far less so, and particularly rare was the industry like oystering in West Sayville, where the richest boss and most destitute worker were from the same quarter of the old world, and possibly the same village. Nearly all Dutch shippers of that date had been brought to America as children, and it is reasonable to assume that Ockers, Westerbeke, and the others, having grown up in Dutch-speaking families, would have addressed their newly arrived employees in their native tongue, and probably in the Zeeland dialect. There must have been some comfort in that for the worker on foreign shores.

As for the labor itself, that was likely to have been less familiar. On the Great South Bay there were no great tides whose ebb left the oysters exposed, so the shellfish had to be gathered from the decks of boats. When the season opened in September, the planters would send their dredgers out to the grounds in the bay. The skippers of these bulky craft earned the honorific "Captain," a most important title in a maritime community and one shared with most of their employers, who had "come up," we remember, as skippers themselves. These were skilled men—some of them, like the Bakelaars, from the northern Dutch Island of Texel and presumably practiced seamen before coming to America.

THE WORK

To appreciate the nature of their task, we must imagine that of a farmer who reaped his crop from ground he could not see but had to know intimately. Such harvesting was difficult enough work when the weather and water were fine, but that was far from always being the case. Whatever the conditions, the task of taking up the oysters was essentially the same. The pilot would steer his vessel in straight lines over the "field," dragging dredges over both the port and starboard sides of his vessel. The dredge was a rectangular iron frame with a toothed blade or bar of iron at the bottom. Anything on the bay bottom would be churned up by this bar and thrown back into the "bag" of iron rings behind (see Plate 5). Having reached the end of one imaginary row, the skipper would turn his craft like a plowman a team of horses, while the deck hands would raise the dredges by means of a motor-driven hoist and tip the contents onto the deck. If everything went well there would be up to 21 bushels of oysters in every such dredge load, comprising many shellfish and probably a good deal else besides. Some of the extras were welcomed: "a good mess of flounders, periwinkles, horseshoe crabs" might be tumbled in with the rocks and shells. Proceeding in this manner, the dredge boat would gather about 500 bushels of oysters from an average cultivated acre, with which load they would turn back toward the shore. In the early autumn, the orders for oysters were not yet large, and a good number of oysters dredged in this period were laid down again closer to the shore. Jake Ockers in particular was shrewd or lucky enough to have secured oyster grounds immediately off his shoreside operations, from which oysters could be taken up more easily in the winter.

It was inside the oyster houses, however, that most of the workers found employment, and there was nothing remotely romantic or seafaring about the life in those shops (see Plate 6). This kind of work had been done mostly by women in Yerseke, but here in West Sayville the women found other employment, and opening and culling were most typically "men's work." But before the oysters were packed or opened, they were "floated," a process that involved placing the shell-fish in floats constructed of old ship masts containing fresh water. The oysters would "drink" (absorb) the fresh water, and the result was a whiter, plumper oyster more popular on the market. The bivalves, having been sorted by size, were next either barreled for shipment as shell stock or shucked and shipped as "open stock."

As of the turn of the century, most of West Sayville's oysters were destined for shell-stock shipment to Europe. For a journey of that distance, the oysters needed a secure home, which they found in recycled flour barrels up until 1904, when the Bayport Barrel Company was founded nearby in order to supply the local trade with its own sterilized containers. Packers laid about three bushels of oysters in each such barrel, hollow shell down, pressing the lot down with a circular weight. When full, each barrel was sealed on top with a wooden lid, hence the designation "double-headed barrels." A full barrel weighed several hundred pounds, so that when the cart outside the plant was loaded with twelve of them its wheels sank into the loose oyster shells with which that and all other town roads were paved. It took strong horses to pull such loads up to the Sayville railroad station, where they were loaded onto special cars to await the daily express ride into Manhattan (see Plate 10).

A goodly number of oysters were opened as well, and the call for open stock seems to have increased markedly during the first decade of the century. Some of the shippers had electric lights installed in their shops in this period, for the express purpose of permitting openers to work a night shift to fill the mounting orders. On a cold winter night one might find thirty or more workers hunched over Ockers's benches, shucking away into the morning. Since for this duty he was paid by the thousand opened, the experienced shucker's hands fairly flew to the task. He would grasp an oyster in one hand and a heavy iron knife in the other, and with two deft movements cut the muscle hinging the shells and dislodge the meat, flipping it into a waiting receptacle. Opened oysters were then packed into wooden tubs, with chunks of ice placed on the exposed meats before the top was affixed, in order to "keep" the oysters until they reached their destination.

Work on the bay and the shore continued through the winter, when the shippers received an increasing number of orders but ex-

perienced mounting difficulty in filling them, for the winter too often
gave vivid reminders that no matter how industrialized the pursuit of
oysters had become the forces of nature were far from being subdued.
Tonging or hauling and dumping the dredges in the miserable cold
was bad enough, but sometimes the fruits of these labors, particularly
if taken from shallow waters, were found dead, victims of the deep
cold. More often the problem was the ice, which made it difficult to
get at the stock. If the ice was deep and extensive enough, the workers
who had tramped the miles to the shorefront in the predawn chill
would simply be turned away. No work, and of course no pay. This
was especially true in the days before the advent of engine-powered
dredge boats, for the small wooden sloops could get trapped in Green's
creek by piled-up ice. A power-driven dredger, however, could have
her prow fitted with metal sheathing and, so armed, proceed into the
bay, breaking up ice as she went. There was a limit to the thickness
of ice such vessels could barge through, however, and the bay was
always a tricky adversary in winter. So shipper Nicholas Vander Borgh
discovered on a January afternoon in 1904, when his steamer made it
out into the open waters only to find that the ice had closed in around
her, snapping off the stearing gear in the process. In that case a fellow
shipper's steamer was able to tow the disabled vessel home, but occasionally the ice claimed a vessel for its own.

Planters could also take up oysters in the winter through the ice
on inshore grounds (see Plate 8). An old bayman still vividly recalls:

That was miserable work—we'd cut away a big slab of ice, and then some of
us would have to stand on it near the edge, bobbing up and down to try to
get the edge of it down low enough so that the other men could shove the
slab under the lip of the ice around it. That's when the men on the slab would
have to jump off and onto the main ice, while others slid the slab right under.
Then we'd lay planks across the opening and we'd stand out on them tonging
in the open water beneath. Well, as you'd guess, sometimes a man would fall
in doing that, and you can imagine how cold the water was. Even if you didn't
go in the water, there was no shelter from the icy winds that would come
across that bay. When we had so many bushels of oysters taken up that way,
we'd load them on a sleigh, which a horse could then draw to the shore and
the packing houses. Sometimes the ice wasn't so thick though as you thought.
Once the horse that was out there to pull in the sleigh broke right through
into about eight feet of freezing water. We couldn't figure out what to do, but
one of the men knew how to get him out—he just dropped a noose around
the horse's neck and pulled to choke him. Well, that horse swelled up like a
balloon and floated right up to the surface, where we grabbed him and pulled

him out onto the ice. The bath didn't seem to do him no harm, 'cause he was out on the ice later that day.

Indeed, the hazards of ice-oystering were many, as a large group of men discovered on that same January ice that had so crippled the Vander Borgh steamer in the winter of 1904. It seems that a good number of men were out on the ice tonging oysters in the manner the old bayman described, when the ice they were working on broke loose and began drifting to the southwest. The calamity was visible from the shore, where a number of would-be saviors tried to make for the runaway ice in their small sharpies. While these boats could not battle their way through the ice choked waters, the Lewis Blue Point Company's steamer could, and that boat succeeded in picking up all the unfortunate castaways before any of them suffered anything worse than "a ducking," as the local paper put it (*Suffolk County News*, January 6, 1904). Thus, the icy winters took their toll on man and oyster, for in addition to killing shellfish and freezing fishermen, a sudden freeze might pile ice onto the shore and up the creeks, smashing oyster floats or even staving in the hulls of small boats (see Plate 9).

With the advent of spring the orders for oysters diminished, and one by one, according to their size, the shippers laid off their workers for the season. A smaller crew was kept for the seeding work, which went on through June. As the schooners came in with their cargoes of seed oysters, they would be unloaded onto smaller boats and from there shoveled methodically overboard onto the oyster lots. For the summer months, the oystery was legally closed, and the shippers either spent their time journeying to their various more distant grounds to survey the progress of their "sets," or turned their attention to the raising or marketing of the other local shellfish, the clam. Cultivation of clams was still minimal though, and most of those shellfish were taken from the extensive natural beds in public waters off Bayshore.

INDEPENDENT BAYMEN

Released from their difficult duties in the shanties or on the boats of the shippers, many a Dutchman headed for the West Bay in this season in whatever size vessel his budget could afford him. On those grounds the company workers were joined by another set of Dutchmen who had, as much as they could manage, followed the bay on their own through the autumn and winter. These were the "independent baymen," remnants of the age just past before the large-scale planters had covered so much of the bay with cultivated lots and the natural growth of the East Bay had begun to wane. In the mind's eye of those who mythologized such pursuits, the bayman of the Great South Bay was "the most independent of mortals."

No more independent individual than the baymen of the Great South Bay exists. He is seen at his best during the winter months, . . . when he dons his working clothes, . . . his yacht comes out with a winter cabin, and his hard work commences. As a class the baymen are industrious and thrifty, and the many little cottages which form a considerable portion of the various villages along the south shore are an evidence of this fact.

The bayman's day of toil begins about 6 o'clock in the morning when he starts out from his cottage for "the shore," where his boat, made ready the night before, is ready for the journey to the oyster beds. The law specifies that oystering shall be done only between sunrise and sunset, so that usually the bayman arrives at the grounds by sunrise.

The process of tonging is laborious. The tongs comprise a pair of handles from eight to twelve feet long, with a double row of steel teeth with which to take up the oysters from the bottom. Usually two men go out in a boat, one tonging and the other culling. As fast as the oysters are brought out of the water by the tonger they are dumped on the boat's deck and there culled. . . . The process of sorting out the good, marketable oysters is considered a good day's work, the oysters fetching on the average about 75¢ a bushel. Years ago the Great South Bay was a Klondike for the baymen, but for many years past, since the leasing of lots came into vogue, $2 a day is considered a fair day's work. In the olden times, forty, even twenty years ago, which were the "palmy days" for the baymen, as high as $25 a day was made by individual bayman. (*Suffolk County News*, February 8, 1901)

Who were these baymen, whose independent life on the water contrasts so strikingly with that of their fellows laboring away on the boats or in the shanties of the shippers? They were to be found, as the article tells us, in many of the small villages along that section of the Great South Bay, and there were certainly a number of them among the West Sayville Dutch. Yet the independent bayman is difficult to distinguish at times from those who worked in the employ of the shippers. There was first the matter of the developmental cycle, as anthropologists like to call it—that is to say, the boy, young man, or new immigrant might be working in the oyster house until he had sufficient capital to purchase a boat or lease lots of his own. While many never reached this stage, remaining in the temporary work for the shippers for many years, the status of independent bayman was still a goal toward which they strived and hence an idea of themselves in whose light their actual circumstances were always interpreted. Such a delusion was anyway encouraged by the continued existence of this class of independent baymen, many of whom were friends, neighbors, or relations of the company employee, and by the persistence of both a "free public bay" and town-owned lands still open for leasing.

Yet it was also clear to the baymen of 1901, as the newspaper article tells us, that things were getting worse and not better for the small oysterman. Most of them relied on the natural-growth beds, which had been steadily diminishing here as elsewhere in America and western Europe. Only in the Chesapeake and farther south did the natural-growth oystermen have much of a future, for the South Bay industry was by that time clearly in the hands of the planters, men with enough capital to lease large amounts of acreage, plant thousands of bushels of seed oyster, and run a fleet of harvesting vessels to reap their bounty in the autumn and winter. Indeed, the small sloop tossing in the wintry waters with wind-frozen tonger perched on the side would have seemed a bizarre anachronism to the oyster shipper from Yerseke, where little middle ground between planter and laborer was left by the turn of the century, or quite a bit earlier in fact. But we also note that the independent oysterman expected to make about two dollars a day working public grounds in 1901, which is precisely the wage, at the time, for a man working on a boat belonging to Jake Ockers. Many a so-called independent bayman found a living thus hard to make and in any given season might find the work for the companies more attractive.

SEED OYSTERING

Yet the image of self-reliance was no doubt reborn for bayman and shoreman alike, as spring brought the winding down of the oyster planters' operations and the renewal of heroic lone ventures "seed oysterin' east." On April 1, Brookhaven Township opened the natural grounds of the East Bay to the residents of both Brookhaven and Islip townships and in the early years of this century, as in many decades before, the baymen of West Sayville raised the sails on their sloops and headed out of Green's "canal" and east into the bay. At this time there were a couple of dozen Dutch crews "oysterin' east" in season, comprising the largest contingent from any one community in the region. In addition to the financial difficulties in equipping oneself for this fishery, the pastime was itself, romantic fantasies of newspaper reporters notwithstanding, far from easy or always pleasant, even when compared to other maritime pursuits. The eastern portion of the bay is somewhat deeper than much of the western bay, and the prevailing sou'westers of early spring blow cold and often rainy winds, churning up waters at times too rough for a small and open "sharpie" or other lesser craft. Even the bayman well fitted out on a good-sized sloop wanted good seamanship in these waters.

More than a good boat and a firm hand on the tiller were necessary for the successful oysterman, and those who managed to make it pay saw themselves as a kind of elite in relation to other members of the maritime community. One old oysterer put it this way: "My father always used to say there were plenty of clamdiggers on the bay but very few baymen. A bayman can always go back to where he was the day before." Indeed, the successful return was critical to the seed oystering. As a look at the map of the bay reveals (see Plate 20) the oysters lay beneath those rolling waters of deep East Bay, not evenly scattered as the clams were in the West Bay but concentrated on the various beds. These beds were "natural," as we have already noted, perpetuated by the spats' habit of affixing themselves to abandoned shells, generations of oysters arising on the remains of their ancestors. By April the spat had grown to seed proportion, under two inches across, and were fair game to the independent oysterman—if he could find them. That job of location, as the words of the old bayman imply, was not as easy as it might seem to the uninitiated. A landsman, equipped with a map of the Bay (Plate 20), might imagine that the oysters on the bay bottom were as easily found as those in the kitchen of a shoreside country inn. Once on the water, however, he would find the map of no assistance, for the undulating surface of the bay tells even the practiced mariner little about what lies beneath.

The bayman found his quarry by means of "ranges." For example, he would know that a particular oyster bed lay beneath his vessel when the lighthouse lay directly off the mid-port side and the old mill chimney was square in his mast. The ranges were simple triangulations— spots on the water marked by the crossing of two imaginary lines emanating from shoreside points.

While these ranges do not seem to have been secret, not all oysterers are remembered as equally adept at remembering or sighting
the markers. A bayman who tonged seed oysters in the 1920s remembered his and his father's generation of oystermen:

There were plenty of 'em couldn't make a living on the bay. I knew fellers
like John, they couldn't catch enough oysters to make an oyster stew. Funny—
they were men who spent their whole lives on the water and still you couldn't
tell 'em nothing' about oysterin'. They just didn't know the ranges, or somehow
couldn't find 'em, so they'd follow someone else to where he was goin' and
lay to alongside.

One might imagine that such close attention from a fellow fisherman
was not always welcome. The oysterman remembers:

My brother Marine and I used to get followed that way, and the S——s were
the worst offenders. Wherever we'd go, as soon as we'd anchor, there they'd
come with their two boats, and they'd lay to one on each side of us. My brother
fixed them one time, though. We had steamed out of Green's Creek and we
saw 'em followin', so Marine just headed way out to Hoyle's Point—that's in
the southeast bay way out by Moriches—and sure enough they followed. We
went all the way out there and then lay to. S—— comes up alongside and
says, "Is this where they are?" Marine answers, "Is this where you wanta be?"
"Yeah—we wanta be where they are." "Good," says Marine, "you can lay here
then," and we started up and went back to the South Great Bed—that's how
Marine was.

That, evidently, was how a great many of them were, for competition and confrontation were central features of the fishery. Reputation as well as income were in the offing, for even if they sometimes
half-seriously account success in the shellfisheries to "a strong back
and a weak mind," the Dutchmen were and are as avidly interested
in evaluating the skills of the bayman as some Americans are of rating
the talents of NFL quarterbacks. The man who related the incident
above, for example, is well remembered by other surviving oysterers
as the bayman who best knew the ranges, and indeed every feature
of the bay and its bottom: "Others of us would have records, logs of
the ranges, but Cos had every one of 'em in his head."

Having found the oyster beds, the oysterman had just begun his
work. Two anchors were set off the bow and two off the stern, loosely
tethering the sloop on long lines. The vessel was thus held approximately stationary, but it could be moved by taking in the lines in either
direction. The two men who normally comprised the crew would stand

on either side of the deck, perched on the narrow gunnels only inches above the water (see Plate 11). The tongs were held directly in front of the body, their tops about head high. The length of the poles depended on the beds being worked. Generally the beds toward the barrier beaches were deeper, requiring seventeen- or eighteen-foot tongs, while the beds closer to the long Island shore took fourteens and sixteens. Standing thus on the edge of his boat, the bayman could reach a bottom only six to ten feet below. When the tongs were closed, he lifted them over the side and dumped the contents on the deck. Along with the young oysters came larger ones, of course, and the shell and other debris on which the oysters had grown. Town regulations required that the shell and full-grown osyters be immediately returned to the grounds from which they were taken, in order to ensure the continued propagation of the shellfish. This task of "pickin'" the seed oysters from the surrounding debris was sometimes performed by the second man on the boat, or among other crews by a third hand, typically a boy, or failing that, a daughter or wife. While few women were to be found on the boats by the 1920s, oystermen remember their presence as far more usual a generation earlier. Certainly the immigrant women, as we have seen, were used to hard labor in the Holland oystery, though typically on shore. For boys this job of pickin' or cullin' oysters aboard the boat of a father, uncle, or neighbor was a typical first step into the maritime life, and perhaps a more pleasant and hopeful one than into the shoreside shanties of the shippers. As for the women, their removal from this task can probably be attributed to the presence of other laboring possibilities in the New World, of which we shall see more later.

Thus working a bed, and moving his sloop along when he had to, the fortunate bayman might fill his hold with bushels of seed oysters by late afternoon, when he turned his craft home to Green's Creek. There he found the shippers waiting to pay him what always seemed an abysmally low price for his hard-won catch. Seventy-five cents a bushel was the price the shippers had agreed on in those years, and there was no point in the bayman's seeking higher prices from any of them, for the Shippers' Association had agreed to pay no more than that for any seed, and there was no market for the seed oyster other than the shippers. So passed the spring for the "most independent of mortals." On the grandest days, an oysterman might have to come in early to unload and then sail back again to the East Bay for more. Those days were rare enough, though, and more often the late afternoon found the oysterman with a few bushels and an aching back, whereupon he battened down a cloth over the exposed hatches and tacked into the headwinds and steep waters west and south, the waves breaking over the low bow and running back over the deck.

The seed oyster season closed legally on June 1, when the bayman would join his less well equipped colleagues on the West Bay. There the "free bay" was rich in natural growth clams, and the warmer weather and shallower waters were less threatening to prospective fishermen. Consequently, the range of vessels engaged in the summer clamming was broad indeed. Literally anything that could float and afforded a reasonably stable perch over the muddy bottoms could be and was used. As residents of Islip Township, the Dutchmen had legal access to the waters off Islip (west of Nicoll Point) and Babylon townships (by reciprocal agreement with that township), and while a large number of them turned out for this fishery, they were far from alone.

CLAMMING

Those baymen who had been seed oystering in the spring took their sloops west for the summer clamming. The Bayshore beds were a good deal farther from home than the East Bay oyster beds, and a difficult sail against the prevailing southwesterly winds. Before the widespread adoption of engines in the 1920s and 1930s, many of these larger craft sailed west on Monday and remained the five-day week in the West Bay clamming, returning on Friday to Green's Creek and home. Having reached the clam grounds, the Dutchmen found themselves surrounded by their less well-equipped compatriots, and a good many others from the Islips, Bayshore, and Babylon. Because of the easy conditions of the fishery, many an amateur mariner was tempted onto these waters in the summer months, hoping for a good return on a minimal investment of capital, if not of labor.

If the clams were a bit easier to find than the more concentrated oysters, there was more skill involved in catching them. Among the Dutchmen, the wooden-head clam tongs were the standard equipment in the first decades of the century. These tongs differed from those used in the oystering principally in the head design. The oyster tongs were flat-toothed, so that in closing the tongs the teeth would slide along the surface of the bay bottom. The clam tongs, on the other hand, had their teeth angled down so that in closing they dug into the bottom, loosing the clams from their burrowed home. Not only did the digging teeth require a bit more push than the oyster tongs, but the "catching" of the clams in the wire bows took a certain trick as well. According to the most successful clammers, the tonger needs a sensitive touch, lightly jerking the tongs upward as he digs out the clams, so that they are thrown just high enough to be caught in the wire bows. Not everybody was so skilled:

It takes awhile to learn how to tong properly. Some people—there was one fellow, Billy "Wacker" we called him. There's a guy who's been clammin since he's a kid and you can't tell him how to tong. He stands there and throws them clams right over the top. He was with me once on the bay, and I said to him, "Bill, you're throwin' them clams over the top o' your bows. I betcha you catch more clams in the afternoon then you do in the mornin'." "'At's right, I always do," he says. That's cause in the mornin' he's full of pep, and he's tired out by the afternoon. A good clammer can feel a dime on the bottom. The light touch is right—we call it "cribbin' 'em in."

As we have already noted, the West Bay is by and large shallower than the East Bay, so the clammer needs shorter tongs. There are, however, some much deeper channels in these waters, whose clams could rest undisturbed by all but the most industrious clammers. There was one pair who are well remembered for, among other things, the length of their tongs: twenty-six feet. Construction of such an instrument was a craft in itself. The tongs needed to be light enough to work, but strong enough, especially above the heads, to keep from snapping under pressure. Their use required special skill as well, an especially sensitive touch combined with something like brute strength. It is said that the owner of the tongs in question had laid them dockside one day, across the tops of four large barrels, when along came an old clammer obviously startled by the magnitude of the instrument. "Do you mind if I lift them?" he said. "No, go ahead," the Dutchman replied. But the old man could not raise them from their perch.

Few men worked in the difficult channel conditions. As if the length and weight of the tongs were not discouraging enough, there were also the strong tides of the channels.

We'd lay out four anchors, two over the bow and two over the stern, and pay out ten feet of line up tide and pull in ten on stern when the tide was running good. You see, the channel clams were always on the edges—so you had to hit them just right. I seen it down there when one guy on one side would get five or six clams in his tongs, and the guy on the other side of the boat would get the tongs full.

While the difficulty of these conditions meant the channel clammer could proceed relatively unbothered by competition, that was far
from the case elsewhere in the West Bay. All was public grounds and
open to every resident of the bordering townships. Sharpies and rowboats of every description found their way out on the bay, good tongers
and bad, and of course the less well respected rakers. According to
the Dutchmen, the rake requires considerably less skill than the tongs,
its head being simply pulled along by a handle and then quickly rocked
back to throw the unearthed clams back into the basket. The rake was
a smaller investment as well, and there were few area residents, no
matter what their other seasonal pursuits, who didn't venture out after
clams at least occasionally. For some of the less well-off, in fact, the
summer clamming with its minimal investment represented a vital
opportunity to fill out a year's poor wages. An interesting case were
the Swedes and Lithuanians who were brought in by the dozens to
work in Islip fish factories. These immigrants are remembered well
by the older Dutchmen for their poor living conditions and the ardor
with which they filled their slack factory time by clamming.

As one would suspect, both the sheer numbers of clammers on
the waters, and the fact that so many kinds of people with potentially
differing understandings of maritime etiquette were involved, made
the summer clamming the frequent site of dispute and confrontation.
When the day's catch was unloaded at the Bayshore or Babylon docks,
all eyes turned to the most successful boats, who could count on being
followed out on the next day. A local Dutchman so inclined to follow
his betters stood a good chance of being labeled thus for life and well
beyond.

Tenile was another one. He was workin' on Hedge's bed down there—there's
three beds like that in a triangle. We were layin' on the south west one. We
lay there and we were the first boat on the bed. 'Long comes Tenile and, plunk,
he throws down the anchor right behind the stern. My brother John says, "Get
that hatchet out a the cabin." "Don't do that," yells Tenile. "I'll move, I'll
move."

Typically, however, a bed seen to be yielding good catches became
crowded beyond the control of anyone.

We worked out here on center bed—clammin. So gosh darn many boats there
you had to push them to get your tongs in between 'em. Nine o'clock, Van
Wyen came out to buy the clams, and they took a load a clams back, but they
couldn't take 'em all off the boat, so they came out again at twelve, and at two
o'clock they come once more and got more than on the two loads before.

Prolific days stand out clearly in the folk memory, but no one seems to have become rich from clamming.

In the age of sail, as we have noted, the West Sayville fleet would sail west on Monday, most of the vessels remaining in the West Bay for the week. For those with smaller craft, however, another frequently used option was open: "the clamdigger's express." Each morning many of the West Sayville men rose in time to walk up to the railroad station and catch the six o'clock train west. Arriving in Bayshore after a short ride, they would disembark and walk the two miles down to the docks, where their sharpies would be permanently tied. Coming in at two o'clock in the afternoon, these maritime commuters would hoof up to the station again to catch the four o'clock train back home. When the first engines began to appear, low-horsepower outboards affixed to the stern of the sloops, the coming and going became decidedly easier, and most men chose to return each night after clamming in the west. As with any technological innovation, there were some older fisherman who resisted the use of the outboard, or at least claimed they distrusted it. Such men were rare among the Dutchmen, however, for if they were conservative in some ways, they were always open to improvement in their way of making a living. Even those who resisted the engine were not averse to hitching a ride, by way of a towline, to the West Bay grounds. Thus a not unusual sight in the years before World War I were lines of sloops heading west into the headwind, linked by towlines and led by an engine-powered craft. For those who depended on sail alone, the ride west was a slow one, and even the return trip might be made in such calm that the baymen were reduced to poling the craft through the shallow waters close to shore. When the winds were good and strong, though, the armada of sloops could be seen on a Friday evening, sails full out and often painted a bright red or blue. Converging on Green's Creek, the West Sayville fleet was an image of beauty that lives yet in the minds of those who came through those days.

Since the fleet did not return to its home port until the end of the week, the clams could not be brought back to West Sayville markets. Many were sold to dealers in Bayshore or Babylon, but the Dutch shippers of West Sayville were not all content to let that particular business slip through their fingers. Two in particular, Vander Borgh and Van Wyen, sent "market boats" west each day to buy the day's catch directly off the clam boats. As one of the above "reminiscences" tells us, on particulary good days several such buying trips might be made, each clearing the holds of the clammers so that they could be filled again without interruption. While the clams were occasionally plentiful, and the demand was typically considerable, the limited buyer's market meant cooperative price-fixing, so that there was nothing a clammer could do but sell at the going rate.

September 1 began the oystering season again, when several baymen who had gone seed-oystering in the spring once again turned their attention to their own leased lots in the west, where seed oysters planted in the previous years might be ready for harvesting. For the rest of the West Sayville Dutch, however, the absence of oyster lots, and the growing cold, left less desirable options. The clams were legal all year, but the wooden head tongs did not dig deep enough for the clams, who began to burrow deeper in the bay bottom as the first cold weather of autumn chilled the waters. Circumstances forced a decision.

Come September, they'd stand in line to get a job, 'cause these clams went to the bottom and they couldn't catch them in the winter. Nine times out of ten, after they got to the shanties in about two or three weeks, the clams came up again, and the fellas that stayed on the bay, they done good till it started getting real cold—then the clams went into the bottom again.

While a few might be tempted to stay on the bay in the hopes of an Indian summer, the oyster companies forced the issue. Naturally enough, they were not interested in a work force whose numbers would vary from day to day according to the weather, so those who wished to work through the long winter months had to sign on in September. Those who waited until the onset of winter might find work if they were needed, but the shippers are remembered as less than compassionate where such tardiness was concerned. So the mass of Dutchmen set aside their clam tongs and lined up for work at the shanties.

SHIPPERS AND BAYMEN

When either the summer clammer or the so-called independent bayman brought in his haul of clams and seed or grown oysters he discovered just how little independence he really enjoyed. The shippers did not compete with one another for their products of the bayman's labors, but they agreed beforehand what they would pay, even as they had agreed on their workers' wages. The bayman's dependence on the shipper might in fact go further than that, for if he was a former or

occasional employee of a shipper he might well have secured a mortgage for his sloop through him. A look at boat registrations for this
period reveals that a great number of West Sayville's independent
sloops were mortgaged by Jacob Ockers and the other shippers. The
Dutch and the non-Dutch baymen alike were in this predicament, and
insofar as both relied on the free bay for their living, their resentment
of the shippers was compounded by the constant efforts of those men
to encroach on the public clams grounds in the west and oystering
grounds in the east. Those who wished to preserve and even extend
the public domain on the bay joined baymen's associations, which
harangued local oyster commissions and the state legislature with
requests and demands. In 1910, for example, a large contingent of
baymen crowded into the Bayshore town hall to voice their opposition
to the local commission there, which was proposing to lease public
clam grounds to private interests.

There was little doubt that artificially cultivated grounds were far
more productive than those left in their natural state, which were at
any rate constantly declining. Occasionally the baymen were able to
convince local officials to put public money to work for the public
interest by purchasing thousands of bushels of seed oysters to be laid
down on the free bay. The shippers were not surprised by the failure
of such efforts to produce significant results. As one of the surviving
Dutch shippers put it, "A man will care for his property. If he has his
own lot, he will scrape it to make sure it's free of parasites, and he
won't take up oysters too soon that would be better left till they are
older."

Certainly even the reported depredations on the public grounds
were frequent. Although dredging was not permitted there, a hand
dredge was easily tossed over the side of a sloop now and again. Taking
seed or grown oysters out of their respective seasons was easy enough
as well. The illicit shellfish were "cribbed" in under a layer of properly
proportioned shellfish, to elude the casual perusal of the bay commis-
sioners, whose unenviable task it was to patrol these waters in search
of offenders. The shippers were evidently willing enough to purchase
such illicit oysters.

Such violations on the public grounds were undoubtedly self-
perpetuating, for if one bayman realized his neighbor was taking more
than he by illegal means, he was apt to feel a fool for keeping to the
rules. But the large-scale depredations were aimed at the oyster or
clam-laden lands of the shippers, for there the baymen could be sure

of taking a rich harvest, while at the same time striking back at his perceived enemy. The local paper, at least, interpreted such night raids on shippers' lands as quasi-political statements, assertions that the bay could not belong to any one man. Even in these waters, patroled by hired watchmen, it was difficult to catch a thief. When one was apprehended, the incident got detailed coverage in the local press.

One particularly exciting midnight encounter was reported in September 1902. It seems that Jake Ockers had been shown a number of clams by Nick Vander Borgh, who was suspicious of their origin. Hundreds of the clams in question were being brought to Vander Borgh each day for sale, and Nick knew the vendor could not have gotten so many clams each day from any public grounds. Captain Jake took one look at the shellfish and said, "Nick, those are my clams. I'd know them anywhere." In fact, Ockers had been devoting some inshore land to clam cultivation and was able to recognize the particular form of the clams he had laid down there. That night Captain Jake and the sheriff secreted themselves on the shore near these grounds to wait for the suspect. After a few hours their diligence was rewarded by the appearance of the alleged perpetrator who, having anchored his rowboat over Ockers's grounds, immediately began taking up the clams by the hundred. Ockers and the sheriff set out in hot pursuit, quickly overtaking the boat, whose owner jumped overboard and waded toward shore. The sheriff fired the customary warning shots after the fleeing criminal, and the culprit made it safely to shore, but not before he had been positively identified by his pursuers. Besides, they had the boat and clams as evidence, the former being the registered property of the suspect. When confronted by Ockers the next day, the man in question denied the crime, claiming that someone had stolen his boat. "He then went home," the article concludes, "and after bidding his family goodbye literally took to the woods and has not been seen or heard from since" (*Suffolk County News*, September 12, 1902).

Such forays on planted grounds seem to have been very common according to contemporary newspaper accounts and complaints, the current bayman's memories of a golden age of honesty not withstanding. Typically, the incriminating evidence was less easily assembled than in the case reported above, and most went unpunished. Perhaps the juries, as the newspapers intimated, were not really convinced that theft of the products of the water was as real a crime as theft of those of the land. In all this, the scene in the Great South Bay was the same as that in maritime regions all over the world. Whether tenure is legal or customary, the definition of various rights of access to bodies of water and their resources is always a sticky problem. For those who doubt that, let them try to start lobstering off the shore of any Maine village. However many warning shots were fired over the waters of the Great South Bay, things seem never to have gotten quite as bad as in some other oystering regions. In 1890, off Ocracoke Island in North Carolina, for example, there transpired confrontations fierce enough to earn the title "oyster war," wherein the people of that section "became enraged at the depredations of oyster men who have been operating in grounds there and have routed them with shotguns" (see McCay, n.d., for a general discussion of such conflicts).

In the waters of Islip and Brookhaven no amount of thievery would detract from the ultimate victory of cultivation and the notions of private property on which such methods were based. There were also some men among the "free baymen" who probably felt more ambivalence on the question, who were not so sure that the retention of large areas of public water and grounds was a good idea, for if the retention and even proper cultivation of public lands might ensure a fair living for all independent baymen, it would also limit the possibility of any one or few of them rising beyond a certain point. Wealth was not to be found on the public grounds; one got rich by planting one's own lots and by eventually shipping oysters oneself.

This ambivalence shows up in the remarks of veteran Dutch baymen today concerning the careers of Ockers and the other successful shippers. There is certainly much resentment in many of their memories of these times, but it is rarely unmixed with a kind of admiration for the shrewdness of enterprise the shippers exhibited. Such men represented an ideal to which the Dutch immigrant bayman could aspire. Moreover, that entrepreneurial view was supported by other aspects of life in the Dutch-American village, as we shall see in the next chapters.

Such hopes were not, however, just culturally nourished illusions. In the early years of the century, there was still land available for leasing, and the market for oysters was ever-expanding. There were also the recent examples of Fred Ockers, T. H. Dykstra, and William Rudolph—immigrants all, whose careers attested to the continuing possibility of success in the bay oystery. Other Dutchmen kept trying, but their path must have been made progressively more difficult by the constant advances of the planting/shipping industry, each of which meant a higher cost and a more organized "establishment" for the prospective entrepreneur. One such bayman remembered his difficulties in the years just after World War I:

Marine and me had some lots of our own we had put together, buyin' them from some of the other baymen whenever they wanted to sell, and we had a good set of oysters laid down there, so one year we decided we'd try and market them ourselves, to see how'd we make out. So we got some fine bushels of our oysters and we barreled them and sent them into the New York market on the railroad. Well, they all came back, with a note from the market that said, "We don't buy wild oysters"—that's what they called 'em, "wild oysters." Why, they wasn't wild oysters, they was grown on our lots. I'll tell you what it was, it was the shippers had made a deal with the market there in New York not to buy any other oysters.

While such allegations are not documented, other would-be entrepreneurs report similar problems, and all drew the same conclusions. A few men finally succeeded in surmounting this barrier by sending their oysters to Philadelphia dealers, over which local shippers must have had less influence. But that was after the appearance of the truck on the scene, which gave more choices of market than the railroad had.

OTHER MARITIME PURSUITS

If oysters and clams seemed, by the turn of the century, to offer little opportunity for advancement, there were finfish available in the bay and beyond in the ocean. A number of baymen who went for seed oysters in the spring tried their hand at fishing rather than clamming in the summer—some only now and again, and others to the exclusion of shellfishing.

With a little adjustment, an oystering sloop could be fitted out for fishing as well, and if the market for fish was better at any particular moment, the enterprising bayman did not hesitate to go after them. An old bayman described one style of fishing in the bay:

Around the first of December we went flat fishin' with a drag net off here in the bay, and we sent in the fish to the Fulton Market. We used the same boat as we did for oysterin', but we put a mast into 'er and a boom onto 'er for the drag net. We didn't have a "heister" so we used a block and fall—we'd heist 'er [the net] as high as we could and then we had what they call a snatch on the other end to bring 'er over. Sometimes you'd drag for twenty minutes and the net would be full of seaweed. When we'd go with a drag net, we'd go down to leeward and cast our line off the stern. We'd swing around then and pull in the bridles. I would pull up one cuttin' board on the bow and then my brother would pull the other one on the stern, and we'd put the sweep line along the rail and scoop the darn seaweed out, otherwise we couldn't heist the net. Dragging down there in the bay you'd catch flounder and crabs too. We were down there one day, right the west of South Island in that cove by Toby flat, we were draggin' and the cuttin' boards on the net came together fast as that. Well, John said we hit them damn mussels we knew were out there. We hauled up and we had thirteen barrels of crabs in that net! Naturally, we turned around and hit 'em again, and we hauled up and had nine barrels more! They were paying one dollar a barrel for crabs then [1920s] so we were glad enough. Usually we'd get two bushels of nice flounder on Toby flat (worth about one dollar a bushel), but that time the mussels out there were starting to die on the edge of the flats and all those crabs were there eatin' them. But there weren't many doin' that sort of fishin', anything that was hard work the Dutchmen done it. Damn fools and Dutchman, that's all you can say.

Indeed, if the South Shore baymen had a reputation for being enterprising souls liable to venture out on any maritime pursuit if the mood and market were right, the Dutchmen of West Sayville were well known for going farther and faster than any other group. If oysters, clams, or finfish looked to be running better in Connecticut or the North Shore of Long Island, the locals of those areas could expect a fleet of Dutchmen to turn into their cove or inlet. Some even started spending the winter fishing Florida's waters.

Such enterprise was probably not always appreciated by other fishing communities, and a certain amount of antagonism is certainly remembered by both sides. The Dutch style of fishing, as well as their ethnic self-image, is revealed in the reminiscences of a bayman recalling the one fishing implement popularly called "Dutch":

There was a thing we called the Dutch eel spear, which wasn't like an ordinary spear that you'd use by hand. There was a long pole, thick and cut in an oval shape, which was set on the bow of the sloop. On the bottom of the pole there was a big iron blade, like a plowshare, and above that two rows of long, sharp spikes. The sloop would push the spear through the soft mud, the blade would dig out the eels that was layin' there, and they'd all get caught between the spikes. You shoulda seen it in the winter. The Bohemians would come down to the creeks on the shore to get some eels. They'd wade out in their boots with their hand spears, and along come the Dutchmen. We'd just turn our sloops right into the creek and churn up them eels and get 'em by the thousands while the Bohemians stood by and watched. Now I think about it, it's a wonder we wasn't killed.

There were, however, also some full-time fishermen among the Dutchmen, men who had as little to do with oystering and clamming as possible and who today are prone to show a little disdain for those "grubbing" activities. "Trap net" fishing in the bay was one fairly popular form. Driven into the mud just off the shore would be a line of poles on which would be affixed a net that ended in a "trap" also supported by poles (see Plate 14). Eels would follow the wall of net and then find themselves trapped by the hundreds. Fishing "companies" formed for the operation of such nets along with other gear for fishing other fish in other seasons.[2] At the turn of the century or just after, there were at least three such associations, each composed of from three to six men, the membership varying with the circumstances.

The greater amount of capital necessary to purchase and maintain several eel traps, ocean pound nets (which were built following the same pattern as the eel traps, but were larger and set in the ocean for the catching of schools of ocean fish), and other sorts of nets and equipment, as well as the boat, encouraged men to pool their resources. But an economic incentive is not usually sufficient to get a number of typically stubborn individualist fishermen to incorporate in that manner, and "companies" on this level are not at all typical of the maritime scene. In that regard it is interesting to note the composition of these companies, for most of their members seem to have been related to one another through marriage. That is to say, a fishing company was often composed of a group of brothers-in-law, men who had married a set of sisters, or each others' sisters. The contractual basis of that relationship will bear closer scrutiny in following chapters, but it is worth remarking at this juncture that while some of the two-man crews were composed of brothers, this was neither the necessarily expected arrangement nor the typical one. Indeed, there is a folk expectation that brothers will not get along well together on the water, and such wisdom is usually illustrated with one or two well-known examples of quarreling siblings.

There remains one other maritime activity of great local importance to be discussed, and that is yachting. With the closing years of the nineteenth century, West Sayville and the surrounding region grew not only as a center of shellfishing but also as a summer resort. A good number of well-heeled New Yorkers summered in the area, some had their own boats but needed them captained and crewed by able-bodied seamen thoroughly familiar with the hazards and beauties of the local waters. Naturally, they could do no better than the Dutchmen. There were also many more casual tourists who were anxious to go yachting on the bay but had no boats of their own. Here too the Dutchmen were ready to oblige, and the only difference between an oystering sloop and a yacht was a good bright coat of paint. Some of the local bayman took so much to this kind of boating that they abandoned the more grimy maritime pursuits, and some of these became well known on the yachting circuit from Long Island to Rhode Island, where they crewed on America's Cup vessels.

Thus did the cycle of the seasons, and the stages of his life, bring the bayman through a variety of maritime activities and experiences. In some of these he worked for others, and in some he was his own master. What distinguished West Sayville most from neighboring communities was the degree of commitment to the maritime pursuits. The *Suffolk County News* observed in 1910:

That the bay is the medium of employment for the greater part of the population of this village is a patent fact. But one not familiar with the village cannot form an adequate idea of the extent to which the "following of the water" for a livelihood really does enter, until they pay a visit to Green's canal at this season of the year [winter] when the boats are nearly all laid up because of the ice in the bay. At the present time there are upward of 75 craft of all description moored in the canal, hauled out on the bank or on the railways. The sight presented by the forest of masts reminds one of gazing at a portion of the waterfront of a big seaport. And these are not all of the boats. There are the oyster boats at work and more than a score of smaller craft tied up in the basins. . . . Without an actual count it is estimated that more than a hundred boats are owned in this village with a population of scarce 1,200 souls.

There were also the many not directly involved in the various fisheries but still dependent on them, such as the builders and repairers of boats and engines, the carters who took the barrels to the station, the schooner captains who carried the seed oysters as well as other cargoes in and out of the local waters, and the peddlers, small and large, who hawked the products of the fishermen's labors.

This great common interest did not mean that harmony reigned among those 1,200 souls insofar as things maritime were concerned. Of course, antagonisms characterized relations between shippers and baymen. The shippers too, however, clever enough to cooperate when it served their interests, sometimes suspected one another of "crossing lines," that is, of allowing their dredge boats to reap from the neighboring planters' fields. And if the Dutch baymen seemed clannish and uncooperative to the baymen of Sayville or Patchogue, then these "stubborn Dutchmen," as they would often call themselves, were not likely to maintain amicable relations among themselves, on the water or off.

There is, however, an important difference between conflict and nonassociation. And while the Dutchmen may have kept their distance from their non-Dutch neighbors on the water, and even more so in other affairs, the competition and conflict within the community in many ways drew them together.

8

THE
SOCIAL CONTRACT

In 1890 a reporter visiting West Sayville for a New York paper, *The Sun*, wrote of "the happy Dutch colonists."

On the shore of the Great South Bay, just fifty miles from New York, is a community which viewed from both economic and moral standpoints is about as near perfection as any community can ever hope to be. It has less than 500 inhabitants yet it has two flourishing churches, and not a bar room or other place where intoxicating beverages can be procured. It does not have a policeman, sheriff, or magistrate, because nobody ever breaks the law there or is noisy, disorderly, unreasonable or quarrelsome. It has no street cleaning department because every man keeps the street in front of his own place in order and every street and highway is as neat and clean as brick and stone and earth can be made. It is a flourishing place, because every family man in it owns his own house, free and unencumbered, is out of debt, and has money ahead. It is healthful. . . . Its inhabitants are the descendants of Americans who settled here many years ago and a large and prosperous colony of Hollanders. The Hollanders are sturdy, energetic people of great earnestness of purpose and strength of will. They came to this country poor, because they were told wages were high here, and today every one of them is prosperous and a property owner. . . . The Hollanders are clannish. They have large families and the young folks marry young. They generally select mates of their own nationality. . . .

While some of this report is accurate, much of it is quite wrong (at one point, for example, the author asserts that the Hollanders had no experience with oystering in the Netherlands). The article, however, is no doubt generally true in one respect at least: as a record of the honest but superficial impression of an outsider guided by his own romantic projections of the American dream. Nevertheless, the impression of a kind of order prevailing in the community was not without basis and has always been striking enough in West Sayville to earn the remark of the passing visitor. The streets were, in fact, always clean.

The author's mistake was in assuming that these external signs of order betokened a perfect harmony within the community. As we have already seen in the account of life on the water, "perfect harmony" is not the phrase one would choose to best characterize local interaction. On land things were not very different. Although serious crime was rare (there were, however, at least two murders between 1865 and 1910), open and sometimes bitter conflict and confrontation was common indeed, and perhaps nowhere more so than in those symbols of moral order—the churches.

The puzzle, then, is why a community in so much ferment could have appeared clannish and calm to outsiders, even to those living as close as Sayville. The answer, which will be fleshed out in the following pages, can be stated simply here: (1) conflict and confrontation of the sort rampant in early West Sayville produces a kind of order rather than disorder, and (2) the conflict among members of the community was a relationship that bound them together in the "contractual community" and obscured other, more damaging oppositions. Between the community and outsiders, the boundary was drawn not so much with hostility as with nonassociation and distance.

These characteristics of West Sayville life and behavior are properly understood as emanating not from some abstract individual character of the person but from a socially constructed Dutch culture adapted to American surroundings. There is an important difference. When we use the word "character," we tend to imagine a set of attitudes that reside within the individual. When we speak of "culture," although we still talk of individual attitudes and behavior, we are also led to think of the group, for culture is always a group phenomenon and, as such, arises from the interaction of people in institutional settings. All of which is to say that if people acted in a certain way in West Sayville, particularly after the passing of the first immigrant generation, it was because organized life taught and encouraged those cultural forms. That life was neither purely Dutch nor purely American. The immigrants and their children forged their own adaptation, blending Dutch and American institutions, as they went along.

We have already seen how the process of adaptation worked with the earlier immigrants, but what of the many more who arrived in the 1880s, 1890s, and early 1900s? What happened to the contractual community? To answer that question we must examine, insofar as we are able, the character of daily social interaction in the nonmaritime settings, for if the latter immigrants found a fully formed maritime industry, they also discovered a social world where formal and informal patterns of association already followed established patterns. The population of West Sayville, however, more than doubled between 1890 and 1910. The effects of such an increase might be considerable in two respects. First, the new arrivals may have come from circumstances considerably different from those of their earlier compatriots, and thus brought with them different views and expectations. Second, the sudden increase in population might have placed a strain on the functioning of important local institutions. To assess the actual impact, we need to look first at these newer immigrants and the world from which they issued.

THE NEW ARRIVALS

Holland's population rose rapidly in the late nineteenth century, even as her chief occupation, agriculture, began to decline. Agricultural depression meant that small farmers who could no longer afford to farm their land lost it, and that agricultural laborers therefore became unemployed. The many other pursuits indirectly dependent on those of the land suffered as well, and a fair number of Hollanders began to seek relief and opportunity on distant shores. Even at its peak, in 1882, however, the number of emigrants that left Holland for America did not compare in either absolute or relative terms with those of the real centers of European emigration. One difference was the existence of other possibilities within Holland, where if not prosperity then at least a living could be found. One such place was the very area of Zeeland from whence had come all of West Sayville's earlier immigrants. The oyster industry in Yerseke and Bruinisse began to boom in the same years that agricultural depression beset the farming population of Holland. As a result, the new and labor-intensive industry attracted landless people to such towns as Yerseke, which saw a veritable population explosion between 1870 and 1890. Not only did this sudden growth put the strain of numbers on the town's institutions, but the fact that these labor migrants came from diverse regions and backgrounds must have weakened the hold that local traditional authority could have had on them.

Contemporaries described the Yerseke of those days as "Klondike" or "Sodom and Gomorrah," depending on their moral orientation. Local historian Van Ysseldijk (1973) has reconstructed, through records and the memories of survivors, a view of life in that town that contrasts markedly in some respects with the picture of West Sayville drawn by that *Sun* reporter in 1890. Drunkenness and licentiousness evidently abounded, and the excesses of the annual fair, in particular, were enough to strike fear in the hearts of many honest citizens, some of whom tried to enforce its cessation, though without success. Stories of drunken sea captains dancing naked on the pool tables of the "Oester Bourse" are still a part of the local folk memory, and one man remembers getting up the morning after fair day to find blood on his family's front door.

From this "wild" town many later immigrants came to West Sayville, and according to the collective memory of those remaining in Yerseke, those who left were the poorest and the worst. "Many of them were criminals," one old man confided, "fleeing the law." One would expect that such a rambunctious crew would have wreaked havoc on the bay as they arrived, family after family, through the 1890s. Of course, they did no such thing, and although several of those who left Holland in general, and Yerseke in particular, could well have been escaping the law, most were simply escaping the poverty that Adriaan Daane describes (see Chapter 7). Moreover, if Yerseke was a wild town in many ways, it must be added that it is remembered as such by a community today known as one of the more religious and conservative in Holland. In the period of economic depression that reached Yerseke in the 1890s and early 1900s, there were signs that the authority of the Reformed churches was reasserting itself. If the state church was issuing food relief, as Daane remembers, that would certainly have served to strengthen the hold it enjoyed over the local populace. Adriaan draws a picture of a Yerseke around 1907 which was far from being out of control:

Every town had five or six policemen who patrolled the streets daily. They informed the people about any violations. Every family was expected to sweep their street and sidewalk daily. Every Saturday the street had to be washed, also the windows and outside walls of the house. A steamboat also patrolled the waters in the vicinity of the island. Any infractions or violations were punishable by imprisonment for a few days or a fine if you could afford it.

This pattern of municipal authority was common in Holland, and the right of the community to insist on conformity in cleanliness and moral behavior was generally accepted. By 1912, when the last of the immigrant families was leaving Yerseke for West Sayville, most conservative Reformed sects of Holland had joined together under the banner of the *Oude Gereformeerde-Gemeinte*, known colloquially as the "strict ones." It was, in fact, the minister of one of these Reformed sects in Yerseke who led the movement that resulted in the founding of the conservative political party, SGP, one of the political wings of the *Gereformeerde* churches today. This party, although holding very little national power, polls very well in Yerseke these days and tends to fill up offices in local municipal elections. Yerseke of the twentieth century has been as famous for its religious and political conservatism as it has been for its shellfishing, and most of the emigrants with which it supplied West Sayville were far from being anything like a morally disruptive element in their new American homes.

By no means all new immigrants hailed from Yerseke, however. Bruinisse continued to send her sons and daughters as she had first done in 1849 when DeWaal and Hage had crossed the sea, as did other Zeeland villages. There was also a considerable contingent from the northerly reaches of Holland in this later migration, in particular from Friesland and the North Holland island of Texel. The route that led such northerners to this American-Zeelander settlement was often more circuitous.[1] Arie Schaper, an old fisherman who left his native Friesland village of Nyaga in 1905, learned of West Sayville only after having lived for a year near Paterson, New Jersey, where many Dutch immigrants were employed in textile mills:

I hated that work. One day another Dutchman who was working there alongside me said, "Schaper, you don't like this work. You want to be a fisherman like you were in Holland. Why don't you go to West Sayville in New York. There're a lot of Dutch people there and they're all fishing for one thing or another." So my brother and I went up there. . . .

Many others were to follow this pattern of coming to West Sayville after spending some time elsewhere in America, sometimes in Michigan but more often in New Jersey, around Paterson. So came the

Dykstras and the Schapers, the Bakelaars and others. Many of them, like Arie, were accustomed to life on the sea, and after an unhappy time in some factory or on a farm, most were grateful for the opportunity to follow some sort of maritime occupation while still living among their compatriots in America. Perhaps less familiar with the oystering than the Zeelanders, many of these northerners apparently preferred to follow the water in other ways, either as dredge skippers for the larger planters, like the Bakelaars, or as bay and deep-sea fishermen like Arie.

Wherever they came from, the new immigrants to West Sayville had characteristics in common: they came seeking a livelihood on the water, and they came through personal connections. Very few Dutchmen, if any, just wandered into West Sayville hoping to find a home. Unlike the Michigan settlements or the factory region of New Jersey, which by this time had attracted thousands of immigrant Dutch, the little ethnic enclave in West Sayville was completely unknown back in Holland except to those with personal connections to its residents. Even Arie, though told of West Sayville by a fellow factory worker, moved there only after having discovered that a neighbor relation from the old country was already there.

As we saw in the case of Daane, there were several reasons why this network immigration pattern would have been favored. Coming from Holland, prospective immigrants needed money for passage. They got it in one of two ways: from relatives in Holland or through relatives in America. Given economic conditions in Holland, few were able to exercise the first option, and more often it was from already settled relatives that the money came. Whether such funds came from savings or were borrowed from local employers, shopkeepers, or whomever, the effect was always to bring the new immigrant to live alongside the older one. Thus they came to West Sayville, very often through the bond of women, who no doubt were more likely to keep writing to one another even though separated by an ocean.

The cumulative effect of this network pattern of immigration is important. Even as the population grew rapidly with families (many of them like the Daanes with very many children) arriving weekly through the 1890s and early 1900s, there were literally no strangers in West Sayville. Everyone arrived already connected to at least one, and by virtue of that one, probably several, or even many, families. The incorporation of all new immigrants into the existing network of kinship meant that even if they included among their number the odd ruffian malcontent, or even criminal, such people found themselves subject to the social control of a village into whose social organization they already fit.

This contrasts with the boom Yerseke itself had experienced in the 1870s and 1880s, when their population had also climbed along with the oyster boom. In the case of Yerseke, this new population arrived from the surrounding and more distant region, all these destitute Hollanders pouring into a town where employment was to be found. They lived in rooming houses, and though subject to the law of the town, they were not easily controlled by the less formal means so important to most communities. Neither wide circles of kin nor church, of which there were too many in Yerseke in those years for anyone to exert much moral authority, effectively controlled these new individuals. In West Sayville, on the other hand, the oyster boom also led to a population surge, but one that was by and large limited to those who were filtered through the social relations of the existing population, so that they found an immediate place in one of the two churches and in the other formal or informal associations that so regulated local life.

When they did reach West Sayville, new families faced the basic problem of accommodations. Those who arrived alone or in small numbers, like Arie and his brother, might find a room in one of the larger West Sayville homes that served as a rooming house. Others would let the upper floor of the house of a relative or any other Dutch family in West Sayville looking for extra money. It was not unusual for a family with a good number of children to pass their first years in West Sayville thus ensconced in a few very small rooms above the only slightly more commodious accommodations of long-time residents. Their goal was always a home of their own, and this kind of arrangement was viewed as a stage in the expected cycle. The numbers of immigrants being what they were, a census taker come to West Sayville in those years must have had a considerable difficulty getting accurate assessments of the number, names, and relations of the residents. According to contemporary informants, a surviving map from the period (see Plate 21) omits a great number of these oddly placed families.

By 1910, when Daane's family reached the area, such accommodations were difficult to find in West Sayville:

So we found one in Sayville on Smith Street which was known as "Tin Can Alley." This was well named because we noticed our neighbors always threw out plenty of garbage—there were many flies, rats, and mice. This was in the days before garbage collection. . . . Our neighbors were Americans, Germans, Polish-Bohemians, and Italians. Most of them were friendly, but we just couldn't understand what they were talking about.

Although residing on the edge of Sayville and thus surrounded by foreigners, the Daanes and the other Dutch families that settled in such peripheral areas were nevertheless very much a part of the West Sayville community. The neighbors with whom they could not communicate did not grow very close. Adriaan's father, as we saw in the last chapter, found work along with everyone else on the West Sayville shore, where he was always surrounded by fellow Dutchmen, many of them fellow villagers. As for his mother, she naturally sought out those of her own country, women with whom she had language and the concerns of daily life in common.

WORK AND COMMUNITY

The first concern of all the Dutch families, newly settled or old, was work, and the particular labor that was chosen or befell the various family members had important consequences in terms of their respective social relations. The associations of work can either strengthen or weaken communal bonds. We can sort out those effects by following the lives of the residents, beginning with those of the children, for work began early in life, and school itself was no easy task.

It is not difficult to imagine the nervousness of the Dutch immigrant children clomping in their wooden shoes toward the school in Sayville the first Monday after their arrival in their new home. Children feel their own oddity much more quickly than adults, but if these West Sayville children were slow to grasp their peculiarity, the Sayville children were there to remind them. While truly harsh ethnic epithets are not remembered by West Sayville's older residents, for a small child it is enough to hear, "Hey, look at them Dutchies" or "Here come the dumb Dutchmen." Older children naturally tried to divest themselves of any external signs of their differentness, and such obvious markers as wooden shoes were restricted to home use as early as possible. But to come from West Sayville and to be known as a Van-something-or-other was enough of a mark. There was nothing unusual in any of this, nor did the Dutch children of West Sayville experience anything like the bigotry and violence that have made the adjustment of some other ethnic and racial groups to America so painful. But the children growing up in a small village had only their own and their fellows' experience to judge by, so that their sense of persecution was not lightened by the fact that others were far worse persecuted than they were. On the positive side, the ethnic boundary drawn by the American children served to reinforce the Dutch children's sense of membership in the West Sayville community, for they were forever being reminded of where they belonged. That membership was ritually acted out on the battlefields of childhood, as one Dutchman born in West Sayville of immigrant parents in 1890 remembered:

They used to call Green's Creek, that runs between Sayville and West Sayville, the Mason and Dixon Line. Lots of times there'd be fights there, and especially in the winter—big snowball fights between the Dutch kids and the Sayville kids. Others might tell you such things never happened, but I'm tellin' you they did.

Others were more reticent about ethnic animosity, for most West Sayville people like to remember their rapid assimilation and are understandably proud of being Americans. But many did recall the epithets of their early childhood, or other difficulties that confronted them once inside the schoolroom. Adriaan Daane remembers:

The first Monday we were told to go to school. This was really something. We wore cast-off American clothing that relatives and friends from Yerseke living there in West Sayville had given us, and wooden shoes. Six of us were old enough to go to school—Marine, Gert, Anna, and I were placed in the third grade. Pet and Nell were placed in the first grade. We just sat there like bumps on a log. That English was really something. We couldn't understand a damn word. Luckily one young boy in our class could speak both Dutch and English, so he interpreted for us. After a while, we picked up the drift of the English conversation, and by the next September, when school started again, we had it made and were put in the class we belonged in.

When school was out for the day or the year, the children did not remain idle. In addition to household chores, many young boys and girls did what they could to contribute to the family budget. "During the summer some of us made a few dollars picking huckleberries or selling vegetables or fish. We were allowed ten cents for each dollar that we made for spending money." If his father had any kind of a small boat, an older boy might spend the summer on the West Bay, away from his mother's wary eye for days at a time. When the family was large, as it so often was, older girls spent much of their time assisting in their mothers' considerable labors, and when a teenage girl found herself helping her mother clothe and feed what might amount to a small company of seamen, she presumably suffered from few delusions about the ease of married life.

Before she entered into that life herself, however, there were other kinds of work to perform, some of which brought the young woman into contact with those outside her domestic circle. Few boys or girls remained in school past the age of fourteen, and since there was little work for women on the shore, they went elsewhere, for the local American environment provided other employment for young women. There was much "housework" to be had in the better-off homes in the area. A few Dutch families would take on a young girl to help in household chores, but it was more typically American doctors, lawyers, and other middle-class professional families of Sayville who could and would hire one or two servants from the nearby pool of willing young Dutch. A woman who arrived from Yerseke at the age of twelve in 1900 remembered:

I stayed home four or five months—then they sent me right out to work. I was thirteen years old. I worked for a family, and they had boys and that's how I learned the English language. I never went to school here. I worked also for an architect for eight years as a maid. The woman there was nice to me. When it got to be Christmas or something like that she might make a dress for me. My sister did the same thing. She worked for another family. He was a lawyer. When I first worked that way I got five dollars a month, and my board, of course. I came home every night, but I got my meals there, and much better meals than I could get at home, because them people were better off than we were.

It would be a mistake to assume that the girls and women who worked in such capacities learned to see themselves as belonging to a class beneath that of their employers. Such work was simply work, and while performing such household duties at least one Dutch girl was dismayed to be treated "like a servant":

I worked for a doctor, and he was all right, but not her. It was Thursday night, I had made pies and they had lamb chops and then she said to me, "Well there's some soup left—you can have it." When they were done with dinner— they had a pantry, and she put the rest of the pie away—you know, I was a young kid about seventeen and I liked a piece of pie as well as the rest of them. She locked the door, I didn't get any—then she says, "Make yourself an egg." I didn't stay there. We were poor, but I didn't stay there. It was easy enough to get a job.

A very different sort of service could be found in other homes. Since the mid-nineteenth century a number of extremely wealthy New Yorkers had carved out huge estates in the Oakdale area. Chief of these was Vanderbilt, whose own Dutch ancestry seems to have given him no feeling of kinship with the local immigrant populace. He and several others, like F. G. Bourne and later his daughter, Mrs. Hard, did provide employment to a large number of local women as domestics. Working in such capacities, young women were not likely to interact as one of the family as they might in the smaller American homes. Thus, the first sort of "housework" probably brought Dutch girls into much more frequent interaction with local families than the latter "domestic" work. Neither, as shall become apparent, seems to have extended their networks sufficiently to include prospective husbands from outside the community and ethnic group.

If they did not find work as "domestics," many West Sayville girls of that era were likely to find themselves in the Patchogue Lace Mill.

I only worked there for about a year and a half. I hated it. Three dollars and a half a week, and we had to ride a bicycle all the way from here to Patchogue and back. After that they had a sort of a buggy—a stage they used to call it— one man drove it—and a sleigh in the winter. You wouldn't have a hairdo by the time you got to the mill! For a few weeks we stayed with a man who used to come around and peddle coffee—I think it cost as much as we made to stay there. The work there wasn't much fun either. We had to stand up and pull the lace curtains they made across the big tables and tie a knot wherever there was a "bullet"—a hole in the lace. There were ladies that would sit and mend these bullets, and they got a little bit more money.

Ideally, when a young woman got married, and especially when she began to have children, she restricted her labors to those required to feed and care for her family, which because the number of children was typically rather large were considerable. But some found it necessary to do additional work:

When I was having my children—I had seven children and raised six—then I wasn't going out that much. I washed home or somethin' like that—did laundry at home—and I went one day a week, sometimes two days a week, to one house. The woman came and picked me up.

Work at home followed a typical routine: one day for washing, one day for ironing, and so forth. Then there was the garden, chickens, and pigs to care for in season, the preserves to be put up, and the constant cooking: potatoes and slowly stewed vegetables, fish and heavy breads, and perhaps an Edam cheese from Van Wyen's store. From that shop and the two others of the area came those foods the family did not grow itself. By the early years of the century, Sam Green's still popular grocery store was joined by a number of small Dutch-owned establishments, as befit a people who searched out every entrepreneurial niche. There was Van Wyen's down on Atlantic Avenue, near the shore; Van Essendelft's up on Rollstone, north of Main Street; and Van Popering's confectionary shop right across from Sam Green's on Main Street itself. In addition to groceries, the first two of these carried a variety of dry goods and hardware necessary for life at home or aboard the boats. All these shops carried their customers on credit, and many are alive today who gratefully remember being able to get groceries through long periods of unemployment, or securing a loan to bring their families over from Holland.

The housewife's day was also broken up, no doubt, by the arrival of her groceries, for most shops were in the practice of sending out a cart and driver daily to deliver the regular purchases of their customers. Delivery boys brought welcome news along with the groceries. But news and the strangeness of more foreign quarters was also brought by a year-round stream of peddlers and traveling salesmen, profering everything from beer to organ music. A woman born in West Sayville in 1890 remembered her childhood as one of many children raised by a widowed mother:

There used to be a lot of peddlers around here, some Italians with notions or hurdy-gurdy men with monkeys. There was an old English couple—the man grinded the organ and the wife would sing and jig—they would come once a year and get breakfast. My mother always invited peddlers in for some bread, which she baked every Saturday. One time an Italian grinder came and showed colored slides in a box, and we thought the world of it. He sat under the grape arbor where there was a basket of fresh-picked vegetables. Mother said he could pick one, and he took a cucumber, shined it, and ate it like an apple. The Dutch peel and salt cukes. They think it "takes the poison out," so Mother was so scared because she thought he was poisoned. She was sure glad when she saw him around some time after that, still alive.

Such were the entertainments in a hard life made much harder by the early death of a husband. There was poor relief to be had through the churches, but pride prevented many from taking any. "The greatest fear was to end up in the poorhouse in Yaphank," and most women tried to manage as best they could, displaying their control over the situation in lines of washing hung out neatly according to size on the appropriate day.

Most men found a life "following the water," but there were also those who decided, as the locals like to say, that "all you get from the bay is a wet ass and an empty gut." For them there was a variety of work ashore. In addition to the pursuits subsidiary to the oystering fisheries—such as carting, peddling, and shipbuilding—there were jobs on neighboring American farms or estates. If they did not captain or crew on the yachts of wealthy employers, they could always labor in their gardens or in their fields. Many young men and immigrants viewed such work as temporary, taken up only as long as it took to put by enough money to purchase a boat of their own or find a place on that of another. But plans do go awry, and a good number spent their working life ashore. For those who did make it out on the water, this sort of farm work provided an important stopgap for times when either market or seasonal conditions made work on the bay unprofitable.

PLAY

The Dutch like to think of themselves as hardworking people, as indeed they were and are, but even they found time for occasional play. Besides the solitary diversions offered by the traveling organ grinders, there were the other home pleasures such as making wine or root beer. For the men there was the mixed work/pleasure of hunting ducks (market gunning) or deer in the surrounding woodlands and marshes.

For the youth the shops and stores also offered opportunities for fun, and the confectionary of Dingman Van Popering was an important social center, as his daughter remembers:

Saturday night was the big night. We girls had to help our father. The boys would sit around on boxes and eat peanuts, tossing the shells on the floor, and smoke cigars and eat watermelon. They would buy candy for Sunday and buy pennies to put in the church collection.

The teens were even resourceful enough to figure out a way of socializing most of their parents could not object to. On Sundays, after having spent most of the day in two local church services, a number of local youths would head out to Sayville's Methodist church for the evening service. The walk to and from provided valuable opportunity for courting. Others, with or without their parents' and elders' approval,

went to dances held at the firehouse and even as far away as the
ballrooms of Patchogue. Such escapades were much easier for young
men to carry off successfully than for young women, and in their search
for the fun so hard to come by they sometimes crossed considerable
cultural boundaries. To the north of West Sayville was the immigrant
settlement of Bohemia, whose populace were Catholics and, as such,
anathema to most of the Dutch Reformed. But the Bohemians were
well known for their wild beer-hall parties, and the lure of that sort of
revelry was enough to draw at least a few West Sayville men into such
dens of iniquity. One Dutchman smiled as he remembered sneaking
shoeless up his parents' stairs in the wee hours of the morning after
such nights among the Bohemians.

But with all this sneaking about, little in the way of permanent
association seems to have come of it. Though there was an occasional
marriage between the Dutch and others of the local populace, up until World War I such unions formed only a tiny percentage of the
total. Even since, it can hardly be said that ethnicity has ceased to
be a factor. With a total population of around 1,000, and with ever-
increasing interrelationships among those, the reader may reason that
a marriageable partner among the local Dutch was not always an easy
find by the early years of the century. If West Sayville was thus isolated
from the surrounding region, it was not so far from other Dutch settlements, particularly those around Paterson, New Jersey, from whence
a number of immigrants were then coming.

In the early years of the century, the shore around West Sayville
was a popular summer resort area, with bustling hotels and other
vacation accommodations. Those were for the middle class; the rich
summered in their own or their friends' estate houses. The Dutch
people of Lodi and Paterson, however, sought relief from the airless
factories of New Jersey in the homes of relations in West Sayville. An
old bayman remembered:

I can remember them New Jersey people all comin' up here in the summer.
You shoulda seen my grandmother's house all cram full of them, sleeping on
the floor or anywhere. You see, they would come up here on their vacation,
they'd come up for the salt air. You'd see them everywhere dressed in their
white pants and straw hats takin' that salt air, and it must've given em one
hell of an appetite, 'cause you shoulda seen what they'd eat. They would invite
us to go down there on our vacations, but they didn't seem to understand that
in those days a bayman didn't take anything like a vacation—he was always
working. We'd go down there once in a while for a short trip, maybe when

we were selling fish in Newark. But if you visited and took a cup of coffee, you were done for—we had a saying here, "One cup of coffee in Lodi is worth two weeks in West Sayville." That's how they were.

MARRIAGE AND CONTRACT

The interaction with New Jerseyites may have been strained by the problems of reciprocity, as the old bayman's complaints seem to indicate, but it may have been through marriage that the exchanges were ultimately balanced, for a good number took place between the two groups. "We used to say, 'Go to New Jersey and get yourself a Blom.' That's 'cause so many West Sayville men got wives of that name down there.'" Actually the local church records reveal a variety of Dutch-immigrant spouses of both genders from Lodi, Passaic, and other New Jersey towns. The effect of such marriages was not only a preservation of ethnicity—the nature of which was in some ways ephemeral as English became the dominant language—but also the easy incorporation of new spouses into the major organ of local social control, the churches. Even the few marriages contracted with local Americans or Germans often brought the spouse into the bosom of the church, especially if the couple chose to remain living in West Sayville. Those who married outside the group and left the community did nothing to alter the local social world, so that the only real threat to the community's understanding of itself were those mixed couples who broke from the community institutions but remained resident in the village. The relatively few who followed that route have some hard memories, and years of relative or absolute exclusion have left them bitter about the "narrowminded people in those churches."

Within the community, marriages forged important contractual bonds, but rarely in the sense that they sometimes do elsewhere. Among the poorer families, there was no such thing as a dowry, and the new husbands and wives, typically in the their early twenties, brought little if anything in the way of economic resources to the marriage. Nevertheless, the "affinal relation," as anthropologists term those bonds of kinship forged through the marriage alliance, were both socially and economically important. A good number of men report having secured mortgage or boat loans from their in-laws, and we have already noted that the fishing companies were often composed of a number of men linked by marriage. Some such groups of men were related by virtue of having married a group of sisters, and such links were important in immigration networks as well, for reasons already noted. Brother/sister exchange marriages were also regular features of early life in West Sayville, resulting in especially strong bonds between the participants (See Appendix B).

While it is not really possible to establish the importance of affinal relations in the lives of the West Sayville people in the period under discussion, the ideological significance of affinal relations is more apparent, and in some ways more interesting. Marriage was evidently viewed as a contractual relationship that, having been forged, allowed for further contracts to be made—the forming of fishing companies, the borrowing of money, and so forth. At the same time, we hear folk warnings about forming business partnerships between brothers, and reminders about the difficulties that brother-partners have often experienced. Perhaps the affinal relation was understood as one that brought two individuals together in an atmosphere of preexisting trust and association but free of the vague and pervasive demands of actual family relations. A person could trust a brother-in-law, but was not uncomfortable spelling out a contractual exchange with him, for such relationships were explicitly contractual and rational. The account book of the Long Island Fishing Company, one comprised of six such brothers-in-law, records every nickle telephone call, every activity of every partner.

Given our argument about the contractual community, it is not surprising that such relationships should have had a certain appeal for the West Sayville Dutch. Even within the family, contractual relations seem to have made an unusual headway. Having reached an age of retirement, for example, the father offered to sell his boat to his son. They would agree on a price and shake hands on it. In effect, the son agreed to pay for the boat on time, so much a month based on his expected income. While many readers will find nothing outlandish in this exchange, it is well to consider that there are other and more common alternatives. For example, in other parts of the world such basic economic tools are often handed over to one or several sons at the point at which the father retires by way of inheritance. Where this happens, the sons so blessed will probably be obligated to contribute to their retired father's sustenance with money, goods, or labor. In such cases there is no perceived element of choice; each actor simply does what is traditionally expected of him. It may be argued that what transpires in such cases is not materially different from the West Sayville situation. Either way, a father gives up a boat and is paid for it. The fact that the West Sayville people chose to *perceive* their exchange as contractual is of great significance, however, for insofar as it was contractual, the exchange was freely entered into by independent individuals, unconstrained by "tradition." Now it may even be the case that on some level fathers are obligated to offer to sell their boats to their sons, that a father who offered such a boat to someone else first or for a better price would have been thought odd or wrong. A vital semblance of independence in action is preserved, however, by a contractual way of talking or thinking about what is being done.

Such conceptual evasions are important when they contribute to a general world view that always emphasizes the free individual as an independent actor. In his travels in America in the 1830s, Alexis de Tocqueville was impressed with the extent to which Americans managed to maintain just such a view of themselves, no matter what the circumstances.

The Americans are fond of explaining almost all the actions of their lives by the principle of self-interest rightly understood: they show with complacency how an enlightened regard for themselves constantly prompts them to assist one another and inclines them willingly to sacrifice a portion of their time and property to the welfare of the state. In this respect I think they frequently fail to do themselves justice; for in the United States as well as elsewhere people are sometimes seen to give way to those disinterested and spontaneous impulses that are natural to man; but the Americans seldom admit that they yield to emotions of this kind; they are more anxious to do honor to their philosophy than to themselves. (Tocqueville 1945, 2:130)

What Tocqueville speaks of here is the contribution that culture, as a collectively held world view, makes to the social order, for on many occasions he remarks that the self-view this ideology sustains contributes to the particular success of American social and economic endeavors. That line of thought has had many heirs, as we noted in the Introduction. Anthropologist Evans-Pritchard found that among the Nuer, cattle-keepers living in extremely simple material conditions in the plains of Africa's southern Sudan, individuals came to live in a particular village and performed certain acts for a variety of absolutely egocentric reasons, but they consistently represented their decisions to others and to themselves as having been motivated by a patrilineal morality. They argued that they always did what they did as good members of their lineage. Evans-Pritchard called this way of talking and thinking in terms of such obligations a "lineal idiom." Even if they

See also pp 14 ff

acted for selfish reasons on many, if not most, occasions, it was important for the Nuer to think that people in general acted on the
obligations of kinship, for they saw their society as depending for its
order and stability on just such behavior (Evans-Pritchard 1940).

We might then apply this kind of argument to Tocqueville's find-
ings and say that Americans like to think in a contractual idiom which
represented individual action as generally free from the constraints of
status. As with the Nuer, the American idiom is important because
Americans feel that the larger group, be it community or nation, is the
natural and orderly result of just such cumulative action. Such an
ideology permits individuals to act consistently in their own selfish
interests and remain convinced that by doing so they are contributing
to the maintenance of the social order.

As for the West Sayville Dutch, this "American" ideology and idiom
was probably close to their own. What difference there was may lie in
the extremity of the Dutch case. Their nineteenth-century American
contemporaries often saw these immigrants as a purer version of themselves—such is the tone of the 1890 newspaper article with which we
began this chapter, and that is the sentiment one meets again and
again in American views of the Reformed Dutch of this period. They
were the Puritans returned; the Ideal Type incarnate.

VOLUNTARY ASSOCIATIONS

While family, street, and shop interaction were all important contexts
for the expression and construction of this local world view and self-
image, the Dutch immigrants were also much drawn to that other vital
aspect of American social life—the voluntary association. All such organizations had the virtue of reinforcing an essentially egalitarian and
contractual idiom, even while they operated as organs of social control.
If the Union made the mistake of defining itself as status-bound, that
was not the case with the secret societies, such as the Masons and
Forresters, which as we shall see later were so anathema to the more
conservative churchmen. In all such organizations, class divisions were
masked to some extent, and in some voluntary associations—even
those borrowed from American society—the boundaries of the immigrant community were reinforced rather than blurred. The churches
were the most important of these and will be treated separately in the

following chapter, but among the others, there is no doubt that the West Sayville Hook and Ladder Company provided the principal arena of local life.

THE VOLUNTEER FIRE DEPARTMENT

"On October 1, 1891, a meeting was held in the store of Dingman Van Popering for the purpose of electing the first officers of the West Sayville Hook and Ladder Company. . . . The meetings were held for some time thereafter in Cornelius DeGraff's barn on Main Street." By 1892 the thirty-two members were installed in their own firehouse, a building that served as a new and vital social center in the community. Although the members contributed subscriptions as well as small initiation fees and annual dues, large purchases typically came only with the help of important patrons like Bourne and Hard. Smaller gifts for specific purposes came occasionally from the more well-heeled members, such as shipper Westerbeke. While the primary function of the organization was fighting fires, no one reading the department's minutes would conclude that fire fighting was either the most frequent or the most socially significant of the association's activities.

After the mid-1890s, the membership included such shippers as Jacob Ockers, Wolfer Van Popering, John Westerbeke, William Rudolph, and Nicholas Vander Borgh—the major employers of the community, and in Vander Borgh's and Westerbeke's cases the pillars of the Dutch Reformed Church. Other members included the proprietors of local stores and the run of baymen and other ordinary folk. With such a cross-section of the local Dutch community on its roster, it is interesting to note that the department's records do not make any reference to the class or management/worker oppositions in the village. Indeed, the entries from 1900 through 1903 make no mention of any union or strike. What did concern these men, insofar as the records reveal those concerns, were the periodic tournaments in which the West Sayville Hook and Ladder Company competed against rival departments in other communities. These bouts and holiday displays of local virtuosity and speed always attracted large audiences; the number of trophies housed in the firehouse indicate that the local crowd was not often disappointed. Such events were a source of new secular rituals of community, and if the fire department was a quintessentially

American institution, the members were known as "the Flying Dutchmen."

The character of interaction in the firehouse, and the less official matters handled there, was probably at least as important to the structure of life and relations in the community as formal department business. Reading the minutes of the meetings, one is struck by the amount of rule-making that went on, complete with a set of fines—usually of around twenty-five cents—for late arrival or profanity. Department funds were also spent on cigars and beer for the less serious firehouse moments, although general sobriety seems to have been the rule. While no details of firehouse conflict are offered by the secretary's minutes, the number of blackballs, resignations, and dismissals is large enough to indicate that various contentions found opportunities for expression in this voluntary association. This sort of interaction in many ways reinforced the immigrant community; even with the occasional German or American member, the rolls of the fire department were, up until World War I, overwhelmingly Dutch. Insofar as other kinds of groups' activities and celebrations were organized from this center, these as well were identified with the circumscribed local world. As we have already seen, the ideology of volunteerism—of the corporate voluntary association with elected officers and constant contention— was quite a comfortable one for the Dutch as well.

In other ways, however, the fire department was probably the greatest institutional agent of American enculturation. While voluntary associations were familiar enough to the immigrants, this one was not only specifically American, it also served to tie the local firehouse into a county and state organization of departments whose relationships were occasionally reinforced through fiscal dealings and regularly through ritual competitions. The specific activities organized through the firehouse were quintessentially American: Halloween balls, Fourth of July picnics, clambakes. The charter members of the department were all young men—most in their twenties and the eldest only forty-one—and all were either born in West Sayville or immigrated with their parents as very young children. Whether Dutch was the language in the home it is impossible to say, but the minutes of the firehouse meetings were kept in English only. One suspects that the language of conversation there was mostly English from the start.

In structure as well as cultural content, the fire department competed with the single most important Dutch social institution in the community: the churches. As we shall see in the next chapter, language was a religious issue in itself, but the dances, balls, and general Americanization that went on within the department must have been upsetting to the more orthodox members of the community. By the 1890s most of these had withdrawn into the newer Christian Reformed Church, and in the early days there appears to have been some trouble between that church and the Hook and Ladder Company. One particular drama, remembered by an elderly woman, was over the desire of the department members to come in uniform into a church funeral for a fellow fireman. The church officials evidently did not feel that such pomp had any place in their service, and hard feelings resulted. Whatever the occasions of contention, it is obvious that those who wished to retain a strong religious/immigrant identity would have seen the firehouse for what it was, a corrupter of old values, a place where the young danced and played cards, and where they certainly became increasingly unrecognizable to their immigrant parents. Aside from what transpired within its confines, the firehouse represented an alternative social forum to those of the churches, an alternative and essentially secular definition of the community.

If one asks either neighboring Americans or the Dutch of West Sayville themselves to say what made this community culturally distinctive, they nearly always answer "religion," for even though the form of Protestantism that these immigrants brought with them to America had close cousins in various American religious bodies, the isolation of the community gave the church a social and cultural force in West Sayville that it rarely enjoyed in neighboring American communities. There also was and is a peculiarly Dutch cultural form that characterized church relations and that has always ensured a central cultural role for religion among those immigrants. In our investigation of how individual Dutchmen sustained a particular view of themselves—contractual and entrepreneurial and at the same time strongly bound to a larger moral body—the operation of religion within the community offers the last and most important key.

9

THE HONEST WAR

"The church is a very big part of people's lives here. They came here because of the bay . . . but they stayed together because of the church." So spoke an elder of the Christian Reformed Church in 1979. His words resonate with one great tradition of sociological thought about the role of religion in providing the moral glue necessary to the survival of social systems. There is, however, an old Dutch proverb that throws an altogether different light on the effects of religion on communal cohesion: "One Dutchman—a theologian. Two Dutchmen—a church. Three Dutchmen—a schism."

On Wednesday, September 13, 1876, eight "separatists" met in the house of Arie Beebe, where, with the help of two schismatic ministers—the Rev. Rietdyk and the Rev. Vanden Bosch—up from New Jersey for the occasion, they confessed their newly-found faith and formed a congregation of the True Holland (later Christian) Reformed Church. This schism so calmly noted in the Dutch Reformed Church consistory records followed years of apparently bitter disputes between factions and individuals. Such battles, in a hamlet of 150 to 200 culturally isolated immigrants, should have left deep scars if not festering wounds. The first Hollanders had arrived twenty-five years before, but the church and settlement which was to be called West Sayville—the community, in other words—was not yet a decade old when thus acrimoniously rent asunder. The Dutchmen were apparently divided into two hostile camps determined to pursue their internecine theological struggles amid their puzzled or unconcerned American neighbors.[1]

The schism of the Dutch Reformed congregation in West Sayville was a local event, but certainly not an isolated one, as the presence of the outside agitators (as they appeared from the nonseceder perspective) attests. In fact, the split was national,[2] begun in New Jersey with the founding of the True Holland Reformed Church in 1858, but soon spreading to the various Dutch immigrant communities across the country. Why should such schisms have transpired, so often splitting small, struggling communities in two? What can an exploration of these disputes in a place like West Sayville add to our understanding of the special character of the contractual community?

From the point of view of the separatists themselves, there is no puzzle about the reasons for the schism. They were, for the most part, straightforward disagreements about right doctrine and practice. The dissatisfied among the immigrants complained of "the neglect of preaching each Sunday from the Heidelberg Catechism, a tendency to ignore the doctrine of predestination, tolerance of membership in the Masonic Lodge, participation in other church services, a preference for hymns over psalms, neglect of catechetical instruction, choir singing (which discouraged congregational singing), and the baptizing of infants in consistory chambers and in private homes, rather than in the presence of the congregation" (Lucas 1955, 511). Several of these issues were raised in West Sayville's church disputes, yet in neither the national nor the local cases can we presume that confrontation and conflict expressed in theological terms necessarily have their roots only in religious matters. If the immigrants were happy to receive the help of American Reformed ministers and congregations, once they had settled into their new life some of these Hollanders, particularly those who had been "seceders" in the old country, began to grow less satisfied with an American church they felt suffered from many of the same faults that had driven them from the established church in Holland. Yet there was more to it than that, as an examination of life in the immigrant churches reveals. An identification of ethnicity with religion permitted Dutch Americans to translate general cultural tensions into religious issues. Those who were less at home in the encompassing American society might focus their anxiety on the relationship between their congregation and the governing American church hierarchy. This, as we shall see, was very much the case in West Sayville.

There is a difficulty with explaining this schism as solely due to the stresses of life in America, for churches in the Netherlands were undergoing their own great upheavals through the nineteenth century. Although their problems were not directly connected to those of the American Reformed church, they took much the same form; in Holland too, various brands of separatists claimed a more orthodox Calvinism and sought a Covenant at once more democratic and totalitarian. Whatever causes are elicited to explain events in the American context should apply as well to the Dutch case.

Beyond that, the American schism did not take whole immigrant communities out of their church so often as it rent them in two, thus pitting Dutchmen against Dutchmen. Why were some of these men and women attracted to the schismatic sect, while others remained in the Dutch Reformed Church? Historian Robert Swierenga (1980) has recently proposed an answer to this problem, based on a statistical treatment of the Dutch regional origins of the immigrants. He argues, with the aid of sociologist Merton's categorical dichotomy "locals"/ "cosmopolitans," that those Dutch who joined the new and more reactionary True Holland Reformed Church were more likely to have come from the less urban-influenced areas of Holland, where the populace was "local" in cultural outlook. Those who remained in the Dutch Reformed Church, conversely, he shows to have been more often from regions where city influences encouraged a more "cosmopolitan" world view. This approach locates the causes of the schism outside the American context and thus may shed some light on the Dutch schisms as well.

The static dichotomy "locals"/"cosmopolitans," however, is only a system of labels and is not much help in explaining the dynamic process of constant internal fission characterizing Dutch Reformed religion in both Holland and America. Verrips's (1973) account of intracommunity factions in a modern Dutch town, and the example of West Sayville, suggest that whatever labels we attach to the individuals choosing one church over the other there is also a community dynamic involved in church fission and factions. The nature of that process is manifest not through a consideration of the individual characteristics of the immigrants[3] but through an analysis of their interaction—and that is revealed in part at least in the records of the church consistory, where a number of colorful social dramas were acted out.

These scenarios lend themselves nicely to Turner's extended case study method (see Introduction and Appendix A), which promises not only to reveal something of the structural roots of disputes and schisms in this and similar churches, but also to shed some light on questions of even more general concern in the anthropology of religion.

Ever since French social theorist Emile Durkheim (1915) argued that religion provides the moral and conceptual framework that society requires to work, anthropologists have focused most of their analytic attention on the contribution made by systems of religious belief and action to the stability of social systems. Shared religious ideology and common ritual interaction have been typically understood to knit together the social fabric, most especially when it threatens to unravel. Thus, for example, the life crises that interrupt the order of social and personal life are marked by "rites of passage" (Van Gennep 1960) which assert the ability of the culture to control these processes. Further, group and individual conflicts that arise in all realms of human experience may often be resolved by religion, especially on the ritual stage, according to analyses of numerous anthropologists (see esp. Turner 1968). By actively reaffirming the ideal moral order, ritual functions on both a psychological and social level, simultaneously providing both individual and group with a conceptual order that guides and makes sense of experience and interaction.

Apparently the religious dogmas of the Reformed faith equipped the individual with a means of making religious sense of disparate experience, as is certainly apparent in the memoirs of Bastiaan Broere (see above, Chapter 2). The relation of religious belief and practice to social interaction in a community like West Sayville, however, presents a challenge to social anthropological theories of religion in two respects.

First, the beliefs of the Reformed faith entailed a central contradiction, or at least conflict: pitting the notions of predestination and personal salvation against the absolute moral authority of the church-community. While the latter may have been a centripetal force pulling the community together, the former was equally centrifugal. If Bastiaan Broere did feel it necessary to seek the fellowship of other Christians, his tireless self-concern made cooperation with his newfound fellows difficult. Church dogma seems, therefore, to have been potentially as much a source of antagonism as of social solidarity.

This apparent contradiction between the independence of the individual in theological (as well as economic and social) affairs, and the moral authority of the church community, was addressed in the ideal realm through the Calvinist doctrine of the "Covenant," a union of free, saved individuals bound together by a kind of holy contract which was affirmed in stages. The confession of faith was a rite of passage which made the adult a full member of the congregation, binding him or her finally and completely to the God-directed will of the community, a bond that was periodically reaffirmed by the only other acknowledged ritual left to the Reformed community, the Lord's Supper. Authority in this community of believers was invested in a "consistory" of elders and deacons, elected by the assembled congregation. That congregation of household heads also "called" or elected a minister (*dominie* in Dutch) from a slate of candidates furnished by the classis, the regional governance body. These consistory officials were supposed to have absolute authority over those who covenanted with them.

Moreover, the bond of the covenant further implied the right and duty of each member of the community to report the moral transgression of fellow members. Anyone's sin, after all, threatened the moral integrity of the group and therefore had to be expunged. One might imagine that such independent-minded people as we have already seen the Dutch men and women to be would not always have been happy to bend before the communal will, especially when embodied in a particular neighbor. One might expect conflicts to ensue.

That brings us to the second challenge that this religious form presents to analysis. As we have already noted, anthropologists expect that wherever conflict arises, religious ritual should provide a formal means for its symbolic resolution, or at least suspension. But ritual was not an obvious feature of the Reformed faith. In challenging Roman Catholic practice, nearly all the Protestant creeds removed authority in varying degrees from the ritually sacred altar and placed it in the deritualized, secular pulpit. This amounted to an attack on the symbolic separation of sacred from secular time and place. Calvinistic creeds were especially concerned with breaking down this barrier, and bringing every action and thought under the governance of a deritualized religious faith.

Calvinist idealization and Calvinist practice, however, may be two different things. If we want to find out when and how dogmatic contradictions produced conflict, and what sorts of resolutions religious practice offered, out best strategy is an ethnographic one. We must look at what people actually do, not only at what they say they should do. A close analysis of what actually went on in one particular church-community should reveal aspects of the dynamic social character of this religious faith not apparent in textual or statistical studies.

The Dutch Reformed Church

The Sayville Dutch Reformed congregation was formally organized in 1866, and the consistory records reveal that serious difficulties were not long in arising. Even the simple matter of Sabbath violation, the most common offense brought to the consistory's attention, rarely proceeded smoothly.

An entry in the consistory records for April 2, 1868, reads:

"Special meeting was held; the Consistory learned that the following members [five names followed] were guilty of violation of the Sabbath day, by going to the bay on Sunday, March 22, to be at work at their boats. Notice was given to these members to appear before the Consistory.

As it turned out, two of the culprits "acknowledged their guilt and confessed that they had not done well." A third man informed the consistory that he was unable to attend the meeting but would the next. As for the other two, they were issued the following letter:

Sir:
I have to inform you that at the meeting of the Consistory . . . it was resolved to give you notice that you are not permitted to partake of the Lord's Supper and that for the following reasons: I. You are guilty of profanation of the Sabbath, II. Because you have refused to appear before the Consistory, notwithstanding you were ordered to do so. In case you have something to say in defense or excuse, opportunity is given you to do so, before a meeting of the Consistory. . . .

By the Will of the Consistory,

L. G. Jongeneel, Pres.

These two men remained unregenerate for quite some time, even with the threat of exclusion from the Lord's Supper. This sort of escalation of what began as relatively minor offenses, with the incurring of greater and greater acts of censure on the part of the consistory, was far from rare.

Ideally, fear of exclusion from the community should have brought the various offenders around, but if the offender could not contest the right of the community to enforce its will on him, he could question either the validity of the accusation or the fitness of the particular officers to represent the communal will. In resisting the orders of the consistory, he might claim either that he was not guilty of the crime or that the consistory or any of its several members were not morally pure themselves. In the first case, the accused took the charge of misconduct as an opportunity to turn communal attention on his accusor, so that what might conceivably have begun as competition or private argument between two individuals was soon raised to the rank of a public religious contention with suit and countersuit. In the second case, by questioning the right of the consistory to act in the community's behalf, the violator in effect claimed that the whole covenant was in a sorry state, as evidenced by the character of its officers. He was, furthermore, likely to find supporters in that claim, for various circumstances ensured that a portion of the community was always unhappy with things as they were.

In the Dutch Reformed congregation, however, it was the minister, or *dominie*, who was most often eventually found to be the underlying cause of whatever ailed the moral community. Today the ministers may be remembered as an unbroken line of eminent elders whose passage down the village streets was faithfully met with doffed hats and respectful nods, but the early church records reveal a different picture.

The first minister, a Reverend Jongeneel, arrived at the founding of the church in 1867 and remained until 1871. In those few years he was the frequent subject of open and angry accusations. In particular, the dominie was found wanting in the strictness of his interpretation of God's word. Early in his tenure one of his elders reprimanded Jongeneel for "preaching wrong doctrine" and for approving of the dropping of the word "Dutch" from the title of the national church. Later he was again found to be teaching "false doctrine" by a whole coterie of congregation members; even one of his own elders was heard to remark that the reverend "was better fit for farming than for preaching."

Jongeneel was replaced by Van Emmerick in 1871, but the new dominie faired even worse than his colleague. On the evidence of a young girl, Van Emmerick was accused of sexual adventures with a local teenage girl. While officially cleared by a classis committee, the minister was never to recover from the suspicions unleashed by that case. He was the subject of constant complaints concerning doctrinal matters, and many began to withdraw from the congregation. On the occasion of a visitation from an elder, one dissatisfied woman remarked, "So long as that guy is minister here, I am not going to step into that church." Van Emmerick was vilified for every possible offense, but most of them were linked once again to what some members of his congregation viewed as the growing laxness of the moral bonds of the community. In 1886 he left the church, having finally secured the salary he was owed by the congregation. His replacement was a Reverend Crousaz, who fared no better than his predecessors. Reverend Schilstra, dominie from 1900 to 1910, recorded these remarks about both Van Emmerick and Crousaz:

Rev. Crousaz behaved indecently and came home drunk now and then from Sayville. He held company with persons in Sayville and spent the evening playing cards and drinking. Afterwards it came out that the minister had a debt of $700 for beer and drink. When this unexpected behavior came out the love and respect for the minister was lost and then they let him go from the church. He went west and we never heard from this unlucky family. Dominie Crousaz was a principal in the Netherlands and probably had to leave that country because of his behavior. This was now the second minister who behaved in this church in the same bad way. This is what happens when runaway vagabonds and bandits like Van Emmerick and Crousaz can come here without decent preparation and looking into and are put for candidates by the classis.

As the Rev. Schilstra argues, the problems of the early ministers cannot be attributed to their personalities alone. Schilstra blamed the classis for sending "vagabonds and bandits" to the immigrant churches, and some of the local congregations' trouble certainly arose from their position as immigrant churches uneasily incorporated into an established American Reformed hierarchy.

If the language of church dispute was always religious, the underlying issues often seem to bear out this interpretation. There was, for example, the problem of money. According to the ideals of the Reformed church, the congregation should have been financially independent, paying the salary of its minister and building its own churches and facilities from the subscriptions and special donations of its own members. Poor immigrant communities, however, were rarely in a position to do so, and West Sayville was no exception. While the arguments between members were typically phrased in a religious idiom, the occasion for such fights could be the raising of money for the dominie's salary or other church expenses. The resentment felt for this financial strain could easily lead people to see the "unfitness" of the minister, a man who after all was living off a financially embattled and very hardworking congregation.

Again in common with many other immigrant congregations, the West Sayville Dutch found themselves uneasily placed in an American hierarchy of classes and synods on which they were financially dependent and from which they were separated by sometimes considerable cultural differences. Language was both an element and symbol of this cultural gap.

By the mid-ninteenth century the Reformed church in and around New York City was English-speaking, and the classis officials who oversaw the installation of the fledgling congregation in West Sayville expected the consistory minutes to be submitted in English. That was difficult enough, but when the classis officials further demanded that these English minutes be signed by the members of the consistory, the Dutchmen absolutely refused, saying, "How can we sign something we do not understand?" Such a protest may seem reasonable, but at several points it becomes obvious that in not signing the immigrants were expressing a more generally felt resentment against the English language—not so much as the tongue of the society into which they had moved, for that they could understand, but as a language of the church and religion.

In the context of the church, language and doctrinal issues were inseparable. The Rev. Jongeneel was the subject of considerable criticism for having supported the national church's intention to drop the word "Dutch" from their official title. But Jongeneel was also accused, in almost the same breath, of preaching "false doctrine." Language and the title "Dutch" were evidently more than ethnic flags; many suspected that the pure Reformed doctrine could be preached only in "the Holland tongue." The defenders of the language were of course correct in assuming that the use of English would open their church to the influence of other doctrines, for once the Dutch Reformed congregation began holding services in English, relations with neighboring churches, like the Congregationalist, became possible, and in fact took place.

The most threatening source of doctrinal pollution, however, was not any of the surrounding American congregations but the mother church into which the young Sayville congregation was incorporated. The tension along this cultural boundary served only to aggravate the issue of financial dependency, having the cumulative effect of creating and maintaining a hostility and resentment between the hierarchy and the local congregation into which any uneasiness the immigrants might feel toward their surrounding American environment could be channeled and expressed.

No wonder the minister got the worst of this tension, for he stood in an unenviable mediatory position between the local congregation and the hierarchy, both of which groups demanded obedience to conflicting doctrinal and cultural standards. Early ministers were always too Dutch for the tastes of the classis, while for the congregation they were never Dutch enough.

This sort of structural tension between the immigrant congregations and their American church was naturally also felt among the other Dutch communities in the Midwest and the east. As soon as the hardships of the earliest years of settlement were overcome, widespread dissatisfaction with the American Reformed church began to be felt. That church, the immigrants discovered, had fallen as far from the strictest standards of doctrinal purity, as had the state church back in the Netherlands. If other more secular difficulties were behind this uneasiness, as was the case in West Sayville, it was nevertheless in the language of religious practice and dogma that these problems always found expression.

What most of those doctrinal issues had in common was a concern for the authority and boundedness of the covenant community. They bespoke a desire to withdraw from the nefarious influences of the outside world as represented most directly by the American version of Reformed Christianity, but as embodied more generally in American culture. To withstand these enemies, a tighter covenant had to be formed, a new church of more inwardly-focused communities, each protected from the surrounding cultural wilderness by walls of non-association. Accordingly, as we have noted, in 1858 a number of immigrants withdrew from the Reformed Church in America to form the True Holland Reformed Church, whose name was changed eventually to the Christian Reformed Church. In West Sayville the split came in 1876. In the Netherlands, however, other schisms took place through the latter part of the century, and there too, tighter covenants were formed by the seceders. In either the Dutch or the American case, the schisms could be interpreted following Swierenga (see above, p.143)

as reactions by "locals" to the pressures of modernization, industrialization, and urbanization. The fact that in both nations this reaction could find religious expression may be attributed to the existence of a dogmatic form that lent itself to such uses.

What about the West Sayville immigrants? Certainly this pattern of cultural withdrawal is apparent from the outset, and the respective church records reveal that the Dutch Reformed congregation was more cosmopolitan in its cultural orientation than the Christian Reformed. Attributing this difference of orientation to the regional origin of the communicants, however, is problematic. The early immigrants were mostly from Zeeland, in fact from the two villages of Yerseke and Bruinisse. These towns were certainly influenced early on by markets and other modernizing influences, especially later in the century. At the time of the early immigration, however, there were potential seceders among the first settlers. Furthermore, it was in the wake of the boom of cosmopolitan influences in Yerseke late in the century that the more reactionary churches there made such headway.

Even after the West Sayville colony was joined by immigrants from other areas of Holland, particularly Texel and Friesland, church membership does not reveal any significant tendency to join one congregation or another according to point of origin in Holland. Zeelanders and Frisians are found on both sides, and what is more not a few families and individuals changed congregations or split between them.

The difficulty with Swierenga's theory is that it, like the American-adaptation explanation of the schism, blames the conflicts within the church, and the ultimate separation of the two churches, solely on external influences. The implication of his reliance on the "cosmopolitan"/"local" dichotomy is that this sort of religious form is inherently conservative unless disrupted by the external forces of social change, which are seen as emanating from the city. But if the Reformed faith's emphasis on the covenant made it essentially conservative, did not its equal stress on individual predestination contribute directly, as Weber argued, to the entrepreneurial ethos of the city (see Introduction)? In other words, do not these "cosmopolitan" forces find as much support in this variant of the Protestant Ethic as do the forces of "localism"?

Certainly the community in West Sayville produced its own "cosmopolitans"; they did not have to be imported. As soon as various individuals found that their economic or social interests required a wider circle of associates, they managed a liberal enough interpretation of the covenant. Jake Ockers was the most extreme case, for he married an American Methodist and joined her congregation. The other big shippers, Westerbeke and Vander Borgh, remained in the Dutch Reformed Church, and both families produced a series of "pillars" in that congregation. When the split came, however, a proportion of the community sought a more restricted church, and this more closed and more visibly Dutch church attracted many among the newer immigrants arriving toward the end of the century.

If we are right in supposing that entrepreneurial cosmopolitanism is an *internal* product of this sort of community, then the separation of the two congregations should not have produced anything like perfect harmony among those who withdrew into the True Holland Church in 1876. There too the internal contradictions of orthodox Calvinism should have produced their very own disruptions, schisms, and threats of schisms as new cosmopolitans arose with their more open attitudes and their opposition retreated behind even stronger covenantal walls. Further, as we shall see, the interactional character of this more covenantal church assured that conflict would be even more frequent than it was in the Dutch Reformed congregation.

THE CHRISTIAN REFORMED CONGREGATION[4]

Two structurally based sorts of conflict within the Christian Reformed congregation can be distinguished. One genre we may call "problems of boundary maintenance." Fights arose from a kind of border tension developing between those who responded to the more individualistic teachings of the church and those who sought tighter bonds in a closed community. The other type of conflict arose from the same structural opposition and typically followed the occurrence of boundary disputes. These "crises of authority," as we will call them, were more frequent in this congregation than among the Dutch Reformed. Ideally their reaffirmation of the absolute moral authority of the community should have readied such transgressors as were reported to accept the communal will as represented and expressed by the consistory. While in this regard the rights of the church were more authoritarian, the Christian Reformed doctrine was also more democratic, so that the sinner might always suspect that, after all, he himself was right and the particular individuals holding office were sadly unfit for their sacred responsibility. In this church, those individuals were less likely to include the dominie.

The dominie was less important in the Christian Reformed congregation (in those years), first because for much of the time there was no one resident. From 1876 until 1890 the small, financially struggling congregation made do with periodic visits from New Jersey ministers whose authority in disputes was minimal. From 1894 until 1899, the communicants were once again without a religious leader, during which time political as well as financial difficulties made the "call" of a new dominie difficult. Even when the dominie was resident, his reduced role is evident in two opposite but mutually dependent ways: He was less powerful politically, and he was less likely to be used as a scapegoat for the conflicts of the community or to be perceived as the source of moral corruption. The dominie's relative lack of authority is precisely what made him less useful for that sort of symbolic role than his counterpart in the Dutch Reformed Church. That being the case, large-scale conflicts were more likely to find their way to the other consistory officers, as the only suitable symbols of the collective authority of the community.

The greater concern with one's neighbor's behavior is evidenced in the consistory records by a far greater number of reported sins. One must conclude that the Christian Reformed community contained either more sinners or more "reporters" than the Dutch Reformed. Given the covenant ideology, one inclines toward the latter explanation.

Whereas the Dutch Reformed consistory concerned itself most often with very public Sabbath violations, the Christian Reformed consistory was somehow able to gain knowledge of far more private infractions. The very intention to get a job which would lead one to work on Sunday, if heard of in private conversation, would somehow turn up at consistory meetings. Thus, for example, were John, Willem, and Leendert brought before the consistory on three separate occasions because one church officer or another had heard that these men intended to "go yachting" in the summer, which employment "would lead them to violate the Fourth Commandment" (work on the Sabbath). On an earlier occasion yet another communicant was brought in and asked, "Is it true that a drunken tailor entered your house last Sunday?" The accused man replied, "That is true, but the tailor was let in by my son Jan while I myself was taking a Sunday afternoon nap."

Reported infractions of the commandments were by no means limited to Sabbath violations. No less than five separate cases of adultery were brought up between 1890 and 1910, several cases of theft (always involving shellfish), and a large number of such minor lapses from moral purity as drunkenness and card playing. A committee was even sent to investigate reports that a well-respected member of the community had "behaved badly on the occasion of celebrating their daughter's wedding—there was dancing in the house until the early hours of the morning." Neither were the difficulties between married couples only their own affair. Twice the consistory assumed a mediatory position between estranged couples, attempting to reconcile them for the good of the moral community. What distinguishes all these cases from those reported in the Dutch Reformed Church records is the greater penetration into the domestic domain of the Christian Reformed consistory. Nearly all the sinners brought to account in the Dutch Reformed Church had transgressed in public. Members of that community were less likely to report lapses within the household, and their consistory was evidently less prone to penetrate into that inner domain.

The most significant incidents the Christian Reformed congregation felt it their duty to handle were those interpreted as "border violations," actions that threatened to blur the line of nonassociation that ideally separated the covenanters from the outer, sinful world and thus threatened the covenant in another way. The most obvious of these, and one of the most troubling to the West Sayville congregation, was the issue of secret societies. In particular, the Forresters lodge had attracted a number of communicants, who were forced to choose between membership in the church and membership in that society. The union, of which we heard so much in earlier chapters, though not officially forbidden by the consistory, was actively discouraged. The question was raised for the first time in March 1902: "Is it permitted to be a member of the church and a member of the union at the same time?" The dominie responded, "This has been discussed many times at classis and synod meetings, and one has to take into account how and why the union originated and manifests itself, but that the consistory holds as its opinion that is shouldn't exist and it is extremely condemnable if violence is used."

Even where members of the community did not join secret societies but rather merely associated with groups whose interests were seen as opposed to those of the congregation, they might be censured. One man was known to have gone "on quite a few occasions" to services at the nearby Congregationalist church. There was, as well, the ambiguous issue of membership in "insurance associations," which were objectionable both on grounds of association and because subscription was understood by some at least to evince "a lack of faith in God's help." Closely related to the issue of preventing association with outsiders was that of keeping up the internal associations of community members. The consistory was particularly concerned with church attendance, of course, but also frequently reprimanded those whose children were not showing up for religious instruction.

In all these cases of reported lapses, the consistory's policy was to send a committee to investigate the matter, and/or require the presence of the alleged transgressor(s). As with the Dutch Reformed Church, the procedure was to require a confession of guilt from the sinners, in lieu of which they would be placed under greater and greater stages of censure. Rarely did major offenders merely submit to the will of the consistory without any sort of fuss, but one can usefully distinguish between those crimes whose punishment incurred some conflict because of the individual's unwillingness to bend before communal authority, and those which were in fact only ammunition in continuing conflicts between individuals and factions. The latter conflicts are the more anthropologically instructive, because they offer occasions through which to view both the structural strains besetting the community and the kind of authority that existed to resolve those strains.

A particularly revealing case is that which involved a member of the consistory, whom we shall call Jan Smit. The trouble began when elder Smit was renominated for that office in the annual election of 1891. Several families were reported to be "unsatisfied" with Smit's candidacy, and the dominie had accordingly gone with Smit to visit them at home and hear their objections. The first of these visits went very badly indeed, for the family in question, whom we shall call the S——s, sent Smit and Dominie De Vries from their door. The H——s were "more calm" and managed to communicate their objections to Smit in the appropriate religious idiom, "Is a member of the church, and an officer, allowed to do nightwatch work during the nights before and after Sunday?" This ambiguous question of Sabbath violation was brought by the minister to the classis, who decided that Smit's behavior as a night watchman was compromising enough to render him unfit for the eldership. Smit confessed his guilt in "sinning against his elderly profession" but did not want to be conceived a "Sabbath violator." That, however, was far from being the end of the matter.

A year later, in the autumn of 1892, once again the elections for church officers came around, and once again Smit was nominated.

The same two men who had complained the previous year raised their voices again and were joined by a third, a deacon by the name of K——. In addition to the fact that too little time had elapsed since his confession, these men felt Smit was unqualified for eldership because he had in the past divulged consistory secrets to nonchurch members and because he had spread slander about the dominie. This time Smit "accepted nothing of what they brought up against him." A big fight ensued, splitting the consistory, and once again recourse was had to the classis officials. Smit confessed that he was wrong, but was allowed to stand for the eldership and was once again elected. The other elder and deacon elected, however, declined their posts. Their replacements evidently accepted Smit, because the records tell us "no further objections among the Consistory, but there are some problems in the community, some are unsatisfied about Smit's eldership and the Consistory has decided that the Dominie should announce from the pulpit that the Consistory wishes to be spared from unsigned letters."

Smit was at the center of various controversies over the next few years, sometimes as elder and sometimes as member, but in every case he was identified with a more "cosmopolitan" interpretation of church doctrine, and his opponents, to judge by their alignments on other issues as well as against Smit, can be characterized as "locals." He was, for example, accused by one couple of having advised their daughter to go out to one of the American churches on Sunday evening, and of having complained to her of the "coercive" nature of their own church.

The full assault on Smit came when he was reelected to an eldership in December 1896. The consistory meeting of that December 18 began with Smit's announcing that some people will come to raise objections. Three men then entered the room, all of them strict interpretationists on doctrinal issues. S—— began, "When a man's wife goes to another church, can that man become an elder in his church? Also, is it Christian to ask money for serving as elder, as Smit has done in the past? Can any man be trusted who has been accused and confessed so many times?" K—— repeated these charges, but added that "Smit visits the Congregational church on Sunday nights and kneels there like the others." The final charges came from van Y——, who referred to a letter he had already given the consistory in protest of Smit's election. In that missive, van Y—— had cited the biblical passage 1 Timothy 3:1–7, which relates the qualities necessary to be a bishop in the church and states: "He must manage his own household well . . . for if a man does not know how to manage his own household, how can he care for God's church?"—evidently referring to Smit's wife's not being a member of the church.

Things got hot enough for the visiting Reverend Koster to say "that he will conclude and leave and that he doesn't want to get ill here." Referring to the problem of language understanding, Koster pointed out that is was not unusual for the wives of functionaries not to be members. It seems, however, that although Mrs. Smit was American-born, she had grown up with her Dutch-speaking grandfather in Grand Rapids, Michigan, so that it was unclear to Smit's opponents why she would be unable to understand the service. The dominie tried to mollify Smit's accusers on the Congregationalist church issue also, whereupon he earned the vituperative response from vander E., "Do you believe that these 'Children of God' follow the hints of the devil, and if they do so premeditatively, are they not even more sinful?" More angry words were exchanged, and once again Dominie Koster threatened to leave them to their own devices.

The final issue against Smit was one that especially raised the hackles of the contenders. Van Y. said that Smit was "an agent for a life insurance company," and added, "Isn't it terrible that everything is allowed to take place in our Church? If I had known beforehand that such a thing would be approved of I wouldn't have become a member." Smit, meanwhile, explained that he did not sell insurance, but merely acted as an interpreter for the company. That was a distinction too subtle by far for his opponents. On this issue the dominie and another consistory member were, however, even more supportive of Smit. The latter fellow allowed as how he was considering taking out insurance himself, while the dominie asked Smit's enemies to show him "where in the Bible or in the Church order it is forbidden." "Our ancestors," vander E. replied, "Couldn't have imagined such a thing. If everything is tolerated I will ask for my 'attest.'" Insurance, according to Smit's opponents, was a sign of lack of faith in God. The God-fearing member of the covenant, after all, needn't fear want, for the "deserving poor" (to borrow a more contemporary phrase) are always well provided for. The recorder tells us that the dominie decided at this point that he was unwilling to "sicken himself any longer in Sayville. He foresees a schism and regards himself as unable to set right this case. He doesn't want to become the cause of a schism." The schism, in fact, would not come for some time. Smit retained his office after all, and the controversy subsided for another two years. When Smit was up for reelection in the fall of 1899, however, the whole process began again.

It will not have escaped the reader's attention that the crimes of which Smit was accused in these various confrontations nearly all involved perceived violations of the integrity of the covenant: "border violations" by a "cosmopolitan" which threatened to destroy the barrier between the closed Dutch community and the outside American world. The fact that Smit was periodically reelected to eldership testifies to the existence of a fair number of "cosmopolitans" sharing his view, as the constant and concerted opposition he met shows the strength of the reactionary "localist" element in the community. The Smit disputes constitute a particularly glaring example of this sort of attack and counterattack (for Smit was able to take advantage of some embarrassing lapses in the families of his opponents), but it is by no means the only lengthy contretemps. "Cosmopolitans" were pitted against the "locals" individually or severally any number of times and over any number of issues.

If one believes the language of the conflicts themselves, then one is led to believe that Smit's opponents were simply religious people appalled at their neighbor's transgressions. Could their close attention to Smit in particular be explained by the fact that he alone was so often sinful? More likely it was because of his structural position as an elder who represented in his actions one particular internally produced danger to the covenant community. The two opposing world views and social strategies represented in these disputes were equally the product of this particular variant of the Protestant Ethic. Further, the democratic/authoritarian government and idiom of the Christian Reformed Church made it certain that neither variant would lose sight of the other, and the lack of a strong minister further assured that the consistory officers, directly elected by factions within the community, would be left as the principal actors and targets in the resulting disputes. By this theory, the other congregation—the Dutch Reformed— suffered fewer upsets after the 1890s, not because it contained fewer sinners but because the private behavior of its members was less threatening to the community's vision of its own sanctity, and because the more symbolically important dominie provided a convenient target for all manner of scrutiny and accusation. The Dutch Reformed Church could see itself through a very difficult period by periodic purgings of its minister. The Christian Reformed Church, on the other hand, was constantly riven by individuals and factions pitted against one another.

RITUAL RESOLUTION

Might not such conflicts, even if abetted by religious ideology, have been overcome, as anthropologists often find, in communal rituals that reaffirmed the solidarity of the group? There was, after all, the Lord's Supper, the Communion rite which symbolically and dramatically acted out the sacred bond that ideally linked all communicants together and separated them from those outside the covenant. The record reveals, however, that the rite presented an opportunity to express hostility as often as solidarity. There were, first of all, communicants who were conspicuous by their absence, who by dint of consistory censure were barred from the Lord's Supper until they had confessed their sins. There were also those not kept away but choosing to stay away, thus demonstrating by their absence disapproval of the current moral state of the community, and particularly of its symbolic representatives, the consistory. In a community of this size and constitution such a strategy was quite effective. If someone stayed away from the communal ritual for long enough, that person would be assured a visitation by a consistory committee, on which occasion he or she would be provided with an opportunity to express disapproval dramatically in the appropriate idiom, replete with biblical allusions. Even presence at the Lord's Supper did not assure a person's ritual "oneness" with the community, for if someone did not approve of that day's sermon, he or she was always free to express that disapproval by not shaking hands with the dominie on the way out of church.

The shaking of hands was a religious ritual in itself, a symbolic reaffirmation of the binding covenant, the Holy Contract. When two individuals fought and then repented, the consistory officers would direct them to shake hands, or in the language of the church "to give one another the brotherhood." If the intention of this act was to apply a little ritual glue to such social bonds, the adhesive did not prove very strong. Those who gave one another "the brotherhood" one month were likely to be at each other's throats again a month or two later. Many were these ritual confessions of guilt, but the deep-rooted conflicts, as we have seen, outlasted a hundred such confessions.

If all these more or less official church rituals were of so little effect in counteracting the conflicts so often pitting the covenanters against one another, by what means did religion resolve these self-generated difficulties? By no means, one is tempted to answer. After all, the difficulties in the Dutch Reformed congregation led to fission: the schism of 1876 which split the church community into two antagonistic camps. Further, within the Christian Reformed Church, at least, schism seemed always imminent, and in fact did finally come to pass in 1911, when a number of communicants from that church founded the Netherlands Reformed congregation of West Sayville. For if the Dutch Reformed had their shared dissatisfaction with whomever happened to be dominie to hold them together, the Christian Reformed were only later supplied with dominies, and even then, as we have seen, such men were not as symbolically or politically powerful as their Dutch Reformed counterparts. Without such scapegoats the unfortunate congregation was left with only one another, but most especially with their neighbors-raised-to-religious-rank, the elders and deacons.

Was schism, however, tantamount to the permanent fission of the community and thus a signal of the final failure of the religious form to contribute to the solidarity of the local social system? We must take a closer look at the character of association both across sectarian lines within the community and between persons within them. Following the teaching of the social theorist Georg Simmel, we must be careful not to mistake conflict for nonassociation. Nor should we exclude the possibility that conflict itself can exist as a kind of ritual, both formal and informal. Ritual combat, after all, may be as ancient a form as ritual communion, although the latter has certainly received the most scholarly attention.

Let us first take up the matter of the schisms. What sort of continuing relations marked the two congregations after the split in 1876?

There was, of course, the hostility one might expect to issue from such a schism. The Dutch Reformed congregation saw the newer church as comprised of dangerous heretics and troublemakers, malcontents who separated themselves artificially with "man-made laws." The Christian Reformed Church, on the other hand, perceived the others as reprobates who had fallen away from the covenant under the evil influence of the surrounding liberal environment. A few older locals still remember confrontations between the two congregations: "If a crowd was goin' down the road on a Sunday to the one church, and another group was comin' up by them toward the other, they'd each stick to their path and so try to force the others off the road. They'd fight with their choirs as well—the one trying to drown out the other." These near-ritual confrontations do not seem to have ever become violent, nor indeed should they be taken as an indication of a necessarily strong hostility between the individual members of the respective congregations. While separated on Sunday, members of the two congregations mixed on other days and in other contexts, and there is no indication, for example, that the oyster houses were segregated according to church membership.

Beyond that, however, individuals not infrequently shifted their allegiance from one church to another. It is difficult to separate religious from nonreligious motivations for these shifts. One old woman whose marriage left her outside and somewhat embittered toward both Dutch churches commented, "They're just like hoppy-toads down there—goin' from one church to the other. Why there was one fella, a carpenter, who was in the one church and when he didn't get the job of doin' the roof on that church, he left and joined the other."

Thus whatever the individual motivation for moving between the two congregations, their existence within the bounds of a single isolated ethnic community permitted a strategy of internal adjustment, both to the pressures and attractions of the surrounding American environment and to the interactional difficulties arising from the confined and competitive life of the community. Although relatively more "cosmopolitan," the Dutch Reformed Church was still, up through World War I at least, very much an immigrant church, and communicants could certainly feel anchored in the Dutch community there even if their field of activities brought membership in the Masons or the Forresters as well. As an alternative, the Christian Reformed congregation offered the refuge of further withdrawal from the outer world.

But what of further schism within the Christian Reformed congregation? It is first important to note that even with the intense quarreling besetting that congregation from its organization in 1876, and despite the fears of visiting dominies, the schism of the Netherlands Reformed group was more than forty years in coming. Many of the more conservative members of the Christian Reformed congregation threatened to leave when things were not going their way, and some withdrew individually or as families from the church. But many of them returned after a brief interim, and the fact remains that in cases of conflict like those involving Smit, the combatants seemed quite willing to wage a constant seesaw battle over the decades with no victory for either side.

In fact, those who did finally leave to form the Netherlands Reformed group were very few in number, a mere handful of men who ostensibly departed over the appointment of a dominie of whom they evidently did not approve. So, far from creating a permanent rift between those who left the church and those who remained, the wives and children of the men who "separated themselves" remained in the Christian Reformed Church. That is not to say that this was not troublesome for at least those families. For them, the Sabbath became a day of combat rather than communion. The son of one of the Netherlands Reformed vividly remembers:

Sunday was the day I dreaded. All week it wouldn't be that bad, but on Sunday my father would get up in a foul mood and everyone in the house would be upset, waiting for the time for church, when my mother and us children would go off in one direction and my father would go off in the other. Sometimes my parents would fight dreadfully over the church and sometimes they would just be silent with each other. My father held to that church until his dying day, but then, thank God, he repented his ways. . . . He said he realized that it was the devil leading him that way, and we were joined together in the end.

While thus traumatic enough within the few families so affected, that schism hardly fissioned the entire community as the first had done. More important was the threat of schism which seemed ever to hang over the proceedings of the Christian Reformed consistory. Schism was the ever possible event, the abetting of which you could accuse your enemies, or the threat of which you could use to curb the hubris of those in office. To withdraw from the covenant when it had lost its sanctity was an understood right within the contractual idiom of the church community. "Protestants," in the words of one battling deacon, "were allowed to protest," to voice independent religious opinions and interpretations.

Indeed, in this religious form at least, Protestants were not only allowed to protest, but they availed themselves so often and in so many contexts of this right that we must conclude that the religious conflict itself was the major ritual form. Not only on church grounds, before the members of the consistory, but anywhere in the community, the individual was able to turn a secular situation into a sacred one merely by using the appropriate language.

Once again, Evans-Pritchard's notion of "idiom" is useful here.

The prospective combatant turned to his textual repertoire as provided by the Bible and church law and found within them the appropriate passage to turn whatever problem he faced into a moral/religious one. As the church records indicate, once this religious idiom was initiated the combatants were constrained to remain within it. Thus, if formal rituals in the church did little to relieve the conflicts of the community (the Lord's Supper was, in fact, not even held during periods of intense strife), then the absence of a sacred arena for acting out religious values only succeeded in turning the entire village into a religious forum. In breaking down the boundary between the sacred and the secular, the Calvinistic creed left each man and woman to his or her own theological devices and made all the world a stage for their confrontations. The ritual nature of these confrontations is evident not only in their symbolic expressions and adherence to understood rules, but also in the people's ability to live with and between these often fierce battles.

Even when faction and schism were the apparent result, confrontation acted to draw the community together in that "honest war," as an early minister called it, whose contenders knew that the greatest gulf lay not between opposing combatants but between soldiers and civilians. It is thus possible to see an integrative dimension to these conflicts; with the aid of church doctrines and associations, entrepreneurial attitudes and clannish communalism could exert their opposing forces as long as the ensuing conflicts were allowed open expression in religious language and on the broad religious stage.

EPILOGUE

Social change did not cease after the first decade of this century, nor did the Great South Bay lose its position as the economic heart of the community. From about 1910, however, the oyster industry began to suffer setbacks on several fronts.

Those Connecticut interests of whom the Blue Point shippers were so wary around the turn of the century proved even more dangerous than expected. Sealshipt Carrier Company, as the "oyster trust" designated itself, had made continuous inroads into the South Bay fisheries through the first decade of the century, but their major coup took the Dutchmen by surprise. A large share of bay grounds had been awarded by civil suit to "the Smith heirs" in 1899 (see above, Chapters 4 and 6), and most of this land was leased by Dutch planters, several of whom were utterly dependent on those underwater acres for their livelihood. Those hardy self-made men were shocked to hear that the more-or-less anonymous forces of distant capital, in the guise of the Connecticut oyster trust, had managed through secret negotiations in 1910 to purchase all these grounds out from under them. Given notice that their leases which ran out over the next year or two could not be renewed, many of the West Sayville planters sold their operations to Sealshipt, whose goal was to capture the entire Blue Points industry. The Dutch entrepreneurs did not take this defeat lightly. There was much public and private railing about the injustice of it all, but when push came to shove, those who could not run their businesses without the Smith heirs' lands capitulated. Younger members of these families were often left in charge of the operations, now plant managers for Sealshipt, but the older planters chose to retire.[1]

The "king oyster planter" managed a better arrangement. Ockers owned or leased thousands of acres outside the Smith heirs' grounds, and indeed outside the bay, and was thus in a better position to deal with Sealshipt. In 1912 they concluded a partnership which left Ockers president of Sealshipt-owned Blue Point Oyster Company and still owner of water acreage further afield. He remained in vigorous control of his interests until his death in 1918 at the age of seventy-one.

From the workers' point of view, these changes on the shorefront brought improved working conditions through mechanization in the shanties, but such changes also threatened to eliminate jobs. As things turned out, however, Sealshipt's move proved unpropitious, for the great day of the oyster on the world market had come to an end. Many people became convinced of the hazards involved in the eating of shipped shellfish, so that the total demand began to diminish. The South Bay industry was peculiarly dependent on export, however, and World War I brought an almost complete cessation of shipping to the lucrative English market. The end of the war brought resumption of this trade, but never at prewar levels.

The final blow to the local oyster industry was struck by Nature, who has a way of reminding us that even our most advanced technology does not free us from her whim. In the 1930s a series of extremely powerful hurricanes rocked Long Island, destroying hundreds of thousands of shellfish and breaking new inlets through the barrier beach that separated the bay from the ocean. The increased salinity of the bay which resulted seems to have so encouraged the growth of "drills" that young oysters could no longer survive in those waters.[2]

If the 1930s brought the end of the oyster industry, it by no means brought the end of the baymen. In the words of one of them, "God took away the oyster, but he gave us the clam." In fact, the very ecological changes that had proved detrimental to the oysters proved perfect for the growth of clams. Confined to the West Bay in the prehurricane years, these drill-resistant shellfish spread through the East Bay after the 1930s so that the entire Great South Bay became a valuable clam ground. The constant increase in the value of that bivalve has made that resource a precious commodity, amounting to a hundred-million-dollar-a-year industry.

Today many of the children and grandchildren of the Dutch men and women met in the preceding account continue to follow the bay. Some of these are the descendants of simple baymen, and in those cases only a small engine distinguishes the methods they use now from those of their grandfathers and great-grandfathers. Their pursuit of natural growth clams has ensured that the old disputes between the baymen and the "planters," who are interested in cultivating clams on a large scale (principally Blue Points, Ockers's old operation, now owned by American Can Corporation), over the extent of the free bay are as important as ever. Growing population and environmental concern has also tended to limit clamming, so that the independent clammers are apt to resist either sort of enclosure as restricting livelihood. At the same time, however, the arrival of thousands of part-time clammers every summer has tended to redefine in local minds just what is meant by a free bay.

West Sayville has continued to produce its share of entrepreneurs as well, on the bay and off. The advent of trucking opened markets further afield, and several new shippers have been able to rise since World War I. Only one of the nineteenth-century planter families remains in the shellfish industry, the Vander Borghs, now in their fourth generation of planting and shipping shellfish. Prosperity in other pursuits, however, has attracted many of the descendants of the immigrants, and many have found employment distant in place and form from that of their forefathers.

Nor were clams the only quarry sought after the passing of the oyster. Eels and finfish are still caught by fishing companies in the bay and in the ocean beyond. And scalloping, important in some seasons, became particularly lucrative in the 1920s. Those who scalloped in the ocean just beyond Fire Island, in fact, sometimes managed to secure other kinds of valuables in the process. Those were the years of prohibition, and the West Sayville scalloper, passing in and out of the inlets to the open sea, was in a fine position to make rendezvous with rum-runners. Several among the West Sayville Dutchmen are reputed to have made some money in that pursuit, although it is claimed that competition with organized crime proved too much for such independent entrepreneurs. Those days are occasionally recalled when a clam dredge brings up a case of vintage illicit whiskey along with the usual debris, contraband tossed overboard while fleeing the authorities.

While maritime pursuits have continued to be a central concern for those who have remained in the community, as we saw in Chapter 1, contemporary West Sayville is hardly the isolated ethnic enclave it once was. Locals say that the wars did the most to break down that isolation, especially World War II. For many soldiers coming from such insulated worlds, the armed forces provided a rite of passage that allowed them, for the first time, to see their home world as a relatively limited one. We would be making a big mistake, however, to assume that the distinctive community we have seen through the preceding chapters is no more. Indeed, the story of West Sayville will go on for a long time yet.

CONCLUSIONS

THE CONTRACTUAL COMMUNITY

While much has been said through these chapters about a small corner of the world, our view of that place has also been very much restricted. Myriad facets of daily existence are not touched on here, and it is certainly the experience of anthropologists that any social world, once looked into, is infinite. The focus of this book has been guided not by any desire to catalog every aspect of the Dutch immigrant experience in West Sayville, but by a concern to understand both the particular and general role of community structure in the process of social change.

The particularity of West Sayville lies in its Dutchness, in the peculiar structure and exigencies of shellfishing, in the legal and technical traditions of the surrounding Americans, and in its Reformed religion. All these factors may be seen as contributing to the particular path followed by the community through the decades of industrialization and change. On the other hand, the American reader is struck more by West Sayville's familiarity than by its strangeness, for the overall structure of the community, and of interaction within it, is more an extreme version of our own view of ourselves than a contradiction of it.

That perception has led us to consider not just the peculiarity of the community, but its possible representativeness as a case study of a community type, as vital to recent Western history as it is unstudied (at least from an anthropological perspective). For the contractual community, of which West Sayville has been taken as an exemplar, is the local social world that structures and maintains the contradictions of what we are pleased to call modern life. These concerns have determined which aspects of local life have drawn our attention, namely, those that contributed most to the structure of social relations in the community and that provided the institutional settings, or stages, most important to the expression (and hence creation) of the local culture.

THE CASE IN PARTICULAR

The sea and shorefront provided a most vital set of backdrops to the continuously changing dramas of this maritime community. But the roles acted out there were partially scripted for other communal stages, and it is all these local dramas, and their interrelations, that must be understood. West Sayville was not just a passive reactor to externally originating transformations; the dynamic community was itself a source of change.

The early immigrants were both baymen and entrepreneurs, following the variety of seasonal pursuits that characterized the local adaptation, but seeking out entrepreneurial opportunities with noticeable vigor and success. Why? From a rational-economic model of human behavior, it can be argued that as landless immigrants with small amounts of capital and less opportunity for investment in land, the early immigrants like Cornelius DeWaal, Bastiaan Broere, or Dirk Van Wyen were simply making the most rational choices in investing time and capital in transporting oysters. Yet it must be admitted that their social and cultural experience in Zeeland helped them to see the choices in that way. While certainly "uprooted," as Handlin put it, these immigrants when it came to an entrepreneurial self-view were "more American than the Americans," and that view was sustained by their new communal association on this side of the Atlantic.

As individualistic as their new neighbors, the Dutch had retained more of the communalism which had once characterized at least the Puritan variant of American life. Furthermore, the strength of the communal institutions that dominated local life in West Sayville, both as agents of social control and as constructors of the world view, greatly affected the local reaction to the transformations accompanying industrialization toward the end of the century. If the "localism" and suspicions of the more orthodox church kept its members out of the union, then the "cosmopolitanism" of the other church was equally antithetical to what is typically meant by working-class consciousness. These were two sides of the same cultural coin, an antithesis whose conflict could be eternally acted out in the confrontations of church and other voluntary associations more supportive of the contractual idiom than any union.

In the Netherlands, this tendency to internal schism, particularly along religious lines, is identified by the Dutch term *verzuiling*, translated as "pillarization" (Goudsblom 1967, 118–27). Although it divides much of the Dutch population into distinct and often conflicting groups, this pillarization, according to Goudsblom, is ultimately integrative in that it encourages a common agreement on both the terms and goals of the competition between the various groups. *Verzuiling* also contributes to the unity-in-conflict of the Netherlands insofar as it joins people in association who might otherwise be divided according to other interests more threatening to society, for example, class interests. It is interesting to note that communist movements have had extremely limited success among Holland's working class populations, among many of whom the loyalties of their respective "pillars" exercise competing and evidently more powerful attractions. Even the labor movement in industrializing Holland experienced grave difficulties in those regions like Yerseke, where other forms of association and competing ideologies offered other ways of expressing conflict.

This latter role of pillarization is reminiscent of the particular problems the Oysterman's Union had in recruiting the West Sayville Dutch to its banner. Not only were the Christians among the immigrants as yet unable to relinquish hope in a "kingdom come when they too would be capitalists," but their religious associations competed indirectly (in the case of the Dutch Reformed Church) or directly (in the Christian Reformed Church) with such an affiliation.

From a Marxist perspective, this pillarization may seem a form of false consciousness, and one particularly helpful to the interests of capital. It did provide a format and language with which the Dutch could ride out the tidal wave of change they encountered in their American environment between mid-century and World War I. The religious form was equally adept, however, at handling the threats of civilization as they were felt back home in Holland. In all cases the Reformed communities reacted to a modernization they themselves had helped to create, by translating the threat it presented to the community into particular issues of doctrine and practice which could then be argued and fought, though inevitably lost, at which point another symbolic issue would arise to replace it.[1]

THE CASE IN GENERAL

Pillarization, at least in its extreme form, may be peculiarly Dutch, but its manifestation on the local level may be a more widespread phenomenon, symptomatic of what we have called the contractual community. In its structure of competing voluntary associations, the pillarized community provides the social contexts for the expression of that particular brand of individualism which so struck Tocqueville.[2] It is the home of the contractual idiom, an ideology which assures that self-interest and the commonweal are not only unopposed but mutually dependent—for such a world view seeks to eliminate the contradiction between individualism and communalism. While its historical roots go deeper, I suspect, than the Protestant Reformation, it is an ideology that was probably given its first formal religious expression in the doctrines of Calvin. The most explicit and eloquent secular version may be found later in the work of Adam Smith, who wrote, "But the study of his own advantage naturally or rather necessarily leads [one] to prefer that employment which is most advantageous to the society. . . . By pursuing his own interest he frequently promotes that of society more effectually than when he really intends to promote it" (Smith 1909, 333, 335).

Social theorists have long been concerned with the origins of this world view and of the modern rational, calculating individual in whom it is embodied. In a recent study, Macfarlane (1978) has challenged the classic views of this problem, at least as they apply to England. In contradiction to Marxist and Weberian theory, Macfarlane finds no great transformation of the traditional peasant community in the sixteenth or even fifteenth centuries. The origins of English individualism, he argues, cannot even be discovered as far back as the thirteenth century, where records reveal that

England was as "capitalist" as it was in 1550 or 1750. That is to say, there were already a developed market and mobility of labour, land was treated as a commodity and full private ownership was established, there was a very considerable geographical and social mobility, a complete distinction between farm and family existed, and rational accounting and the profit motive were widespread (Macfarlane 1978, 195–96).

Indeed, some anthropologists experienced in fieldwork among the world's peasantry and tribes might dispute the absence anywhere of some sort of calculating individual. If, for example, the Nuer system of reckoning descent is "ancestor-centric," they are also able to express a set of egocentric relations even more relevant to their daily associations and decisions. Yet there is an important difference between the world view and behavior of the Nuer and that of the Puritan, and if Weber was wrong about how the latter arose, he may have made the most important contribution to the problem in defining the central issue as one of culture.

Having accepted a romantic definition of "community"—a form of association whose material existence, not just in pre-sixteenth-century England, is questionable—Macfarlane sees the symptoms of a well-developed rational individualism as evidence for the absence of any kind of significant communal association. In other words, he follows classical social theory in opposing, historically and logically, "community" and "the individual." Yet, unless we accept such individualism as the natural state of humanity stripped of a culturally reinforced traditionalism, we must search for the equally cultural sources of that rational individualism. Marx may well be correct in pointing to various "systems of production" as the roots of such cultural forms—but the ideology in question needs support from social forms which present constant reinforcing opportunities for its expression—for the repeated "social construction" of a capitalist reality.

Tocqueville understood that American individualism was maintained in the voluntary association, and a more recent French visitor to America observed,

The citizen must, first of all, fit himself into a framework and protect himself; he must enter into a social contract with other citizens of his own mind. And it is this small community which confers upon him his individual function and personal worth. Within the association, he can take the initiative, can advocate his personal political views and influence, if he is able to, the line of the group. (Sartre 1962, 113)

Such associations which serve to define and reinforce a form of individualism need not be, and are no longer typically, in America at least, confined to the local community. When local communities are expressly defined in terms of such a *contrat social*, however, they may (as evidenced in the case of West Sayville) exert a moral force that binds members as much to their own individualism as to their community.

In West Sayville the Reformed churches played the most critical role in defining that social contract. Such a religion, however, is not a source of moral stability in a static social world, but an extremely flexible orthodoxy that reacts to any and all threats by symbolizing them in a form in which they can be handled. Thus it would not be correct to say that the traditional culture of the Dutch immigrants in West Sayville resisted the overwhelming forces of change by which they were assailed through the late nineteenth and early twentieth centuries. Nothing could be further from the truth or do less justice to the real strength of that community. More remarkable was the community's ability simultaneously to embrace and resist those forces by bringing them into the common arena. The covenant survived by always adjusting the symbolic threat to one appropriate to the times. That is a very elastic sort of conservatism, and one which struck me most clearly in the course of conversation with an elderly immigrant woman. "So you live in Pennsylvania," she said. "I went there once on a trip organized by the church [Christian Reformed], to the Amish country. Those were very godly people, but I don't understand why they have to be so backward. Why I have a cousin out in Michigan who's a farmer, and he's got the latest kind of tractor with all the gadgets—and I'm sure he's as good a Christian as anyone."

APPENDIX A

METHODS

In commenting on the growing appeal that anthropology seems to have for historians, Natalie Z. Davis (1982, 12) listed four features that make anthropological writings useful for historians: "close observation of living processes of social interaction; interesting ways of interpreting symbolic behavior; suggestions about how the parts of a social system fits together; and material from cultures very different from those which historians are used to studying." It might be added that anthropologists have been increasingly interested in the work of historians as sources for an expanded background for their ethnographic studies, but also, and more significant, for a fundamentally diachronic view of social and cultural reality. Attempting to see "structure" as the temporary artifact of continuing "process," many anthropologists have been led to expand their time frame, either through a reconstruction based on some mixture of oral and written sources or by means of the work of historians who have already done so. When they follow the former course, as I have primarily done in this work, they are anthropologists writing history. The concerns that motivate, and the methods used in, such a study (if attractive on the grounds Davis lists) are likely to make the result irritating to some historians, who will find the work too narrow with respect to certain aspects of local life and overbroad in its grasping after theoretical generalities. The perspective that animates this work is open to such charges; it arises from a shared disciplinary tradition that has defined certain problems as more "interesting" than others, as well as from my own peculiar research experience.

My previous fieldwork was conducted in a bilingual (Gaelic/English) fishing community on the northwest coast of Ireland. There I was concerned with both the historical formation of the community in a colonial setting (Taylor 1980a, 1980b) and the relation of fishing to contemporary social organization and ideology (Taylor 1981). Pervading all these topics, however, was a more general interest in the nature of "community," a category of social life which if once naively assumed in its romantic definition is lately in danger of being defined out of existence by some anthropologists. On the one hand, those concerned with day-to-day social life in local settings have been increasingly apt to approach behavior from the atomistic perspective of "symbolic interaction" and network formation. On the other hand, Marxian or Marxoid anthropologists have been advocating attention to the political economy and world system which surround and shape the little world in which the anthropologist does his or her work.

These respectively microscopic and telescopic adjustments of anthropologists' view of their subjects are extremely valuable corrections to what in some cases were simply wrongheaded versions of social reality. Yet the question of levels of social and cultural actuality persists. Should the ethnography of communities be abandoned in favor of the study of systems both above and below it? And does a concern for history also require a rejection of any local focus on any middle ground— what, as Gluckman (1964) asked, should be the "limits of our naivety"? The proof of the value of any particular approach is in its ability to illuminate something otherwise left in the dark. In the case at hand, I asked myself whether, in considering the "community" as a real social field, I could explain something of the contrast I perceived between different parts of Ireland as they developed through periods of great social change.

There was something else about the notion of community—the people themselves seemed to use it. They designated, by its use in particular contexts, aspects of self and a central category in their picture of the surrounding social world. When anthropologists cease to pay attention to what the people they study tell them about what is important, they lose the most important advantage ethnography enjoys over less interactive modes of social scientific research.

If the nature of community was intriguing in the Irish case, it was more so in the Dutch-American village of West Sayville. Several things impressed me on my first few days of talking with people in the community. First was the self-conscious "individualist hardworking entreprenuer" self-image of the people I met, and the strongly Christian attitude of a fair number of them. Struck by the obvious contrast between these "Dutchmen" and the Irish fishermen I had known, I was naturally, and rather forcibly, reminded of Weber's thesis in *The Protestant Ethic and the Spirit of Capitalism*. At the same time it was also plain that the "community" as represented in certain institutions and interactive settings, and as embodied in an idea "toward which," as Weber would say, "people acted," was if anything even stronger than it was back on the northwest Irish coast.

That juxtaposition of individualism and communalism seemed to lie at the heart of an understanding of the particular configuration of life in West Sayville, yet since that dichotomy also lay at the center of a specific type of community which has played a particularly important role in American history, West Sayville presented an opportunity to see once again whether a focus on the community could contribute substantially to an understanding of the forces of history and social change.

METHODS

The methods used in this study involve sources and modes of interpretation. While both are, to a certain extent, artifacts of what happened to be available, they are greatly influenced by the theoretical concerns outlined above and apparent throughout the course of the study.

The focus on the decades around the turn of the century is also the result of both practical and theoretical considerations. The industrialization of the oyster fishery, and its consequent social impact, was most pronounced in this period. But it was also a time when immigrants were still arriving in large numbers and when the social and cultural boundries of the community were still well drawn. Oral sources can take us no farther back, and the most important written sources, fortunately, also illuminate this period.

ORAL SOURCES

I will admit, as an anthropologist, to a preference for living people, and I doubt that I would have been drawn very far into the documentary study of West Sayville had I not first met some of its residents. Although I had grown up in the nearby South Shore community of Blue Point, I knew the clammers of West Sayville as a youth only by the occasional dark references of fellow and more experienced followers of the bay than I was. They were the "Dutchmen," held to be expert baymen and rather unfriendly toward outsiders. Returning to the scene as an anthropologist, I found their local image unchanged. "They are terribly clannish," a Sayville merchant informed me. "You won't get much out of them. They don't like outsiders and they won't tell you anything about what *really* goes on." In fact, the vast majority of men and women I had the good fortune to meet and talk with in West Sayville were willing and marvelously able to talk with me—to share their personal experiences, their view of the history of their community.

In seeking after certain types of information, anthropologists often find that several "expert" informants are more valuable than a representative sample. There are other matters, in fact, which by virtue of their sensitivity are not likely to come up for discussion on the first meeting, but which can be broached and may be dealt with candidly after some trust and rapport has developed. This again favors repeated sessions with principal informants, rather than random sampling. I have tried to do nothing in these pages to violate that trust, although I have let the study be informed, where appropriate, by such revelations. The list of principal informants follows. Others contributed to my general understanding of the point of view and experience of the Dutch immigrants and their descendants, but those that follow were sources for major portions of the picture limned in the preceding chapters.

1. Ninety-three-year-old male, born in a small village in Friesland. Immigrated with his younger brother in 1905 to New Jersey, and came from there to West Sayville in 1906. Told in great detail of his early life and family circumstances in Friesland, his coming to America, and the ups and downs of his life as a deep-sea fisherman in this oystering town.

2. Ninety-four-year-old woman, born in West Sayville of immigrant parents. Daughter of the owner of a shop that was

a principal social center, she was able to give valuable accounts of the interaction of youth in such settings.

3. Sixty-year-old woman, born in West Sayville, daughter of a fisherman, was able to tell in detail of her father's fishing company and its maritime pursuits.

4. Seventy-one-year-old man, born in West Sayville of immigrant parents, an oysterman and general bayman, widely acknowledged as one of the best on the water. He was the single greatest source of detailed accounts of all manner of maritime pursuits and of dimensions of local life at first difficult to discover through other accounts.

5. Ninety-two-year-old woman, born in Yerseke, immigrated with her parents at the age of twelve. She was a good source on the experiences of the later immigrants, on women and women's work, and on the social life in early-twentieth-century West Sayville.

6. Eighty-one-year-old man, born in West Sayville of immigrant parents. A bayman and, along with his brother, a small-scale planter and shipper who was able to relate a great deal about the struggle of such small entrepreneurs in a West Sayville already well controlled by large shippers.

7. Eighty-nine-year-old-man, immigrated as a small boy from Yerseke. He was an active fisherman and oysterer most of his life and related many of his maritime experiences.

8. Eighty-year-old man, immigrated as a small boy from Yerseke. He did not "follow the bay" but plied a number of trades in the community. In addition to taped conversations, he was the source of an unsolicited handwritten eighty-page "life history" which included much on his father's experiences in turn-of-the-century Yerseke as well as on his own childhood in West Sayville.

9. Seventy-one-year-old man, born in West Sayville, worked for a neighboring estate and talked of that experience as well as of his active life in the fire department.

10. Seventy-year-old man, born in West Sayville, fisherman and eeler all his life, first with his father. He provided an ex-

tremely detailed account of fishing techniques, along with
the log of his father's fishing company (dated 1912).

11. Forty-year-old man, eeler and clammer born in West Sayville,
contributed a younger man's view of what has happened to
maritime life in West Sayville, as well as a detailed account
of his own eeling techniques.

12. Eighty-nine-year-old woman, born in West Sayville of immigrant parents. She provided a detailed picture of a woman's
life in early West Sayville, and the angle of a local who had
married outside the local churches and who in other ways
had deviated from the local norms.

13. Ninety-one-year-old man, born in West Sayville, a direct descendant of Bastiaan Broere and a man who also lived in
some ways on the fringe of the community. A schooner captain for many years, he offered a rare picture of that life before
World War I.

14. Fifty-year-old man, born in West Sayville of a very late immigrant family (1920s). He has worked on and off the bay,
and contributed a view of changes in the community since
World War II, and his own experiences as one who returned
from the war with a Catholic wife.

15. Seventy-four-year-old man, born in West Sayville of immigrant parents, an elder in the Christian Reformed Church
and a good source of the orthodox view of the community.

16. Eighty-year-old woman, born in West Sayville, the daughter
of a store owner and the descendant of an early shipper. She
was a good source of general social life and of the Christian
Reformed Church life in particular.

17. Eighty-year-old bayman, born in West Sayville, a principal
source of detail about early-twentieth-century maritime techniques and the life cycle of the bayman.

18. Seventy-seven-year-old man, born in West Sayville of immigrant parents. He told of his father's experiences as a late
immigrant from Yerseke and of his own as a bayman and
entrepreneur active in clamming.

19. Fifty-year-old nephew of above, born in West Sayville, and

major clamming entrepreneur who told of his experience in that enterprise.

20.   Ninety-year-old man, born in West Sayville of immigrant parents. He was an active bayman and mariner all his life, and provided detailed accounts of many aspects of local life, in particular of yachting for the rich.

21.   Thirty-five-year-old woman, descendant of one of the earliest immigrants to West Sayville and an avid collector and relator of passed-down family experiences.

22.   Eighty-year-old man, descendant of Samuel Green, who was a source of his family's history and their view of the surrounding Dutch community.

23.   Eighty-one-year-old man, born in West Sayville of immigrant parents, and a major planter and shipper of oysters and clams who described that enterprise.

24.   Seventy-year-old man, born in West Sayville, son of a major planter and shipper of oysters who provided an account of many technical aspects of that pursuit, as well as the perspective of the local elite.

25.   Sixty-five-year-old woman, born in West Sayville, the daughter of immigrants from Texel, told of her father's life as a captain for Ockers and of her mother's household rounds.

In Holland:

An important view from the perspective of those who remained behind in Yerseke was provided by two principal informants, one of whom was related to a West Sayville family.

1.   Seventy-year-old man who told much of the religious life and social interaction in the Yerseke of his youth.

2.   Seventy-two-year-old man who had taken an active interest in the history of shellfishing in Yerseke and provided much valuable information regarding that industry and the local view of those who emigrated.

Oral history, as the results of such conversations are somewhat portentously called, is not something that one can automatically gather with only the aid of a tape recorder. For an anthropologist, at least, such information is understood to flow only in the context of a knowledge of the informants which grows up through a variety of interactions in the course of participant-observation. In the real-life conversations of everyday interaction, we interpret messages according to our knowledge of the sender and the context of the sending. Anthropologists in the field do the same thing—well or badly—whether they admit it or not. Determining not only what is true in some objective sense, but also what is true for the speaker, requires interpretation based on the anthropologist's assumptions about the relations of informants to one another and to himself.

The sessions at which most of the oral material used here was gathered took place in the households of the informants. Most often only a husband and wife were present, though on a number of occasions my presence happened to coincide with that of a visiting friend, in which case mutual memory-jogging often led to especially rich accounts of specific events, as well as to revealing disputes about what really went on. Many of the facts and dates under contention could be and were checked in contemporary documentary sources, and while the memories of the informants often proved accurate in detail, it was the attitudes and values revealed in the course of our conversations that most interested me.

My usual practice was to go prepared with a list of general and specific (to the particular life of the informant) questions, the answers to which I would wait for, or seek directly when conversation otherwise began to reach a lull. I was not, however, interested in simply directing respondents to answer *my* questions, since I was at least as interested in discovering what was important to them. I was not disappointed in this tack, and the personal life histories which I was most often offered were as impressive in their omissions as in their choice of topics. The "contractual idiom" of which I have spoken so much in these pages was often striking in these interview situations. Whether as religious as Bastiaan Broere, or as blasé about the church as an old schooner captain, or as embittered as a peripheral widow, these informants all tended to represent themselves as "free-acting," forging their own social relations and cutting their own path through the world. I was again reminded of the contrast with my Irish friends, whose comparable stories were often delivered as veritable litanies of kinship connections.

The presence of the museum sponsoring this research within the confines of this community, and appropriately set on the shore, gave rise to some special effects as well. A number of older men, retired and semi-retired baymen for the most part and happy to be of aid to the research project, took to meeting every other Wednesday at the museum in order to reminisce and offer the museum staff and researchers any aid they might need. These sessions were taped, and over the months they provided probably the single greatest mine of experiences "on the water." Between the four or five men typically present, someone was always able to describe in detail, and make sense of, any past maritime pursuit I had stumbled across in some written source which, as often as not, made no sense as described there.

Such group sessions also presented opportunities to watch these baymen interact with one another, and in that process the language revealed more of the local idiom in action.

DOCUMENTARY SOURCES

I have mentioned that I habitually checked local memories against documentary sources, yet I would not want to leave the impression that I always found the latter the more reliable. Census returns, although an invaluable aid to this sort of study, are not without their shortcomings. Census collectors were quite fallible even when not actually evaded by their informants, and a comparison of those records with church rolls leads one to suspect that a certain number were regularly missed. There is the further confusion of names. Dutch pronunciation is evidently difficult for the English listener to grasp, and the same Dutch name was habitually rendered in a wide number of utterly dissimilar forms, perhaps even by the same collector. Some collectors or informants might decide to Anglicize the name, either by sound or translation, but then revert to a Dutch form in the next census. The results of all this are trepidating for the researcher. For example, Van Popering was also rendered Vonpoform and Fornifioferan, Van Wyen might appear as Van Dyne or Van Wiggen, Scherpinisse as Sharp and then Sharpi, and Groudywaard as Goldsmith or Goldsworth. Only by painstaking checks with other sources, especially church records, could such identities be sorted out. With all its deficits, however, the census returns, supplemented by church records and collected genealogies, permitted a reconstruction of the general form of kinship and marriage relations in the community through the turn of the century. A number of sections of the chart assembled from these data are included as Appendix B in order to illustrate some typical patterns of family intermarriage.

Other elements of social relations and interaction were revealed by church records, though I was handicapped by the availability of marriage and membership records of only the Dutch Reformed Church. An examination of those, however, did reveal something of the marriages with New Jersey and other communities discussed through the text, as well as the origin point in Holland of newly arriving members and of the families and individuals who over the decades either "left us" or "came to us from the seceders." As for the consistory records, which I was fortunate enough to obtain from both the Dutch and Christian Reformed churches, I will discuss their interpretation below.

Township records were valuable sources of the lifeway and concerns of the surrounding American population, and particularly of the shifting legal status of the shellfisheries. The local newspaper, *The Suffolk County News*, published in Sayville from the 1880s, was a particularly good record of the ups and downs of the industry. The local interest in shellfishing ensured detailed coverage of the minutia of that pursuit: the comings and goings of the schooner fleet, the rise and fall of prices, the improvements and failures of particular shoreside establishments, and of course the union, strike, and constant disputes and court cases over the "free bay." This record was particularly valuable in conjunction with the oral history provided by baymen, since the records of the shippers were very sparse indeed. From that perspective the single but fortunately revealing account was the surviving minutes of the Blue Point Oyster Shippers' Protective Association.

Other local written sources included pamphlets produced by the industry, Green's general store account books from the late nineteenth century, the minutes of the volunteer fire department and of course the personal written accounts of Bastiaan Broere, Adriaan Daane, and Almina Hage Terry. While all these used in conjunction with oral history provided a detailed picture of various aspects of local life, for the social anthropologist it is the interaction of people in institutional settings that is most important and most difficult to divine from all these sources. For that reason, the church consistory records were the most compelling of all written sources, providing a view of the confrontation of real actors on a central community stage.

The Extended Case Method or Situational Analysis

One of the assumptions on which situational analysis rests is that the norms of society do not constitute a consistent and coherent whole. On the contrary, they are often vaguely formulated and discrepant. It is this fact which allows for their manipulation by members of a society in furthering their own aims, without necessarily impairing its apparently enduring structure of social relationships. Situational analysis therefore lays stress on the study of norms in conflict. The most fruitful source of data on conflicts of norms is, not unexpectedly, disputes." (Van Velsen 1967, 146)

Not only is there a tension between the individual's own goals and the moral requirements of his society, there are always conflicts between the norms themselves. From this perspective it is dangerous to follow too closely the metaphor that equates the structure of any society's cultural values or norms of behavior with that of a language, with the implication that a set of grammatical "rules" lies behind all observable "expressions," for at the core of the society's rules or of the culturally structured world view lie fundamental contradictions. These contradictions lead to conflict within and between real people in real, and often recurrent, situations. Choices have to be made among the demands of conflicting norms, but therein, as Van Velsen argues above, lies an opportunity as much as a problem. "Vague and discrepant norms" allow for self-interested "manipulation." That is to say, actors can pursue their own goals while maintaining that they are following the rules, and both sides in any dispute involving such structural contradictions are probably able to justify their positions in normative terms. Yet such individual manipulation represents a problem for the group as a whole, whose collective interests are served by the maintenance of a semblance of coherence and unity. That goal must be achieved through another sort of action—the symbolic.

It follows from these assumptions about human behavior that anthropologists attending to a sequence of typical disputes may find opportunities for exploring (1) the underlying normative conflicts that may be generating such observable confrontations; (2) the manner in which individuals manipulate norms in pursuance of self-interest; and (3) the collective, symbolic assertion of a moral order as over against the disorder of real life. In fact, various anthropologists have found different of these possibilities to be the most important or intriguing. Some are enamored of the endless machinations of egocentric actors (e.g., Bailey 1969, 1971), while others (most notably Turner) have been led into a deeper examination of the ritual reconstruction of the moral order.

The church disputes seemed to offer a perfect opportunity for the use of this situational, or extended case method, approach. The particular cultural character of the community made it problematic in some ways, and therefore even more attractive as a test of the general usefulness of the method. The consistory records of both churches were full of conflicts that on closer examination proved to follow certain patterns. Those patterns were dissimilar in the respective congregations, and the differences seemed to be explicable in terms of the interplay between the central contradictions of the contractual community and the respective social organization of the two churches. The description of the conflicts contained in the records were detailed enough to reveal individuals using normative language in defense of self-interest. More important, that language could be understood to constitute a sacred version of the contractual idiom, and thus (it could be argued) offering a symbolic means for maintaining the coherence of a moral order based on contract, where the power of ritual, as it is more typically understood, was much sapped.

If conflict is endemic to all societies and offers a path, as Van Velsen and Turner maintain, to an understanding of social structure and action as well as symbolic processes, then it is particularly vital to what I have called the contractual community. In such social systems, the forms of association that provide opportunities for certain forms of repetitive conflict—so far from being inimical to cohesiveness—may be necessary to the construction and maintenance of the local world view. If in historical studies we ignore such interactive settings as are accessible through the records, we may end up with a picture of atomized individuals, as Macfarlane found in medieval England. That discovery may lead us to the further error of assuming, as a correlate to the strong individual, the absence of a strong community. For the Dutch of West Sayville, as the extended case method shows, the confrontations within communal associations were vital social acts, at once defining a well-bounded community and reinforcing the individualism of those living and acting within it.

APPENDIX B

KINSHIP DIAGRAMS

The following five kinship diagrams are based on church and census records as well as informants' reports. They are included here to give some idea of the extent of overlapping connections in the community created by marriage, particularly in the first generation of marriages in the 1860s, 1870s, and 1880s.

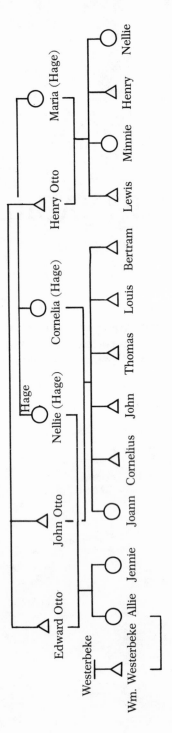

Otto/Hage Genealogy

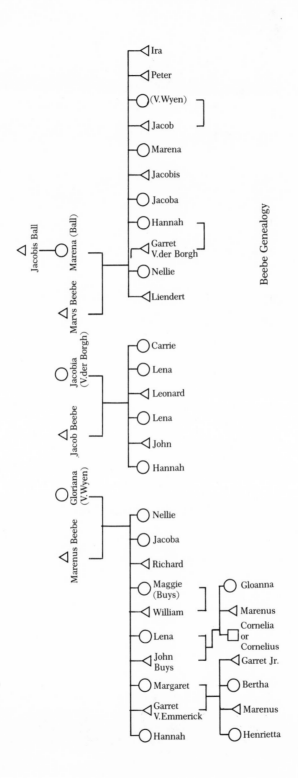

Beebe Genealogy

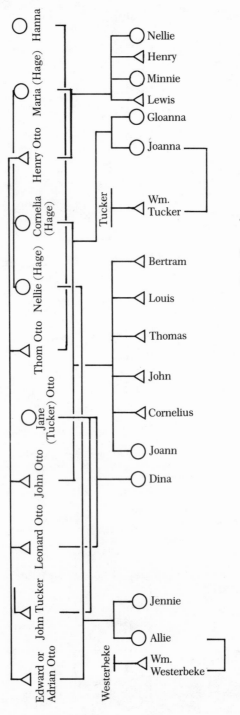

Otto Genealogy

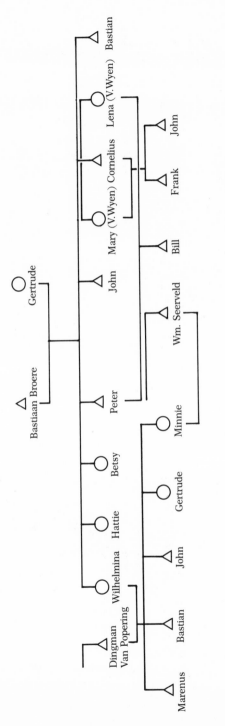

Broere Genealogy

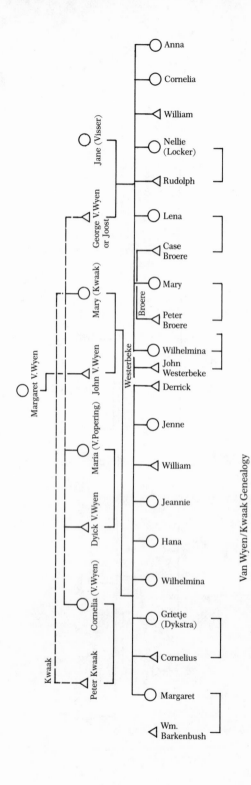

Van Wyen/Kwaak Genealogy

NOTES

Introduction

1. For a more extensive argument on this topic, see Taylor (1981, 1982). The problem rests with the confusion between community understood as a specific type of relationship, as described by Tönnies (1957), and the "local community." Those caught in a Tönnian model would have to call a West Sayville a "little *Gesellschaft*," which label would be very misleading, conveying at best half the characteristics of life in such social worlds.

2. See esp. Turner (1957, 1968) and Van Velsen (1967). For a discussion of these methods as applied in the present study, see Appendix A.

3. It might be argued, from a Freudian point of view at least, that the intensity of such conflicts is better explained if we assume that the "enemy" not only arose from within, but was unconsciously recognized as an aspect of self, a realization of a sensed danger within oneself. Perhaps the more orthodox Dutch Reformed were afraid of the Methodists, as they were, because they saw these American emotionalists acting out a possibility within their own faith.

4. I owe this formulation of the role of ritual, and the suggested parallel with Boyer and Nissenbaum's study, to Anthony F. C. Wallace (personal communication).

5. This approach to the workings of culture, emphasizing as it does the lived and flexible quality of a conceptual framework, is similar to that espoused by literary critic Raymond Williams (1977, 128–29) in his discussion of what he calls "structures of feeling."

6. See Evans-Pritchard (1981, 172) for a brief word on the possible connection of Durkheim's thought to that of Tocqueville.

Chapter 2
The Immigrants

1. "The absolute number of families and single individuals emigrating (between 1844 and 1877), ca. 19,000, reveals that the "distant magnet" of the United States was of limited pull" (Swierenga and Stout 1976, 299).
2. For accounts of the Iowa migration, see H. P. Scholte (1911), L. Scholte (1939), Vander Zee (1912), and Oostendorp (1964). Leonora Scholte's (1939) account is that of the wife of the famous minister and offers an interesting view of life in Iowa.
3. See esp. A. J. Pieters's (1923) account of life in Dutch Michigan.

Chapter 5
The Strike

1. A search in the national office of the AFL-CIO revealed only the charter of this local branch of the union.

Chapter 6
Oyster Is King

1. In addition to local oral history, this section relies heavily on Van Popering (n.d.), a detailed account of the local industry.

Chapter 7
Baymen and Workers

1. For a good account of the technical aspects of oystering in the Northeast, especially in southern Connecticut, see Kochiss (1974).
2. In addition to many oral history accounts of fishing, I was fortunate enough to receive a copy, from Ed Ockers, of his father's daily records (Ockers 1912), which constitute a detailed daily log of all the pursuits of a small fishing company.

Chapter 8
The Social Contract

1. Some of these northerners may in fact have been in touch with Zeelander affairs back in Holland, for fishermen from Texel are reported to have come into the Oosterschelde for young shellfish.

Chapter 9
The Honest War

1. The American commentators on the religious scene were prone to counting up the number of churches—the higher the number, the greater the presumed religiosity of the community.

2. For a summary of the religious issues and the complicated series of events involved in the schism, see Lucas (1955, 511–12). A more detailed treatment of the Christian Reformed Church can be found in Kromminga (1943) and Zwaanstra (1973).

3. Commenting on the social context of the schism and of the further explosion in 1882, when many more joined the Christian Reformed Church in America, Arnold Mulder (1947) wrote, "During those years more congregations, in Michigan, in Iowa, in Wisconsin, and in nearly every community where Hollanders had settled, had joined the movement and the Christian Reformed denomination had become firmly established." For our present argument, the important point is that splits tended to bifurcate small communities and hence should be examined from the point of view of village dynamics as well as personal attributes and religious issues.

4. Quotations are from Hendrick Taatgen's translation of the Dutch manuscript records of the Christian Reformed Church.

Epilogue

1. According to a contemporary newspaper account, the forced retirement of one major shipper left him despondent enough to take his own life a year later.

2. There may be other factors involved in the demise of the oyster, including pollutants that cut off the oxygen supply of the young shellfish.

Conclusions

1. Integrative conflict was the major concern of theorist Simmel (1955) and first introduced to social anthropologists through the works of Max Gluckman (e.g., 1963). Sociologist Coser's (1956) exploration of Simmel's theories is the most penetrating and clear treatment of the topic. Apropos of our concern with the integrative effects of conflict between "pillars": "Conflict may serve to remove dissociating elements in a relationship and re-establish unity. . . . Loosely structured groups and open societies, by allowing conflicts, institute safeguards against the type of conflict which would endanger basic consensus and thereby minimize the danger of divergences touching core values. The interdependence of antagonistic groups and the criss-crossing within such societies of conflicts, which serve to 'sew the social system together' by cancelling each other out, thus prevent disintegration along one primary line of cleavage" (Coser 1956, 80).

2. On the significance of such associations in America, Coser remarked, "It may be that one reason for the relative absence of 'class struggle' in this country is the fact that American workers, far from restricting their allegiance to class-conflict groupings and associations, are members of a number of associations and groupings which represent them in diverse conflicts with different religious, ethnic, status, and political groups. Since the lines

of these conflicts do not converge, the cleavage along class lines does not draw the total energies and allegiance of the worker into a single area of conflict. The relative stability of the American class structure (as compared with Europe) and failure of Marxian or Syndicalist Sorelian attempts to divorce the American worker from nonclass types of allegiance seem to confirm this observation" (Coser 1956, 77).

REFERENCES

Acheson, James M. 1981. "Anthropology of Fishing." *Annual Review of Anthropology* 10:275–316.

Anderson, W. E. K., ed. 1972. *The Journal of Sir Walter Scott.* Oxford: Clarendon Press.

Bailey, F. G. 1969. *Strategems and Spoils.* New York: Schocken Books.

Bailey, F. G., ed. 1971. *Gifts and Poisons.* New York: Schocken Books.

Bell, Colin, and Howard Newby. 1972. *Community Studies.* New York: Praeger Press.

Boyer, Paul, and Stephen Nissenbaum. 1974. *Salem Possessed: The Social Origins of Witchcraft.* Cambridge: Harvard University Press.

Broere, Bastiaan. 1887. *Korte Beshrijving van het Leven van en de Wonderbare Leidingen Gods met Bastiaan Broere, in Nederland en in Amerika.* Amsterdam: J. A. Wormser. (Translation: Anonymous MS available at Suffolk Marine Museum, West Sayville, New York.)

Brooks, Thomas R. 1964. *Toil and Trouble: A History of American Labor.* New York: Delacorte Press.

Coser, Lewis. 1956. *The Functions of Social Conflict.* New York: Free Press.

Davis, Natalie Z. 1982. From "History: 33 Questions." *Institute for Renaissance Interdisciplinary Studies Newletter,* vol. 3, no. 3.

Dobriner, William. 1960. "The Natural History of a Reluctant Suburb." *The Yale Review,* Spring 1960, pp. 399–412.

Durkheim, Emile. 1915. *The Elementary Forms of the Religious Life.* Translated by J. W. Swain. New York: Free Press.

Ennew, Judith. 1980. *The Western Isles Today.* Cambridge: Cambridge University Press.

Evans-Pritchard, E. E. 1936. *Witchcraft, Oracles, and Magic Among the Azande.* Oxford: Clarendon Press.

———. 1940. *The Nuer.* Oxford: Clarendon Press.

———. 1954. *Nuer Religion.* Oxford: Clarendon Press.

————. 1981. *A History of Anthropological Thought.* London and Boston: Faber and Faber.

Glerum, J. 1953. *De Zeeuwse Oester-Mosselcultuur en Kreeftenvisserij.* Meppel: Stenvert and Zoon.

Gluckman, Max. 1963. *Order and Rebellion in Tribal Africa.* New York: Free Press.

Gluckman, Max, ed. 1964. *Closed Systems and Open Minds.* Chicago: Aldine.

Goudsblom, Johan. 1967. *Dutch Society.* New York: Random House.

Handlin, Oscar. 1951. *The Uprooted.* Boston: Little, Brown & Co.

Hill, Christopher. 1964. *Society and Puritanism in Pre-Revolutionary England.* New York: Schocken Books.

Howell, N. 1949. "Islip Town." In Paul Bailey, *Long Island: A History of Two Great Counties, Nassau and Suffolk,* Volume 1. New York: Lewis Historical Publications.

Ingersoll, Ernest. 1881. *The Oyster Industry.* Washington, D. C.: Government Printing Office.

Kochiss, John M. 1974. *Oystering from New York to Boston.* Middletown, Conn.: Wesleyan University Press.

Kromminga, D. H. 1943. *The Christian Reformed Tradition: From the Reformation Till the Present.* Grand Rapids: William B. Eerdmans.

Lewis, Herbert. 1978. "European Ethnicity in Wisconsin: An Exploratory Formulation." *Ethnicity* 5: 174–88.

Lijphart, Arend. 1968. *The Politics of Accommodation.* Berkeley and Los Angeles: University of California Press.

Lucas, Henry S. 1955. *Netherlanders in America.* Ann Arbor: University of Michigan Press.

McCay, Bonnie. N.d. "The Pirates of Piscary: Ethnohistory of Illegal Fishing in New Jersey." *Ethnohistory.* In press.

————. 1982. "Sea Tenure and the Culture of the Commoners: Perspectives on Inshore Fishery Conflicts and Management in the North Atlantic Region." Unpublished manuscript.

Macfarlane, Alan. 1978. *The Origins of English Individualism.* New York and London: Cambridge University Press.

Merton, Robert. 1949. "Patterns of Influence: Local and Cosmopolitan Influentials," in *Social Theory and Social Structure.* New York: Glencoe.

Mills, C. Wright. 1956. *The Power Elite.* New York: Oxford University Press.

Mulder, Arnold. 1947. *Americans from Holland.* Philadelphia: J. B. Lippincott Co.

Nicoll, Henry. 1865. "Annual Report of the Suffolk County Agricultural Society." *New York State Agricultural Society Transactions,* 25:535–552.

Oostendorp, H. P. 1964. *Scholte: Leader of the Secession of 1834 and Founder of Pella.* The Netherlands: Francher.

Pieters, A. J. 1923. *A Dutch Settlement in Michigan.* Grand Rapids: Reformed Press.

Power, Garrett. 1970. "More About Oysters Than You Wanted to Know." *Maryland Law Review* 30, no. 3, 199–225.

Reeves, Henry A. 1885. "The Commerce, Navigation, and Fisheries of Suffolk County." *Bi-Centennial: A History of Suffolk County*. Babylon: Budget Stream Print.

Sartre, Jean-Paul. 1956. "Individualism and Conformism in America" in *Literary and Philosophical Essays*. Translated by Annette Michelson. New York: Collier paperback. 104–113.

Scholte, Henry P. 1911. "The Coming of the Hollanders to Iowa." Translated by Jacob Vander Zee. *The Iowa Journal of History and Politics* 9 (October).

Scholte, Leonora. 1942. *A Stranger in a Strange Land: The Story of a Dutch Settlement in Iowa Under the Leadership of H. P. Scholte*. Grand Rapids.

Simmel, Georg. 1955. *Conflict and the Web of Group-Affiliation*. Translated by K. Wolff. New York: Free Press.

Smith, Adam. 1909. *Wealth of Nations*. Edited by C. J. Bullock. New York: Collier & Son.

Swierenga, Robert. 1980. "Local-Cosmopolitan Theory and Immigrant Religion: The Social Bases of the Antebellum Dutch Reformed Schism." *Journal of Social History* 14:113–135.

Swierenga, Robert, and Harry Stout. 1976. "Socioeconomic Patterns of Migration from the Netherlands in the Nineteenth Century." Edited by Paul Uselding. *Research in Economic History*, vol. 1. Greenwich, Conn.: Jai Press.

Taylor, Lawrence. 1980a "Colonialism and Community Structure in Western Ireland." *Ethnohistory* 27:169–81.

———. 1980. "The Merchant in Peripheral Ireland: A Case from Donegal." *Anthropology* 4:63–76.

———. 1981. "'Man the Fisher': Salmon Fishing and the Expression of Community in a Rural Irish Settlement." *American Ethnologist* 8:774–88.

———. 1982. "*The Western Isles Today* by Judith Ennew." Review in *American Ethnologist* 9:217–18.

Thompson, A. G. 1850. "Annual Report of the Suffolk County Agricultural Society." *New York State Agricultural Society Transactions* 10:301.

Thompson, E. P. 1966. *The Making of the English Working Class* New York: Vintage Books.

Thompson, Samuel L. 1854. "Annual Report of the Suffolk County Agricultural Society." *New York State Agricultural Society Transactions* 14:639–41.

Tocqueville, Alexis de. 1945. *Democracy in America*, vol. 2. Henry Reeve Text. New York: Vintage Books.

Tönnies, Ferdinand. 1957. *Community and Society*. Translated by Charles P. Loomis. New York: Harper & Row.

Troeltsch, Ernst. 1931. *The Social Teachings of the Christian Churches*. Translated by Olive Wyon. New York: Macmillan Co.

Turner, Victor. 1957. *Schism and Continuity in an African Society*. Manchester: Manchester University Press.

———. 1968. *Drums of Affliction* Oxford: Clarendon Press.

Vander Zee, Jacob. 1912. *The Hollanders of Iowa*. Iowa City: State Historical Society of Iowa.

Van Gennep, Arnold. 1960. *The Rites of Passage*. Translated by M. B. Vizedom and G. L. Caffee. Chicago: University of Chicago Press.

Van Velsen, J. 1967. "The Extended-Case Method and Situational Analysis." In *The Craft of Social Anthropology*, Edited by A. L. Epstein. London: Tavistock Publications.

Van Ysseldijk, W. E. P. 1973. *1000 Jaar Yerseke*. Yerseke.

Verrips, Jojada. 1973. "The Preacher and the Farmers: The Church as a Political Arena in a Dutch Community." *American Anthropologist* 75:852–67.

Vlekke, Bernard. 1945. *Evolution of the Dutch Nation*. New York: Roy Publishers.

Wallace, Anthony F. C. 1978. *Rockdale: The Growth of an American Village in the Early Days of the Industrial Revolution*. New York: Alfred Knopf.

Wallerstein, Immanuel. 1974. *The Modern World-System*. New York: Academic Press.

Warner, Lloyd, and Paul Lunt. 1941. *The Social Life of a Modern Community*. New Haven: Yale University Press.

Weber, Max. 1958. *The Protestant Ethic and the Spirit of Capitalism*. Translated by R. H. Tawney. New York: Charles Scribners Sons.

Williams, Raymond. 1977. *Marxism and Literature*. Oxford: Oxford University Press.

Yans-McLaughlin, Virginia. 1977. *Family and Community: Italian Immigrants in Buffalo, 1880–1930*. Ithaca: Cornell University Press.

Zwaanstra, H. 1973. *Reformed Thought and Experience in a New World*. Kampen: J. H. Kok.

UNPUBLISHED SOURCES

Blue Point Oyster Shippers Protective Association—Minutes. 1901–1910. Notebook in Suffolk Marine Museum; West Sayville, New York.

Brookhaven Township Records. In museums at Stony Brook, New York.

Christian Reformed Church of West Sayville. 1876–1910. Consistory minutes.

Daane, Adriaane n.d. "History of the Daane Family." Handwritten account written in the late 1970s by an eighty-year-old immigrant from Yerseke. In Suffolk Marine Museum, West Sayville, New York.

First Reformed Church of West Sayville. 1867–1920. Marriage, baptismal, and membership records.

First Reformed Church of West Sayville. 1867–1910. Consistory minutes.

Green General Store Account Books. 1852–1871. In Ockers House Museum, Oakdale, New York.

Hoffman, Rev. John. 1898. "Historical Sketch of Sayville, Long Island. Typescript in Suffolk Marine Museum, West Sayville, New York.

Islip Township Records. In Town Hall, Islip, New York.

Ockers, Ed, Sr. 1912. "Records of 1912." Handwritten accounts of fishing company. Photocopy in Suffolk Marine Museum, West Sayville, New York.

Suffolk County Census Records. 1850–1890.

Suffolk County News. 1885–1920. Published in Sayville, New York.

Terry, Almina Hage. n.d. "The Pioneers of Oakdale." Typescript in Suffolk Marine Museum, West Sayville, New York.

Van Popering, Marinus. n.d. "The Shipping Industry." Typescript describing oyster industry in Sayville area. In Suffolk Marine Museum, West Sayville, New York.

West Sayville Hook and Ladder Company. 1891–1915. Minutes in notebooks in West Sayville Firehouse, West Sayville, New York.

INDEX

UNIVERSITY OF PENNSYLVANIA
PUBLICATIONS IN ETHNOHISTORY